CELLING AMERICA'S SOUL:
TORTURE AND TRANSFORMATION IN OUR PRISONS

By Judith Trustone

with Muti Ajamu-Osagboro, Jameel Salahuddin, Robert Muhkam Hagood, Tony Harper, Michael King, Anton Forde/Trevor Mattis & Jameel Whitaker

Cover design by Judith Trustone

ISBN 0-7414-1433-3

Published by:

519 West Lancaster Avenue
Haverford, PA 19041-1413
Info@buybooksontheweb.com
www.buybooksontheweb.com
Toll-free (877) BUY BOOK
Local Phone (610) 520-2500
Fax (610) 519-0261

Printed in the United States of America

Printed on Recycled Paper

Published February 2003

ABOUT THIS BOOK

Celling America's Soul: Torture and Transformation In Our Prisons is a journey into Shadow America where the Thrownaway People, the addicted, the impoverished, the mentally ill, and the retarded are warehoused in villages of the damned. Join Judith Trustone, a white middle-class Creative Writing teacher as she encounters first-hand the brutality and injustice of America's penal system, a throwback from the Middle Ages, at Graterford Prison in Pennsylvania. The fifth largest maximum security prison in the country, it is considered one of the toughest in the country with 3300 inmates and 1200 staff.

Not just an expose' of state-sanctioned brutality, this book also celebrates the creative spirits of seven prisoners, some of them innocent, who've managed to transform themselves despite their environment. So far, imprisoning just these seven has cost taxpayers $5,160,000.

Their writing, art and poetry demonstrate the incredible loss of human potential in a corrupt and expensive system that punishes rather than rehabilitates, putting our communities at even greater risk in these days of homeland insecurity. The book puts human faces on "criminals." Their stories are not easy to read, though their transformations are inspiring.

The second part of the book, "Visions Of What Could Be," shows the responses by prisoners, lawyers, teachers and visionaries to two questions:

1) What do you think of the present system?
2) If you had no legal, political or financial limitations, what kind of a new system would you build from the ground up?

For the reader inspired to action, there are recommended readings and resources, as well as twelve things you can do right now to begin to help our imprisoned fellow Americans receive need treatment and rehabilitation rather than the daily torture which describes their lives. Finally, in the "Afterthoughts," those who made this book a possibility share the healing, personal changes and hopes that the project inspired.

ABOUT THE ART

Because cameras are not permitted into the prison, the art in the book is from color copies of prison polaroids of oil paintings, most of them by Muti Ajamu Osagboro, that have been scanned into black and white photographs. The art and photographs are intended to soften some of the harsh intensity of prisoners' stories. The cover is of the Eastern State Penitentiary Historical site. The two SageWriters who chose anonymity are not included in the pictures on the back cover. The pictures of Muti, Anton/Trevor and Muhkam are stills from a documentary, "Unbelievable Isolation" by Glen Holsten of WHYY-TV in Philadelphia. Tony's picture is from his graduation from a G.E.D. class when he first came to prison twenty years ago.

THIS BOOK IS DEDICATED TO:

*** the 6.6 million Americans currently in the grip of a corrupt and inhumane criminal justice system and those who love them.**

*** all those who participated in this book's birth, openly or anonymously, and those who love them.**

*** those caring people working within the incarcerated community for justice, reform, kindness and decency.**

*** those falsely accused and criminally imprisoned.**

*** the victims of crimes, especially those crimes that would never have happened if their perpetrators had received treatment and rehabilitation.**

*** all the political prisoners around the world who dare to speak out against oppression.**

*** those whose spirits have been crushed by racism, sexism, classism, poverty and war.**

*** our ancestors, whose wisdom flows through us, and to those who come after us, all of our childen, that they may know and keep freedom in their lives. May they know a more just and humane world.**

"Judith Trustone accomplishes a remarkable feat in this work. She uses a narrative style and method to debunk the current criminal justice systems' practices and gives an eloquent expose' on how it loses its way in its attempt to fulfill society's mandate. It ends up being an eponym for criminal justice failure. She facilitates the articulated voices of the incarcerated to illustrate her 'travesty of justice' theme that currently represents criminal justice operations. Here's an institution mired in societal regression--blind engagement in accelerated depravity of those (staff and inmates alike) entering the system, a huge contribution to perpetuating the 'reoffending cycle' and an assurance of increasing difficulty of community integration. There's also the escalating cost and waste of both human and financial resources, the growing endangerment of public safety and of course the continued erosion of public trust in the system. This book presents the most cogent need for transformation from the current retributive model of criminal justice to one based on restoration."

Errol McClean, organization
development consultant

ACKNOWLEDGEMENTS

Special thanks to Peter Brigham, Brian Jennings, Douglas Jennings, Jennifer Masse, Rosalyn Payne, Phyllis Cross, Joan Gauker, Sarah Lauenborg, Robert Seidenberg, M.D., Pennsylvania Prison Society, AFSC's Prison Project, The Lionheart Foundation, *Graterfriends,* and the families of the imprisoned who inspired us with their devotion and determination.

Art by Muti Ajamu-Osagboro
Photography by Judith Trustone

FOREWORD

by Joan Gauker,
Coordinator of Volunteers, Graterford Prison,
Founding Editor, <u>Graterfriends</u>

Terrorism is not a new thing to those who live in American prisons. Yet it continues daily because we who are free on the outside stay outside those walls physically, emotionally, mentally and spiritually. Too "busy" with our lives, we rationalize not getting involved in meaningful ways until someone close to us gets caught up in the system. Though quick to move to stop atrocities anywhere else in the world, or to protest when an animal is abused, we are slow to even notice those same atrocities in our own prisons and jails. Fortunately, this book opens yet another door to the truth about the American prison system, and begs us to come inside and look around.

This will be hard, for reading this book makes us uncomfortable since we don't really believe our progressive society has such a degrading prison system. Many think our prisons are "country clubs." Yet those who DO know the system is degrading believe it should be that way. We in the United States assume that a prisoner becomes a person without a family or community, and that treatment for that "alien" is expensive and is "coddling." As if blind to the fact that most prisoners will return to their former communities, American prison officials (with our silent blessings) generally see it as their mission to inflict additional punishment above what the courts deemed adequate, often on a daily basis. Unmindful and uncaring that the real punishment for anyone is **being** in prison, many correctional officers, who are full of their power, become new judges and juries each day for their unwilling charges. Because of America's backwardness, Europeans come to our country constantly with the sole purpose of befriending our prisoners, our own people, whom we abandon. This fact, alone, should call us to a higher plane in our dealings with our fellow citizens.

In the midst of our inhumanity to prisoners, here and there imprisoned men and women rise above the mayhem and violence in which they are forced to live. They find a way to become serene. They take up reading, writing, painting, and music, and find themselves and a piece of a life. They become model prisoners. You'll meet several of them, some artists and poets, in this book. Yet, the American prison system, whose mission is to punish, often cannot abide model prisoners. So they soon find a way to make it difficult for such positive prisoners to write, to paint, to read, and to make music. Then it becomes difficult to exist without being accused of some imagined infraction, which will finally put the model prisoner into solitary confinement in The Hole.
After being immersed in this book, one can no longer turn away from the truth that sensitive, intelligent, thoughtful, decent, perceptive and too many innocent people are rotting

away in a system which could put their talents to use in so many enriching ways for the good of society. After reading the experiences, insights and observations in Celling America's Soul, shame and common sense should propel us to change our system into one that recognizes the redemptiveness of each offender; one that finds a way to probe the intellect and stir the heart of each of its charges; one that encourages forgiveness; and one that promotes restoration – so that offenders can return to society ready to enhance their families, themselves, their communities, and ultimately their nation.

Not just an expose' of the horrors of American prisons, the book also celebrates those prisoners who have managed to transcend their environment to become thoughtful artists and writers, dedicated to giving voice to the incarcerated.

In the second half of the book, "Visions Of What Could Be," prisoners, activists, teachers, visionaries, and correctional staff describe what other countries are doing, and what we could do in this country if we had no political limitations and could think of true treatment and rehabilitation outside the cellblock.

****

"Blessed indeed are we who live among those who hate, hating no one; amidst those who hate, let us dwell without hatred."

"Of hatred and ill will may not a trace remain. May love and goodwill fill body, mind and life."

"Hatreds never cease through hatred in this world; through love alone they cease. This is an eternal law."

Dhammapada, 34,5, 197

"Hidden Innocence" Holmesburg Prison oil on canvas
Muti Ajamu-Osagboro

INTRODUCTION

The day after September 11th I got a call from a former student in my Creative Writing class at Graterford Prison. Attempting a lightness I didn't feel, I said, "I guess you guys are the only Americans not afraid of being bombed."

His voice heavy, he said, "We face terrorism in here every single day."

I couldn't say a word, remembering the tales of deprivation and cruelty they'd talked and written about in class.

Like most Americans, I had no idea what really goes on in our prisons. A human rights activist since high school, I'd worked with court-stipulated male and female offenders at large drug and alcohol treatment centers where I developed programs for the addicted. I was told by staff during orientation at every agency where I'd worked to remember that "All prisoners claim they're innocent." I too adopted that cynical attitude.

Then one day in 1983, I read an article in the Sunday paper about a prisoner, a Lifer at Graterford Prison who'd turned himself around spiritually and created a peer, self-help program with other Lifers to help prepare young inmates to stay out of prison after their releases. (To date, keeping him imprisoned has cost taxpayers $1,050,000.) I was moved by the story to write a letter to the Pennsylvania Board of Pardons supporting clemency for him. I sent a copy of my letter to the inmate, and when he wrote back and invited me to the prison to do a workshop, my curiosity was aroused. Here was a chance to go inside one of the largest maximum security prison in the country, called by some one of the toughest boys' clubs in the US.

Could prison really be as bad as I'd heard and imagined?

While I of course intellectually supported prisoners' rights, I'd never taken the time to learn how few they really have, and the kind of degrading conditions under which they exist. Out of the class of fifteen, seven are involved in the book, telling their stories, some anonymously and some publicly, perhaps putting their very lives at risk for revealing the truth. Muti, Muhkam, Jameel S. and Jameel W. are African Americans, Anton/Trevor is Jamaican, Tony is Hispanic and Michael is white. Most of them have been in there since they were teens, and, due to politicians' testosterone-driven Draconian laws, most of them will never get out. The cost of maintaining a prisoner in Pennsylvania is $35,000 a year; $65,000 for older inmates. Treatment for the epidemic of Hepatitis C in those prisons offering treatment runs an additional $25,000 a year. Just these seven men have cost us so far $5,160,000

Pennsylvania allocates $3,900 a year for educating a child.

Is this how we want our tax dollars spent?

Muti, Muhkam, Anton and Tony are innocent. I've seen the evidence. So far they have cost taxpayers $2.6 million to keep them in cages. For the rest of their lives.

Tragically, Pennsylvania is one of just a few states where lifers can never be considered for possibility of parole. Their only recourse is a recommendation for clemency to the Governor by the Board of Pardons, which has stated publicly its position not to pardon anyone. With a new governor, Ed Rendell, hopes are high that justice will have a chance to breathe a little in Pennsylvania.

My first trip to Graterford was a culture shock. Driving up a long country hill to the fortress with deer grazing peacefully outside its walls, I felt like I was entering another reality. This is one of the places I've come to call Shadow America, where we warehouse the Thrownaways, the poor, the addicted, the mentally ill, the abused and the retarded. It was like traveling back to a time of slavery, stepping into a horror theme park. As I entered, I'd never before experienced a building emanating such pain, despair and rage that it was almost palpable.

According to inmates, this is one of the "better" prisons.

After being searched, stamped and braceleted, I was escorted by guards to the classroom. I passed a sea of men in prison garb, men whose skins were mostly black or brown with an occasional salting of white. Their faces showed a range of expressions from madness and despair to eyes sparkling with fierce intelligence and undaunted spirits. Some seemed lost in the world of the Thrownaways, barely alive, as if their spirits were on their last legs.

Everyone passed through rows of guards, mostly white, standing stiff and frozen faced, as if constantly braced for challenges from their angry, despairing charges. The air was thick with repression, and the noise was deafening.

I was suddenly aware of my gender. My white skin. And my vulnerability.

While I didn't expect a luxurious classroom at Graterford, I was unprepared for the holes around the windows that allowed puddles of rain to pool under the desks. No one but me seemed to notice as we adjusted our seats to avoid wet feet.

I designed a workshop like one I thought I might need if I was ever incarcerated. I included meditation, guided imagery, breathwork and gentle movements as well as class discussions of contemporary topics. The enthusiastic responses of the students kept me coming back as a volunteer for several years. Encouraging them to write, I soon was mentoring several serious writers.

Eventually I was hired to teach Creative Writing at Graterford, which was the beginning of my deeper journey into the heartless soul of a prison. My role model was Hermann Spector, a librarian at San Quentin back in the fifties and sixties who believed in "Bibliotherapy," the healing and rehabilitative power of reading and writing. Through his encouragement, there were so many manuscripts presented for publication one year, over 1500, that San Quentin began charging a 25% agent's fee (this at a time when all other agents were charging 10%.) Among those manuscripts was Eldridge Cleaver's Soul on Ice and George Jackson's Letters from Soledad.

Could there be writers at Graterford who could also have such a strong impact on American thinking?

When Hermann Spector had a heart attack and had to leave his job, prison authorities replaced him with a guard rather than a librarian, and threw out his files, twenty years of work.

In the Creative Writing class, as the students opened up and began to share their experiences and, for some of them, evidence of their innocence, I realized that I had to get their stories out to the public. We formed a working group, calling ourselves SageWriters.com. Our mission statement on our website says "We are a group of free and incarcerated writers, artists and activists dedicated to bringing an artistic voice to justice, liberation, social change and creating a community love ethic." We began to create this book, and sharing and cautious affection began to grow among group members, unusual in a place where trust is as rare as filet mignon.

Our first project was Anton Forde/Trevor Mattis' Contemplations of a Convict: Aphorisms for the Heart and Mind which was published by Infinity Publishing.com in 2001. (By using the alternative new print-on-demand technology, we are able to publish work for $500 that would not ordinarily get a voice. We hope in the future to be able to affiliate with a non-profit in order to apply for foundation support for SageWriters; meanwhile we're looking for volunteer editors and Patrons willing to subsidize a prisoner's book.)

The idea for CELLING came out of the class exercises which you'll read about in the first chapter.

As I listened to their stories and read what they wrote, I was coming face to face with my own stone wall of denial, not a comfortable feeling. I thought of the Black musician I'd lived with for several years who had given me a front row seat to the racism, both subtle and blatant, that Black people have to deal with every day, an experience too few white people can comprehend. I thought of my brief career in real estate back in the 60's when Bill Cosby, a major television star at the time, wanted to buy a home on Philadelphia's Main Line. Every homeseller I questioned said this about selling Cosby their home: "I wouldn't mind, but I couldn't do it to the neighbors."

Then there was a friend's cousin who adopted a baby girl a few years ago. The whole family was thrilled, including her grandfather, the judge. The nursery was done by a decorator, and the beautiful baby was outfitted in the latest in designer babywear. When she was almost three months old, her birth mother went to the adoption agency and tearfully confessed that the baby's birth father was Black.

They immediately gave the baby girl back.

Is it our culture's racism reflected in the educational, health care and employment disparities that has created a $46 billion a year industry that doesn't work? That has 6.6 million Americans, mostly people of color, in its clutches? That punishes rather than providing treatment and rehabilitation? A criminal justice system that only works for the privileged? A system that makes people worse and puts our communities at even greater risk? According to James Gilligan, M.D., Director of the Center for the Study of Violence, "The most effective way to turn a non-violent person into a violent one, is to send him to prison."

Certainly there are those who are too damaged and are a danger to society; they need treatment, not punishment which is all most of our prisons offer, which makes inmates even more violent. Studies show that 70% of prisoners are addicted, 35% are mentally ill or retarded, and practically all suffer from various degrees of poverty, lack of education and health care, neglect and abuse. Despite the stereotype that everyone in prison is getting a free college eduation, in reality there are only a few programs available, and it's estimated that 70% of the incarcerated can't read or write well enough to fill out an application for a driver's license.

Several of the men in this book could only write their names when they first came to prison as children.

This system harms not only all those imprisoned but also the staffs who control and counsel them, most of whom are decent people trying to work under laws, philosophies, structures, rules and regulations carried over from the Middle Ages. One glaring example of this madness was a ruling a couple of years ago from then Governor Tom Ridge that no inmate could have more than ten books in their cell. This to a large population of Lifers for whom books are their only escape into the real world and sanity. Some had almost a hundred books, and had to choose only ten, the rest given away or thrown away, like them, in the trash.

There wasn't a peep out of anyone about this even though I called all the local newspapers. People just don't seem that interested in the bad things that happen to prisoners. Until they find themselves or a loved one imprisoned.

One who knows this best is Graterford's compassionate superintendent, Donald Vaughn. Beginning his career as a prison guard forty years ago because he "needed a job," he's managed to work his way up through the ranks to become the CEO. "We were trained back then not to look prisoners directly in the eyes, to maintain distance," he comments, noting the positive changes he's managed to implement. One of the more progressive minds in an unyielding system, he worries about what would happen to Graterford if he was no longer in charge. He says, "Just because we run prisons doesn't mean we believe in them," echoing what 92% of the country's superintendents and wardens said in a national survey prepared for a Senate sub-committee. The survey respondents also all said that half the people now in prison could be released tomorrow, with no threat to the community.

The system has broken Vaughn's own heart. A few years ago, his son was arrested and sentenced to prison. When Vaughn found out he'd been sent to Graterford, he immediately had him transferred to another prison, where he was beaten to death two days later.

Anton Ford/Trevor Mattis, the Jamaican, one of the innocent ones, was once beaten so badly by 15 guards that he had to have his face reconstructed. Tall, slim and still elegant after twelve years behind bars for a crime he did not commit, he's partly blind and suffers chronic pain. He says, "I've seen quite a few people get stabbed. In here, death is not such a significant event. I've heard screams of "Rape!" in the night. The guards never come. I've listened to one prisoner beating another to death two cells away. I've heard the blood-curdling screams of a man being bludgeoned. I never knew humans could make such a sound. You can actually hear the soul depart in those ghastly screams. I hope never to hear it again."

According to prisoners, though denied by Department of Correction authorities, there is rape and often murder in every prison by either inmates or guards on a regular basis. The California advocacy group, STOP PRISON RAPE, estimates that there are 364,000 rapes each year in prisons. Prisoners and activists say this figure is too low. Sadly, these violent assaults are too often material for comedians and cop shows. As a culture, we accept the possibility of violent sodomy as part of the "punishment" of incarceration, chuckling over "vaseline" jokes. If there was any other system like the prison industrial complex costing taxpayers $46 billion a year that was such an abysmal failure at rehabilitation, it would be abolished quicker than you can say Enron.

The first part of **CELLING** *focuses on the seven SageWriters' stories and testimonies from other inmates at a dozen of Pennsylvania's 28 prisons and their family* *members. One chapter,* ***"Rapes, Murders and Abuses,"*** *describes the daily terrorism prisoners are subjected to. Not all abuses took place at Graterford. Some of the tortures described took place at other prisons. One of them, Holmesburg Prison, was the scene of the gauntlet where guards lined up in two rows and each prisoner had to run between them as they clubbed him. Murder was not uncommon. That prison has been closed.*

Mixed in with the horror stories are prisoners' poetry and art, examples of their spiritual transformations despite the daily terror, and a special section honoring mothers, fathers and loved ones. There is also a part focused on women in prison.

The second part of CELLING, ***"Visions of What Could Be,"*** *is a compilation of ideas from prisoners, teachers, guards, activists, writers, artists, those living and working in Shadow America. I asked people to answer two questions:*

1) *What do you think of the current system?*
2) *If you had no political, legal or economic limitations, what kind of a new system would you build from the ground up?*

Respondents include Ernie Preate, former Attorney General of Pennsylvania, who became a prison activist after his own experience with incarceration for fraud; Bill Ayers, a former member of the 60's Weather underground, now a professor of education at the University of Illinois at Chicago; and Bonnie Kerness, Co-Director of the American Friends Service Committee's Prison Project and co-author of "Torture in US Prisons." The ***VISIONS*** *section also includes information from other countries who view America's criminal justice system and its death penalty with dismay, especially at the fact of those 6.6 million American citizens either in prison or on parole or probation. If studies show that 2/3 of death penalty sentences are flawed, considering it's the same system for non-capital sentences, it* *isn't difficult to extrapolate that 2/3 of the currently 2.6 million incarcerated Americans may have been unjustly imprisoned. Examining the current budget of $46 billion a year (and growing) for an anachronistic, dysfunctional, bureaucracy must surely bring us out of our cultural denial. An industry with such a failure rate should be declared a national emergency.*

At the end of the book, I list resources for those moved to involvement at various levels including "Twelve Things You Can Do Today." Then the seven original SageWriters, whose stories are highlighted, describe in the "Afterthoughts" chapter how writing this book affected them. After getting to know them through their writing, do you still think we need to spend any more than the ***$5,160,000*** *we've spent so far to keep just the seven of them caged? Think of the treatment and rehabilitation that money could have bought instead of financing terrorism!*

*In "****Afterthoughts****," Muti reflects on whether or not I really could know Black reality. No, I can't, anymore than he could comprehend my white, middle class world, though we both try. But I know injustice when I see it. He wondered if I'd be willing to come out of my comfort zone and be "niggarized." I ask the same of you, for reading this book isn't easy. Our sense of ourselves as moral, compassionate people is challenged by the experiences described in these pages. My neighbor and assistant, Jennifer Masse, thought she knew the system and its many flaws. She'd read* ***Actual Innocence*** *before I met her. A white, professional Republican, she began having anxiety attacks and dreams about the imprisoned SageWriters in the book. "I'm not sure I want to know all this," she said one day after commenting about how she just couldn't get these guys out of her head.*

Hopefully your response will be as strong when you acknowledge to yourself the terrible waste of humanity (and our tax dollars) in these 19th Century dungeons.

Escalating harassment and censorship by guards reached an intolerable level when they began another "investigation" of me, their third. By searching me and going through all of my files, they learned I was discussing the inmates cases, a no no, one of many rules and regulations I had trouble taking seriously. Instead of sitting me down and discussing their concerns, the guards treated me like they treat everyone, as a criminal. Despite the administration's opinion of me as a "fabulous" teacher, the only thing they cared about was a rigid adherence to rules. As Ernie Preate, former Attorney General says about prisons, "While the system claims it's trying to rehabilitate, it's really about tearing people down."

(Later I heard of another teacher, a woman who'd volunteered at Graterford for years, who, after numerous "investigations," was strip searched and whose car was gone over by drug-sniffing dogs. She resigned and is now a successful writer.)

I discovered I was not as strong as I'd thought. I'd begun to feel a deep level of anxiety like I'd never known before, a shakiness in my solar plexus that was entirely new. I began experiencing fear as I drove up the winding road on my way to the inevitable interrogations and searches before I got to the class, if I even got there at all, which sometimes happened. For the first time, after going into the prison for nine years, I felt in my being just a tiny bit of what inmates endure every day, some of them for the rest of their lives: what I call Chronic Traumatic Stress Syndrome. Or Battered Prisoner Syndrome. When Director of Activities, Tony Wolf, told me class was suspended pending another investigation, I asked him what about? When he replied, "I can't tell you," I knew I could no longer work under such conditions. I told him I was quitting.

Feeling as if I was abandoning them, I knew I had to resign, confirming the expectations of the most cynical students that "anything good that happens in this place they destroy." I'll never forget looking back into the classroom that final night when I knew I might never see most of them again. In that moment, I realized how deeply they'd etched a space in my heart, which was heavy with sorrow at my own inadequacy. I realized that they'd taught me much more than I could ever have taught them.

A week after I resigned, I was walking with a friend, Bill, a park ranger, around a lake in Chester County. When we came upon a man fishing, Bill engaged him in fishing talk while I gazed out at the water. When the man said he'd just retired as a guard at Graterford Prison, my ears perked up. Knowing about our book project, Bill asked him what it was like for him working there.

We were astonished at his reply. "I hate niggers," he said, spitting into the lake as he adjusted his pole, not noticing our shocked responses. "If I didn't like the way they looked at me or if they didn't obey me immediately, I'd wait until no one was looking, get 'em alone in their cells and grab their balls and hold my stick against their throats and tell 'em if they didn't do what I said when I said it, they might find themselves dead on the floor of their cell."

He continued, describing a contest the guards used to have, a variation of ping pong, where they'd strip a prisoner, put him naked in an empty cell and turn a firehose on him, counting how many times they could bounce him against the wall before he collapsed.

Stunned by his vitriol, I knew in that moment that no matter what the obstacles, I had to write this book.

** Imagine never again seeing a tree or a sunset---for the rest of your life.*

** Imagine having to strip, drop your pants, bend over and spread your cheeks to a stranger every time you had a visitor or walked from one part of your neighborhood to another---for the rest of your life.*

** Imagine not being able to have regular meals because the new $13 million prison kitchen was (reportedly) closed by state inspectors due to maggots?*

** Imagine never again having a private phone conversation without a stranger listening and recording? Or never getting a piece of mail that someone else hasn't read first?—for the rest of your life.*

** Imagine living like the people who were terrorized by the snipers and like the people living with daily violence in ghettos---for the rest of your life?*

** Imagine having your every move controlled by people who hate you and mutter the "N" word to you whenever they can—for the rest of your life?*

** Imagine never being able to sleep deeply because you have to be alert for possible beatings or rapes---for the rest of your life?*

** Imagine never being able to make love again---for the rest of your life?*

THIS IS REHABILITATION?

"The fact is that more than 95% of the people now in prison are getting out some day. If we don't try hard to make a difference with the inmate while they're with us, we're jeopardizing public safety." Secretary of Corrections, Jeffrey A. Beard

There's a Native American saying, ***"Great Spirit, Grant that I may not criticize my neighbor until I have walked a mile in his moccasins."*** *Come into the classroom with me, step into their moccasins and get to know the hearts and minds of your fellow Americans living in Shadow America*

Readers' Guide

Because CELLING includes so many voices, in order to spare you confusion as to whose voice you're reading, if the words are in italics, they're mine.

If they're in bold italics, they're quotes from others.

If they're in regular text, they're the words of whomever is identified.

The dollar amounts are added when I know how long the writer has been imprisoned. Many wrote from across the state in response to a call for submissions that was published in Graterfriends. I don't yet know their individual stories.

Part One
THE VIEW FROM SHADOW AMERICA

IMAGINE

by Anton Forde/Trevor Mattis

Imagine being fed hatred and being fed by hatred.
Imagine spending hours at a time contemplating revenge.
Imagine constantly being prodded, poked, and provoked
to the brink of uncontrollable anger,
but you continuously fight to contain that fury.

What you've just imagined is the life I live.

Imagine the only comfort and solace you have is you.
Imagine the only company and companion you have is you.
Imagine the only person who loves you is you.
Imagine dying a second at a time for fifty years,
And every second you die, you know it and feel it.

What you've just imagined is the life I live.

Imagine not having any hopes or dreams.
Imagine not having any visions or a future.
Just staring, looking, watching, sometimes thinking,
but you stare at nothing, look at nothing, think of nothing.
Imagine just being in here, existing.

What you've just imagined is me.

Eastern State Penitentiary Historical Site, Philadelphia, PA

Chapter One
THE CREATIVE WRITING CLASS

The course started in July in a sweltering room with a feeble fan that was too noisy to use. The fifteen men, several of them Lifers, were mostly Black and Hispanic and a couple of whites. After determining their skill levels and interests, I decided I could best serve them by expanding their minds and bringing a little bit of beauty and normalcy into their grim lives.

They spoke often of the horrible smells in prison where 3300 men eat, smoke, ejaculate, sweat and shit in open toilets. One night in class, I asked them to sit in a circle with their eyes closed while I played meditative music (Audiotapes are considered contraband, one of the many ways I got into trouble.) I walked around the circle and placed a drop of essential rose oil on each of their left wrists, instructing them to breathe in the fragrance and then begin writing whatever came up for them.

Here are just a few of their five-minute responses:

"Freedom to inhale the scented vapor of life beyond this small room. So strong it will be with me the rest of the night and well into my dreams. Comforting and soothing, a pleasure that cannot be tainted or touched by the harsh surroundings of my personal hell, a place I prefer not to return to, but I must. Only now I'm a little stronger and revived, with the vapors of Freedom deep in my lungs, infecting every pore of my being."

"My mind went to the first time I made love to a woman after almost sixteen years in prison. I remember just wanting to smell her body from head to toe. I felt alive again. I felt my senses return. I was free and whole, most of all complete. Oh what a smell!"

"It's as if I was circled by rose bushes out in open space, relaxing without a care in the world."

"The color of light I've seen produced
from the mild fragrance of a rose,
perhaps less real or more imagined.
Blue, lime, deep green, yellow and purple.
The rainbow of my mind?
Or something more or less creative than a moment
of enhanced illusion?"

"Lush, soft, deep, bright, fresh, wild, free, sensual, energetic, enveloping, opening, motivating. Biting, expanding. Outdoors. Nose candy. Excitement. Anticipation. Unpeeled fruit."

They were all visibly brightened and excited at what the olfactory stimulation had opened up in them. When the guard came to escort me out, he sniffed the air suspiciously, and the students had a good laugh, a nanosecond of joy.

During one of the class assignments, which focused on finding beauty in such a place, Anton wrote the following piece, which was published in The Philadelphia Inquirer.

"Last spring, I participated in the horticultural program here at Graterford (now disbanded). I was given an assignment to plant a packet of seeds. I chose a packet that was supposed to be extremely hard to grow outside optimum conditions. The seeds were those of the genus Calceolaria. I took on the challenge and carefully nurtured the seeds to seedlings. I watched as the seedlings grew into small plants. These plants then bore some of the most beautiful flowers I've ever seen. The common name of the plant is pocketbook plant, because the delicate blossoms are shaped like a lady's pocketbook. There were soft pink, blue, yellow and red flowers, and they all sold the first day of our annual plant sale.

This experience taught me a valuable lesson that I think society should heed. Proper nurture and care are Nature's prerequisites for maximizing the potential of all life. It showed me what prison is all about. In here, I see a lot of seeds that grew up without proper nurture and care, and they survived, but now they are wild and hardy. These many young, mostly Black and Hispanic seedlings, are now being further exposed to much harsher conditions and environments. I wonder what type of plants they are going to develop into as we challenge Nature's laws within prisons. Not withstanding that, have you ever seen a cactus bloom?"

****

One week Muti came to class excited about having seen the first rainbow ever in his life the night before one of the many prisoner events, a Runathon, to raise funds for charity.

A REAL RAINBOW
by Muti Ajamu-Osagboro

"It was late afternoon-early evening
and the sea of captured bodies filtered into the night yard.
I shared the obligatory greetings of Freedom.
I was feeling a bit less stressed because of
earlier artistic triumph.
The sky was ink blue-or so it seemed,
the clouds unusually puffy and light,
giant versions of the cotton balls my sister used to
put between her toes until the nail polish dried.

I was tuning in to my inner vibes and the yard felt different.
No specific activity sought-calisthenics and the like,
for I was readying for the Big Run in the morn.

While I was still milling about the overcast sky lit up.
My peripheral caught colors that were most assuredly

alien to this hell haven.
Tilting my head back and fixing my eyes on a special
piece of sky, I saw a REAL RAINBOW!

Not the type in magazines or television screens
nor in electronic games or in my childhood school books.
I'm talkin' a REAL RAINBOW.
Majestic purple, ravishing red, brilliant orange, birth-giving green, highlighting yellow and an unmistakable tinge of pink.
Ah pink! Up until now its high point was that it was one of my often-used colors on canvas in an oil painted creation.
Now this understated pale peekin' pigment warmed my chest and set my mind racin' on a menagerie of blissful scenes.

A REAL RAINBOW from nowhere took me everywhere I wanted to be.
It was as if the Goddess of Creativity plucked the colors
from one of my nocturnal paint storms and arched them across the sky.
It was long and illuminating, wider than an interstate…
Imagine hues being lanes.
The forty foot wall seemed very small as I embraced it all.

Today in a place where dulled senses see old time black and white and grey-the color explosion brought a dire burst
that fed my retinas' thirst."   9/15/2000

****

When I asked Muti how the other prisoners in the yard had responded to the rainbow, he said, "I told them, Look up! Look at that! But they just mumbled Yeah, Yeah, their spirits weary and kept their eyes down."

As the class progressed, we wrote and talked about everything that impacted on them, from violence, police profiling, gun control, fathers and fathering from prison, women, sexism and racism, politics, health and relationships. They wrote essays, short stories and screenplays.

One night, after talking about yet another study showing how many black youth are caught up in the system, I gave them the five-minute assignment to write about what their experiences were like with the police when they were growing up. I was stunned when I read their stories, for the ones who'd grown up in North Philly all wrote the same thing. As pre-teens, the police would stop and make them get into the police cars and then would drive them to an all-white neighborhood, and, laughing, make them get out and find their way home through dangerous gang territory. They soon learned to run when they saw a police car, and of course who do the cops stop when there's a crime? Whoever is running...

I suddenly realized they may have run right by my office at St. Luke's Hospital (now Guiffre) in North Philly where I was hired back in the '70's to set up treatment programs for addicts and their families.

While I'd known for years of the racist practices of the police, (I'd run training programs for them about addictions and dealing with addicts in a non-violent way for two years), reading these stories was the beginning of my deeper level of understanding of how the criminal justice system conspires especially against black males.

One of the most beautiful classes was when I led them in a guided meditation to finding a "Safe Place" where they could feel free. Here are a few of their visions:

FINDING A SAFE PLACE

I was going along with my meditation, left and right brain hemispheres filled with Earthlight, spouting a cascade of sparkles until Judith spoke about drifting beyond these walls to a place of serenity. At that moment, my spirit stumbled, but gradually I found a way to scale these walls in my mind. I was transported to a seashore in the Caribbean. It was night and I was under a coconut tree with my back resting on the curved tree trunk. I was looking at the sky's orchestra of galaxies. The wind, cool and salty, coming in fresh from the sea, cut a constant rhythm. The waves hummed gently as they caressed the seashore and crept up to lick between my toes.

****

Winfield Patterson had never written before the class began. Though not a core part of the book project, his enthusiasm and heart contributed greatly to the group. This gentle soul has been in prison since he was twenty, at a cost to taxpayers of $875,000 so far.

Sanctuary for me is in the midst of a tropical rain forest just after the monsoon rains have washed over every square inch of this lush, green haven. It is so clean and alive. Soft, natural sounds of life sing pleasantly in my ears. Flashes of brilliant colors streak across the sunny sky as tropical birds. Enjoying their gift of flight, they spread their wings to catch the cool breeze of the wind, living ships that sail gracefully in our haven. In this place, I am happy, safe and at peace in my own Garden of Eden in my mind.

BEAUTY IN THE BEAST
by Malik Bey CL 2373

The beast is a huge monster with dimensions that cover 67 acres of land. It is a Leviathan of mega tons. The guts are concrete and steel that if used for a bridge could supply all the material to build another Golden Gate Bridge. Encased within the vast maze are tiny honeycomb caves filled with bee-like creatures that race and scurry about daily. At the extreme end of this beast, I found myself caught in a wonder of nature that shook my senses. I was inside the chapel behind locked doors. A small window was my only view to freedom. The first thing I noticed was snow falling, touching everything and everybody. There were guys in a dog kennel environment attempting to exercise their bodies after long hours of hold time. The snow does not discriminate as man does. As I watched, I saw a side of life that few noticed. I saw two odd shapes moving across the grounds, Canadian geese, just walking like an old, married couple on a morning stroll. My mind was boggled and it reeled at the sight of these beautiful, graceful birds, free to be a thousand miles away. Yet here, today, we are in the same place, a prison. Beauty knows no boundaries or limits. A simple thought and truth stands out for me. It is all a matter of perspective.
NO PRISON CAN HOLD MY MIND!

****

A bright, blinding light reflects off a vast pool of brilliant blue. The sand is momentarily covered by a film of milky foam as the water begins to ebb. Knee high waves usher in the next flow of foam. The water seems to continue on forever as I stare from my seated position amongst the skillions of specs of brown sand. No people. No places to be seen, just the wonderful light and roaring sounds of crashing waves. Time has no place here and I can be everything the world has never allowed me to be. Flying!

****

Heaven on earth. A hidden place thought not to exist, where my senses are alive and light flows into me constantly, healing the negativity that rains down constantly in this hellhole. The air is filled with the scent of roses, lavender and fragrant gardenias. There is celestial music and a feeling of universal love. I am safe.

****

I sit at my mother's kitchen table, just the two of us. We smile as our hearts overflow with the moment. This is something we've both longed for that always seems so far away and beyond the realms of possibility. Oh how long the road leading home has been. After traveling so far and experiencing so much, I embrace the comfort of this place. Here there is shelter, there is love, there is Mother. Snatched away from her and dragged off to a strange and hostile place, a place made of steel bars, concrete walls and evil guards. A place where there is no love, no family, no mother. Everything here is just as I left it; twenty years has not touched the sacredness and sanctity of my home.

****

The rooftop of our building was three stories high and covered with tar. The third floor apartment was abandoned, so it was easy for me to climb out the once-boarded up windows onto the fire escape where I could make my way to the top. This was my private spot. I had a lawn chair in a corner along with some clothes and other things. At night I gazed upon a million stars. This is where I came to be alone in times of trouble. Sometimes I would look down upon civilization and dream of a bright future filled with all the good things of life.

As they began to share their stories, the idea for this book was born.

Chapter Two
A PORTRAIT OF INNOCENCE

By Muti Ajamu-Osagboro
($735,000)

"You must make the injustice visible." Ghandi

At 39, Muti Ajamu-Osagboro could pass for twenty. Tall, slim and athletic, with dreadlocks framing fiercely intelligent eyes that flash with humor, Muti's life was stolen from him when he was seventeen. Sentenced to life in prison for a crime he not only did not commit but attempted to dissuade the perpetrators from committing, he has faced the daily challenges of remaining a decent human in prison with compassion, discipline and integrity.

With an incompetent attorney and a Philadelphia assistant district attorney, Richard Michaelson, who was later found to be a cocaine addict and dealer, the teenager didn't have a chance at justice, especially when one of the real criminals implicated him for a shorter sentence, less than 24 months, for himself. All four perpetrators have either pled guilty or confessed to the crime, exonerating Muti, but ultimately it may not matter. Recently disclosed evidence of his innocence remains clogged up in the judicial system. Without competent, courageous legal representation, which neither he nor his loving family can afford, his petition for freedom may never be heard at all.

Muti has not only survived but flourished, transforming himself, despite tremendous odds, into an accomplished writer, and an award-winning artist and poet.

****

"I was shocked at the number of inmates who had not received adequate counsel."

Former Pensylvania Attorney General, Ernie Preate

MUTI

"I am disturbed by the sentence. It seems unfair when another youth who cooperated in the investigation was allowed to plead guilty to third degree murder and faced only a possible 10 to 20 years in prison. You were not the actual shooter," said Judge Charles L. Durham as I stood before him at age 17 and was sentenced to mandatory life in prison for second degree murder. I was accused of being a lookout in a robbery that resulted in the accidental shooting of Korean grocer Sook Ja Yu in North Philadelphia.

That feeling was the most awful I'd ever experienced in my young life. Not only had I tried unsuccessfully to dissuade the others from their deeds when I realized they were serious, I had left the store and was walking fast more than half a block away when the fatal shot was fired. At the time of my trial, I had no idea that the man who prosecuted me, ADA Richard Michaelson, would soon resign after it was learned that he was a cocaine addict and dealer with underworld ties. The DA's office has never re-investigated his cases, for to do so would no doubt leave them vulnerable to the massive civil litigation that would certainly ensue.

Because of this, I am a political prisoner.

Unlike most of my peers, I had no record, didn't do drugs and had big plans for my life. Despite growing up in the infamous Richard Allen Homes in North Philadelphia, I didn't know that as a young Black male from the projects, I wasn't supposed to dream. I saw no limitations on my aspirations, no small feat in an environment notorious for crushing the goals and spirits of young people. I wanted to be part of the U.S. fencing team at the Olympics (I had already competed in the Junior Olympics). I had visions of being a professional magician (I was so serious I'd had business cards printed up).

My backup plan was to eventually take over my brother-in-law's heating oil company, Brown and Waller. He said I was gifted when it came to advertising. My sister, who ran her own successful business, told me what a good salesman I was, so I wanted to go to college to major in business with a minor in architecture, as designing buildings also fascinated me.

Unfortunately, I rarely applied myself at school because the curriculum, for the most part, was neither challenging nor relevant to the harsh realities I faced daily. I spent a lot of time making my classmates (and faculty) laugh because I always found humor in everyday dramas, (though after twenty-one years in this pit of pain, my sense of humor is wearing thin). Many teachers told me I was going to be the next Richard Pryor. I loved the school atmosphere; I was a sharp dresser and I could out dance anyone at parties and school events.
While everyone around me rode the trolley, I was the only one in my neighborhood with a silver and blue moped. I loved the feeling of freedom. The world was mine.

…while others struggle to remember,
I can neva forget/speedin' on my moped/no helmet on my head/my Ro-Ro in back wit hands around my waist…"
from "MY SWEET FORGET YOU NOT" 9/21/98

"Locked in Love" Oil on Canvas Muti Ajamu-Osagboro

Friends nicknamed me "Professor Rich Boy" because they said I was bright. Curious about a lot of things, I explored knowledge for its own sake. The "Rich Boy" part was because I would often feed them from our well-stocked refrigerator, which was a sharp contrast to their chronically empty ones. I actually believed my family was indeed rich, for the poverty I witnessed at the houses of others was brutal; the fundamental things people need to grow as human beings were missing in most of their homes.

When my mother, a divine woman, learned of my nickname, she laughed, a long, belly achin' laugh, and she said, "Rich, huh? I'm going to take you to work with me so you can see money doesn't grow on trees."

At 3:00 a.m. the next morning we were standing in the dark and cold, waiting for the trolley to take us to her job as a food server at the Youth Study Center (YSC). Once we were behind the steel doors and metal gates of the juvenile detention facility, she said, "I want you to look real good at their (young detainees) faces, because if you don't listen to me, this is what you will look like and where you will wind up."

I believed her.

My mother worked hard to provide creature comforts for me and my eight siblings. My father, in and out of our lives, did what he could when he was around. With a loving family, lots of books and magazines, and always plenty to eat, the abundant life inside my home was in stark contrast to the turmoil right outside the door. Our lives were surrounded by drugs and violence. The fact that my mother was able to maintain her sanity against this backdrop makes me both appreciate and marvel at her success even more.

As I got older, I was ripe for the encouragement of a dynamic community activist, Sister Nadirah Williams, co-organizer of the Million Women March. She convinced me that not only could I help my community, I was duty bound to give assistance wherever needed.

We organized pickets and effective demonstrations against the neglect of Richard Allen Homes by the city. Under Sister Nadirah's tutelage, I counseled the children, fed them breakfast and lunch, and supervised them in arts and crafts. We went to film festivals, nature walks in Fairmount Park, trips to the zoo, the Art Museum, the Academy of Natural Sciences, and local swimming pools. We cleaned up graffiti, painted walls, put out trash cans, swept up broken glass, and planted flowers and vegetables. Our rewards were block parties with bands and cookouts and certificates of service, which instilled community pride.

Sister Nadirah taught me the importance of fighting for freedom and getting in touch with my African roots and identity. I legally changed my name to constantly remind me of my life mission to build a foundation for growth centered in African culture. Muti Ajamu-Osagboro means he who protects from harm, makes his meanings clear and who fights for what he wants. This gives my very intelligent son, who was almost two when I went to prison, a strong, positive cultural identity.

Daily pain, terror and unrelenting suffering were not supposed to be my life.

Here's what really happened that fateful day.

It was a balmy, late afternoon on January 2, 1981. I stepped into the crisp sunshine for the first time that day and went to see a friend, Pierre, who also lived in the projects. Pierre wanted to stay in, so I left, looking for the inevitable party. While I was talking to an acquaintance named Buttons, four dudes walked by that I knew from the neighborhood, Elliot, Goldie, Robinson and Thomas. Elliot was loud and talked fast, one of my competitors in school for class clown. Goldie was shy and quiet. He used to live in the apartment below us, but had moved out of the projects months before and I hadn't seen him for a while. Robinson and I were just associates. Thomas was known in the neighborhood as a hobo sort, with dirty clothes, droopy body posture and a hair full of lint. He was thought to be retarded, and it was rumored he didn't know how to read or write. His older brother had been a member of one of the biggest gangs in the area and had served time at the YSC.

Although dead on her feet from work, my mother always took time when she arrived home to share many experiences of the juveniles that proved why it was important for me to stay away from drugs. She'd tell me all about dudes like Thomas' oldest brother and how I was to be careful around them because they could cause trouble in a blink of the eye.

That day, as the four walked quickly by, I called after them, asking where they were going. Thomas and Robinson ignored me, but Elliot said, "Come on, man." They were on their way to Robinson's house in another part of the projects so I went along having nothing better to do. Once there, Thomas pulled out some marijuana and some stuff in a brown bottle called "locker room" and they all got high. Even though everyone knew I didn't do drugs, he kept offering them to me despite my repeatedly saying no. They began to laugh and Thomas remarked that he wanted to buy my moped when they came back. Then Robinson pulled a gun out from under his pillow and gave it to Goldie. Seeing the gun was no big thing as they were common in the neighborhood. Thomas blurted out something about they were going to get the Koreans, as if they had an inside joke. I took their words and behavior to be a mixture of drug-induced ramblings and neighborhood braggadoccio. In the projects, it's called "frontin'" and you can hear similar chatter in any men's gymnasium or locker room.

I asked, "Which Koreans are you talking about and what are you going to do?" Thomas chimed in, "Just you wait and see." I thought nothing of it because Goldie not only worked for Koreans but was also good friends with some of them. Then someone said, "What time is it?" Robinson replied that it was almost 6 o'clock and time to leave.

I walked with them for about three blocks, and the whole time they were laughing wildly and acting very paranoid. Again, nothing unusual. At the corner of 12th and Mt. Vernon, a couple in a car near the corner called Robinson over. While they were talking, I went into the corner store for something to eat. Inside, I had to wait in line. Mr. And

Mrs. Yu, the owners, were at the front of the store. They were both nice people.

While I waited, Thomas, Elliot and Goldie came into the store. One suddenly had a hood on and another his collar turned up. The three were crouching as if trying to disguise themselves. Like a lightning bolt it hit me that the Koreans Thomas had referred to earlier were these particular people and the time was now! More shocked than scared, I immediately let them know that what they were about to do was wrong. They stared ahead blankly and didn't even acknowledge me. I told them I was leaving and wanted nothing to do with them or their obvious plan of robbery.

Outside, Robinson was still talking to the girl in the car. I turned back toward the projects and started walking fast, wanting to get as far away from them as I possibly could. When I was about half a block away, I heard what sounded like a gunshot, and I started to run, totally shaken. Once I got home at around 6:15 p.m., I stayed in for the rest of the night. I discussed what had happened with no one.

A couple of days later, Goldie came to my house, scared and shaking. Surprised, I asked him what had happened. He said the Korean woman was dead, which was the first I'd heard that someone had died. When I asked him if he'd shot her, he replied that she had hit the handle of the gun and it had accidentally gone off. He asked me what he should do and I told him he had to decide. About a week later, I saw his picture in handcuffs in the Philadelphia Daily News. Accompanied by his mother, he had surrendered to Daily News columnist Chuck Stone and another reporter, Linn Washington, (frequently a guest columnist for the Philadelphia Tribune). Goldie had confessed his crime to both reporters. Nothing in the police report mentions any involvement by me. (Robinson just recently confessed from prison to a reporter as well.)

Thomas, crying and petrified, came to my house for the first time, which was odd, a day or two after Goldie. I told him they should have listened to me and not done it. He said Robinson was hiding out in West Philly and he was thinking of doing the same. I told him just make sure he didn't get my name mixed up in his madness. He then said his sister Gail (a known criminal, police informant and drug addict) was trying to hook something up with the police in order to get him out of trouble. Thanks to a report I received recently from a federal investigator I learned that this was the reason (besides Thomas' being a juvenile) that Gail's name is on every false statement he made to the police implicating me. Thomas received a sentence of less than 2 years.

On May 5, 1981, detectives called my house and told my mother they wanted to routinely question me in the shooting death of Mrs. Sook Ja Yu. My mother said let's get it over with and, with two of my sisters, we drove to the Police Administration Building (the Roundhouse) so I could be questioned. When my mother told the police they couldn't question me without an attorney present, they immediately arrested me and charged me with conspiracy and homicide robbery. In my mother's (and my) worst nightmare, I was sent to the Youth Study Center. Robinson and Goldie had already been there for four months. I was arraigned, given a preliminary hearing and sent to trial. Thomas had implicated me in the crime as a lookout man.

When they first put the handcuffs on me, I was numb and thought how do you go into a store to buy a snack and come out with a conspiracy to commit homicide robbery? Though my mother had been retired for three years, each night when the YSC employees went home, I kept waiting for her to call me and tell me it was time to leave like she had done so many other times. It never happened.

As terrible as it was at the YSC, on my 18th birthday I was shipped off to the notorious Holmesburg Prison. From the outside, it looked like a castle from a horror movie, and from the inside, it made horror movies seem not so bad. The transport van rode over the gray 30' bridge and gigantic steel doors slammed behind me. The sterile silence allowed the boom from the shutting doors to echo and vibrate for several moments, the echo drowned out by a guard barking, "Happy Birthday!" while looking at my file.

The malice in his voice made me wonder if he was human.

Holmesburg Prison was rat-infested, always dank and dreary, cold and monotonous. (It has since been closed as unfit for humans.) Surrounded by so much negativity, I saw that I had to fight with everything I had to remain positive. I took weekly computer classes (there had been none in my high school) to further my education.

I soon learned that the state prison was far more sinister than Holmesburg. Life in prison was the evil twin to life in the projects: brutal law enforcement officials, drugs, violence, unemployment, overcrowding, broken spirits, despair as thick as fog, and fear hidden behind a macho facade. The people that work in the prison hate the people who "live" in them, just like those who work in the projects. Many guards use the prison as their personal fiefdom where they not only play with the lives of prisoners like they are chess pieces, but they also enrich their pockets with everything from petty crime to fraud and extortion. Rape and murder are not unusual.

Though I've witnessed savage brutality by county and state prison guards, the state's correctional officers' sanitized version of crime shocked me the most. They plant knives or some other weapon or drugs in a prisoner's cell to get a "bust" on the prisoner, which is how the guard can get promoted in rank or pay scale. This keeps the prisoner in longer and may interfere with his going home. Some guards are as humane as an inhumane environment will allow, but they are few. Prisoners who are "busted" can't receive visitors and many family members are harassed when they do come to visit. Fathering my son from prison has been challenging; when he and I are able to fight through the relentless and arbitrary rule changes, we steal some joy, however briefly.

"…you don't know the half/captives are raped by correctional staff/lame ass obese negresses ignore the aftermath. Affirmed by the affidavit-that take on and defeat Goliath-'cept dis ain't Biblical/it's literal littering the internal field of dreams/Kafka themes…"

from "RUBIC COUNTRY: THE TRILOGY 12/31/99

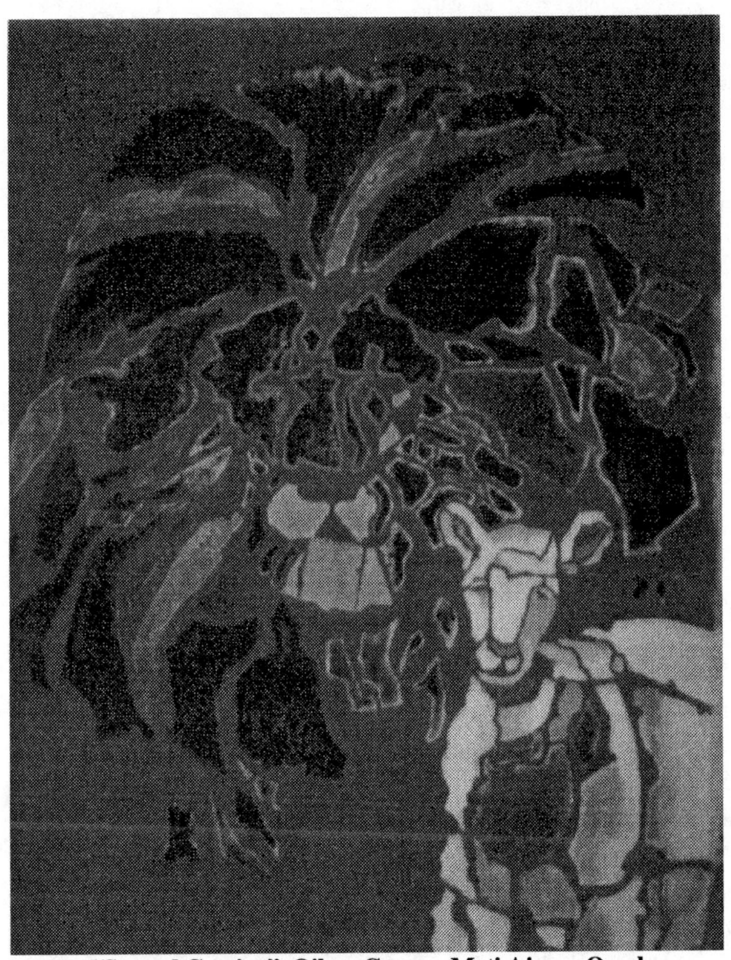

"Second Coming" Oil on Canvas Muti Ajamu-Osagboro

Back to my story. About three years later, I saw Elliot at Camp Hill. He said he'd gotten 5-10 years for the shooting. He apologized for calling me to join them on that ill-fated day. I told him that my grief stemmed from Thomas' lies that I was involved, which he told in order to save himself. When I read the police report interview which he allegedly made of his own volition, the language in his statement is that of an educated person, someone with a basic command of standard English, but not that of a teenager who is mildly retarded, has spoken Ebonics all his life and can barely read and write. (Thomas has since signed an affidavit stating that he said whatever ADA Michaelson wanted him to say.)

My "trial" was a travesty. Prosecutor Michaelson, not only broke several laws but he also violated my constitutional rights in order to get a conviction.

"Assistant District Attorney Richard Michaelson has been suspended without pay from the D.A.'s office pending an investigation by the U.S. Attorney's Office and the F.B.I. into allegation of possible wrongdoing...Sources said that federal officials are investigating Michaelson's involvement in a narcotics case and possibly in drug trafficking."

Philadelphia Daily News, May 27, 1982

"(mob) Drug dealer turned F.B.I. informant Ronald Raiton has told federal investigators that he sold a large quantity of cocaine to Assistant District Attorney, Richard Michaelson, on a Caribbean island...Michaelson resigned Thursday. The Daily News has learned the DA's office conducted an internal investigation of Michaelson in 1979, after he appeared at least twice as a spectator at the Municipal Court trial for (Joseph N.) Disantis, Jr. (mobster) and was seen talking to him." Philadelphia Daily News May 29, 1982.

(This type of misconduct continues unchecked, justified and harbored by current DA, Lynn Abraham, according to a 1997 expose' by Philadelphia Magazine. In addition, a report by the Defenders Association of Philadelphia documents the historic pattern and practice of racial profiling by the District Attorney's office in the selection of juries, calling it "Southern Justice in the City of Brotherly Love.)

Michaelson got Thomas to give false testimony against me to the trial judge Charles L. Durham (now deceased). Thomas testified that the DA's office never promised him anything in exchange for his testimony against me. Actually Michaelson promised and delivered to Thomas: employment, time served, release on bail, warrants from a previous conviction lifted, no penalty for previous violations of probation and suppression of his previous criminal record. He was told he would be home by Christmas if he didn't mention the deal to the judge. In exchange for his false testimony that caused me to be sent away for life without any possibility of parole, the reward he got from Michaelson was less than 24 months for a homicide-robbery he admitted he'd planned.

Judge Durham never learned about the criminal actions of the prosecutor. Had he known, his growing suspicion of the relationship between Thomas and the prosecutor would have compelled him to drop all charges against me. To make matters worse, the prosecutor allowed Thomas to give false testimony about the planning of the robbery, telling the judge the plan was hatched at Goldie's house in Richard Allen on the same day as the crime. Michaelson knew the conspiratorial conversation never took place as Goldie had moved out of that house at least 6 months before. According to the law, by creating my involvement in a conspiracy where none existed, this made me subject to everything that happened after the fact, the robbery-homicide.

My court-appointed attorney, Arlan Mintz Kardon, was grossly incompetent and inexperienced in homicide criminal defense law. She allowed the prosecutor to trample any constitutional rights I had. She coerced me to take the stand in my own defense, and the prosecutor, with deceitful and knowingly false questions, got me confused and I incriminated myself before I knew what was happening. He drew inferences where none existed. My seventeen-year-old naivete' was no match for the raw and well-seasoned misconduct of the prosecutor.

Unbelievably, Ms. Mintz didn't perform basic legal procedures such as researching, investigating and interviewing known witnesses who would have totally refuted Thomas' testimony and the entire basis of the Commonwealth's case. In spite of my lawyer's incompetence and Thomas' perjury, it was the unchecked power by prosecutor Michaelson that put me, an innocent man, in prison for life, and gave Thomas, the real criminal, his freedom after 24 months. This miscarriage of justice could be stopped by the DA's office based on the law and its code of ethics at any point, but that never happens. Only **convictions** go on the resumes of the politically hungry; the DA's office is a proverbial stepping stone to power, only in Philadelphia the stones are melinated flesh and destroyed lives and families.

In a 1992 ruling in the case of Commonwealth vs. Scarfo, the Pennsylvania State Supreme Court, in an unprecedented admission, said about the Philadelphia District Attorney's office, "We are especially concerned that prosecutorial misconduct seems to arise in Philadelphia County more than any other county in the Commonwealth."

To see how prosecutors in Philadelphia routinely circumvent and break the law, listen to former Assistant District Attorney, Jack McMahon, as he instructs new prosecutors about how to select a jury in a training tape entitled, "Prosecutorial Instructional Training Tape." McMahon, now in private practice, after making several racist remarks about Black people and how to keep them from sitting on juries in homicide cases says: "Let's face it, there's Blacks from low-income areas…you don't want those people on juries; in selecting Blacks, you don't want the real educated ones…" He concludes, "The law says the object of getting a jury is to get a competent, fair and impartial jury. Well, that's ridiculous. You're not trying to get that. You are there to win…the only way you're going to do your best is to get jurors that are unfair and more likely to convict than anybody else in that room."

If prosecutors would break the law to deny the constitutional rights of Black, tax-paying, educated citizens who've not been accused of any crime, how many laws will they break to deny the rights of Black defendants waiting to be tried? The answer is breaking as many laws as necessary to get a conviction...justice be damned!

Judge Durham, in a non-jury trial, after hearing only part of the evidence, found me guilty of conspiracy, robbery and second degree murder and then sentenced me to LIFE. He said, **"I want the record to reflect that if I had any discretion in this case as far as the sentencing, it would not be one that the statute provides for. I want that on the record because I think his part in the conspiracy doesn't warrant the type of sentence the law says is mandatory."**

After my sentencing, my world shrank to a 13 ½' by 5' by 8' cage, which is smaller than most bathrooms. I couldn't have gotten through those early days without the continuous support of my family, especially my beloved sister, Rosalyn , whose visits both comforted strengthened me.

> ***...Imagine every night a steel door shut and sealed like a Pharoah's tomb-but you ain't no dead king. Steel windows wit chicken wire-but you ain't no rooster. Stretchin' your arms out and touchin' both walls like a sardine can-but you ain't no fish...Somebody thinks this is a zoo and a cemetery."***
>
> ***From IMAGINE: Y2KAGES" 1/4/00***

"Self-portrait" Oil on Canvas Muti Ajamu-Osagboro

I began to study law, completed my G.E.D., studied electronics and learned how to tutor the illiterate. I developed an Afrikan-centered curriculum for the literacy program to make it more relevant to the students. I earned an Associates Degree in Business Administration and Accounting and additional college credits. (A lot of these educational opportunities have been discontinued so politicians can prove they're tough on crime.) As chairman of the Graterford branch of the NAACP's Press and Publicity Committee, I learned how the media does not seem interested in listening to the voices of the suffering.

My quest to undo the damage done by my attorney and the District Attorney turned me inward. I began a spiritual journey to learn who I was and what my life's mission could be under these circumstances. My independent studies enabled me to tap into my spirituality, which gave focus to my strength and allowed me to better comprehend why and how this was happening. New vistas opened to me as I began to connect with new possibilities. Beautiful things began to awaken and pour out of me, parts of me I thought had been killed in that courtroom. I became a teacher and started helping prisoners learn the law, how to read (a problem for more than half of the imprisoned), how to get a job in order to make parole etc. I discovered a talent for writing, and have created songs, plays, essays, books and poetry. When I started drawing and painting, the creative process was cathartic. I was amazed when I entered my work in several art exhibits and people from all walks of life responded enthusiastically. My work was part of four exhibits in Philadelphia, one at the infamous Eastern State Penitentiary in Philadelphia, now a historical site where horror movies are made. One of my art instructors is Philadelphia's nationally-recognized treasure, Lily Yeh. Another is Kevin O'Neill of the Painted Bride Art Center.

As I devoted my energies to my studies and to helping others, I began to mend the emotional wounds of being imprisoned for something I did not do. It requires strong vigilance to remove the daily, psychological shrapnel that the prison constantly hurls at me; I'm convinced I have Divine protection.

While I was doing my best to blossom without sunshine or spring rain, my sister Rosalyn hired a series of attorneys who were glad to take her hard-earned money without filing a single petition on my behalf. None of them had the courage or integrity to challenge the District Attorney's office.

Muti's beloved sister, Rosalyn Payne

Currently acting as my own attorney, I've filed a Post Conviction Relief Act (PCRA) petition after receiving a package from a federal investigator with proof of my innocence. My petition was "dismissed pending appeal" in February, 2001. I also have two additional petitions pending in the PA State Superior Court. Proof of my innocence is in the cumbersome wheels of justice. I'd feel more confident if I could afford a lawyer I could trust to oversee my petition's progress through the courts.

I see myself becoming free, very soon. Once people learn what is really going on in courtrooms, my unjust sentence cannot stand up under fair, legal scrutiny. When I was first imprisoned, I promised myself I would keep four things: my desire to learn and grow; my sanity; my manhood, and my love for my people. Because of the support I've received, these four qualities are not only intact but have grown in ways I could never have imagined.

Once I'm free, the first thing I want to do is visit my father's and mother's graves. They've both died since I've been in this house of horrors, and the PA Department of Corrections would not permit me to go to either of their funerals.

I look forward to simple things, like going to the refrigerator when I want a snack, swimming and biking. I want to take long, luxurious baths. I want to explore landscape painting, and work on my books. I want to do what I can to help my community, especially the young people, who are so confused. I want to smell freshly-cut grass as I picnic in the park or go hiking in the woods.

Most of all, I want to be free to enjoy life like a man is supposed to

Muti Ajamu-Osagboro	Free Muti Now Defense Com.
AM-6021	P.O. Box 14102
Box 244	Phila., PA 19138
Graterford, PA 19426	RosalynPayne@Comcast.net

****

Ed Coleman is a graduate student at Temple University, who met Muti when he came to the prison to teach a Pan-African Studies course. After getting to know him and learning that both he and Muti grew up in the Richard Allen Homes, he was inspired to write the following poem:

A Blues For Muti in B Sharp

Beaten
Battered
Bruised Bodies
Strewn like discarded crack vials
Once filled with the illusion of freedom
Across a battlefield of
Red White and Blue
C's
Constitutionally castrated

Castigated as three-fifths
Confined as 2.6 million
Beaten
Battered
But victorious Lovers of freedom identified by their scars
Bruised Bodies
Strewn like discarded crack vials
Once filled with the illusion of freedom
Across a battlefield of
Red White and Blue
Ticker tape parades
Across the morning, midday, evening
and breaking news
Reports of pathological criminals laying
in the bush
To enslave innocent men women and
children
For a crime they couldn't commit
When the charge is melanin
Bodies
Beaten
Battered
Bruised Bodies
Strewn like discarded crack vials
Once filled with the illusion of freedom
Across a battlefield of
Red White and Blue
Giving way to Red Green and Black
Bodies
Beaten
Battered
Bruised
But victorious
Lovers of freedom
Identified by their scars

"It is one of the most beautiful compensations of life that no man can sincerely try to help another without helping himself." Ralph Waldo Emerson

Muti at work

"Defacto criminalization of black manhood-under the guise of a tough-on-crime pose, means we have built the foundation of a world without African-American men. We've become used to throwing away these men's lives without making even the first effort at redemption. We've come to see it as normal, part of black men's reality."

Leonard Pitts

"Ka Liberation" Oil on Canvas Muti Ajamu-Osagboro

***"The ultimate weakness of violence is that it is a descending spiral, begetting the very thing it seeks to destroy. Instead of diminishing evil, it multiplies it. Through violence you may murder the liar, but you cannot murder the lie, nor establish the truth…Violence merely increases hate…Hate cannot drive out hate; only love can do that."* Martin Luther King, Jr.**

Chapter Three
PREFERENTIAL TREATMENT?

"MICHAEL KING"
($770,000)

SageWriters, Box 215, Swarthmore, PA 19081

Unlike that of Muti in the previous chapter, the life of Michael King (not his real name) has been filled with poverty, abandonment, sexual abuse and addiction. Son of a deaf-mute mother who was "forced" by his heroin-addicted father, Michael and his sister are the only ones in their family who are not hearing impaired. Encouraged by a step-sibling, he began stealing at age six. In addition to getting him money or things he wanted, the stealing he soon realized gave him a "rush." By his teens, he'd discovered drugs and his stealing took on a new urgency to support his habit.

Now 34, Michael is a handsome man with blond hair and blue eyes, an all-American looking guy. He's a repeat, multiple offender who's spent most of his life in institutions and in trouble with the law. He's stolen and vandalized thousands of dollars worth of property. He has thirteen felony convictions for burglary, one federal conviction and three other felony convictions in other states. Currently serving an amazingly short sentence of three years, he feels once again he's receiving preferential treatment by the criminal justice system because he's white. He has never gone to trial because he's always been caught red-handed.

He's been in many treatment programs, not unusual for addicts, and fears that he may have become "treatment resistant."

Though they write, he hasn't seen his sister for eleven years, and like most prisoners, rarely has visitors. His mother died of cancer three years ago. "I burned my bridges a while ago with my repeated trips to prison and my abuse of drugs. I must deal with the consequences of my actions. In some ways, though visits are pleasant, they can be stressful. I understand the effects my life experiences have had on my psyche, but I don't make excuses for the decisions I've made or who I am, nor will I deny my feelings and desires."

Can he change? Will he continue to be a menace to society?

In the writing class he was excited to discover that he has a vivid imagination and a knack for story telling. He knows he has to straighten up and get his life in order even though he hasn't had much success living on the outside. He hasn't seen his son and daughter in two years, and he wants to improve himself enough to become the father he never had. He's waiting for a place in Graterford's Parenting Program, hoping he can learn to be a good father.

He found the experience of writing his story cathartic.

MICHAEL

It's been said that time is our most precious commodity, but in prison, it's man's worst enemy. Either you're thinking of sex and the good times of the past, or the future, but never the present. Fortunately I have a future, which is more than can be said for the many thousands in this prison. I know several dozen Lifers, and there isn't a day that goes by that I'm not grateful for the breaks I've been given. The truth is I should be doing more time than three years because I'm a multiple repeat offender, and I wonder if the short sentence has anything to do with the color of my skin. The man in the next cell is in for five years for stealing a case of beer, his first offense. Guess what color his skin is?

There is no doubt in my mind whatsoever that if I was put in front of a sentencing judge today and if my skin was anything but white I'd be spending at least twenty years rotting away in this snakepit. Of course if you are a man of means, your chances for "justice" are dramatically increased in your favor.

It's never completely quiet in prison. It's noisiest during the day, but at night there's always the sound of toilets flushing, pipes creaking, or someone crying out with a nightmare. Even in the early morning hours you can hear the radio, which the guards turn up full blast every night, I'm sure to annoy us. After the final lockdown at night is when I find myself through reading or writing.

I have a son and daughter that don't really know me. I've been in and out of their lives so many times that I fear I have caused harm. I've decided that I have to prove I can be responsible for myself before I ask to be let into their lives again. I've had no contact for two years because of their mother. I cannot blame her for this even though I feel bitter and sad inside. By the time of my release, hopefully in 2003, I'll be 35 years old. I'm long past due for being a responsible person. I have skills that I intend to utilize but my top priority will be completing my parole incident-free, which for me means staying drug free, something that has eluded me to this point.

I was born in1965 in Milwaukee to a deaf mute who was a printer by trade. It wasn't easy for her to find work because of her handicap. My older sister, Amy, and I quickly developed sign-language skills so we could communicate with my mother and other family members. Why my sister and I aren't deaf is a small miracle because the majority of the family is, including aunts, uncles and cousins. Amy and I had to be good spellers in order to sign, which I believe gave my education a jump start. Feelings were not expressed, and this probably played a negative role in my emotional development.

By the age of five we were living in an apartment on the south side of Chicago. Our grandmother lived nearby and we stayed there while my mother worked. In the back of her apartment building was a great maze of wooden steps where we'd play for hours. I still get a warm feeling deep in the pit of my stomach when I recall those stairs.

One of the biggest regrets of my life is never knowing my father. I can't begin to explain the bitterness inside from not having the presence of someone I could look up to in my life. I can't tell you how my father walked and talked, how he smelled, whether he was tall and skinny or short and broad. With the exception of a faded black and white photo of him sitting at a kitchen table, I can barely tell you the shape of his eyes or face. I've had to rely on my mother's version of who he was, and she's been dead now for over three years. Her memories weren't pretty. The few times she'd talk about him she said he was a heroin addict and a no good drunk who forced himself on her and I was conceived as a result. When I was sixteen and we were living in east Texas, we were contacted by his family in St. Louis and told of his death. There was no money to attend his funeral.

Since early childhood, I've been in trouble with the law. I'm sure if you lined up ten psychologists and asked them what was wrong with me, you'd get ten different answers ranging from I'm a product of my environment to I'm a borderline personality disorder.

What a bunch of crap. I wasn't that different than many other kids. The bottom line is I've always enjoyed living on the edge, and I'm a creature of my desires. I rarely worry about consequences, and despite my many arrests, I've gotten away with a lot of crimes. Fortunately I've only ever harmed myself, though I've come close to doing something that would keep me here forever.

For a short time in my life, when I was about five, I did have a stepfather. Jim was a deaf-mute like my mother. They met through a deaf bowling league. Jim was tall and lanky with a beer belly like a bowling ball. He had two kids of his own, Ronnie, who was a few years older than me, and Jenny who was a year younger. It was Ronnie who was my mentor in creating my life of crime. Jim worked as a foreman for the Chicago Tribune, and for the two short years my mother was married to him, Jim provided us with a comfortable, middle-class lifestyle in the suburbs.

Gary, another deaf-mute, lived in the basement. Deaf mutes have their own communities just like any other ethnic group. Most deaf mute households keep boarders who are also deaf mutes but suffer from additional handicaps like retardation, partial paralysis etc. These boarders perform household duties and provide additional income from social security or menial jobs in the work force. Gary was slightly retarded and crippled in both hands, which meant he couldn't sign. All the kids loved good-natured Gary, but Jim kept him as a boarder for another reason. Gary was a true hustler and used his handicap to great advantage. Weekday mornings on his way to work, Jim would drop Gary at a designated spot where he panhandled sign-language cards. Even if you didn't know Gary you could tell he was afflicted. Gary made between $200-300 a day, which in the seventies wasn't chump change. Jim got it all, and his bedroom was stacked with hundreds of dollars in rolls of coins.

When Ronnie suggested we steal from Jim, his own father, I'm not sure why I agreed. Jim wasn't a bad man and he'd bought me a ten-speed bike for my sixth birthday. Once I started, I didn't quit. Even at that innocent age, I got a rush from stealing. Jim became suspicious and changed the locks on his door, but nothing stopped us. We always had more money than any of the other kids in the neighborhood.

Each Sunday we were required to go to church, and we'd put in an appearance in our Sunday best and then head for the record store across the street from the church where there were pinball machines and other interesting paraphernalia. We'd spend the time playing games and listening to records. With the exception of Sunday services later during my time at Boy's Harbor, this was the extent of my religious career. I don't believe in a lot of things, but I do believe in man's capacity for evil, and to a lesser degree, good.

By the time I was eight or nine, I couldn't be trusted around anything. My own mother didn't trust me. We moved a lot and were on welfare much of the time. When I was ten, my mother packed us up again, this time for Cedar Bayou, Texas. She had relatives there who would let us live in a trailer they owned. I thought of it as an adventure, though Cedar Bayou and Chicago's South Side were light years apart. Now I was in the land of steers, where football is king and chewing tobacco the nectar of the gods.

My stealing continued until one night I crossed the line and stole my mother's car. When I got into an accident and fled, I denied everything, but people in the other car identified me as the small boy running away. At her wits end, my mother was convinced that I should be placed in a boys' home. I felt totally rejected by her.

Boys' Harbor was by the Bay of Galveston. There were about sixty kids in four cottages according to age. Each cottage had a married couple who were supposed to be substitute parents. Everyone there was either abandoned, a discipline problem or ordered by the courts. For some reason, the two years I was there I kept my stealing to a minimum and I did well in my classes. I was encouraged to do well and for a time I felt accepted. After two years, when

I was twelve, I started to rebel and finally my mother was told to come and get me.

Gary was my mother's latest boyfriend. He looked like Grizzly Adams and drove an old Ford Galaxy 500. He could hear and speak, which was unusual for my mother, as in the past she only associated with deaf mutes. I felt unwelcome. Mom's eyes were full of love for me, but she worried about my future.

Soon I was back to my old tricks and there were nights when I didn't come home at all to sleep on the couch. I had discovered drugs. Cruising the streets, I often ran across other kids like myself. Mom and Gary knew I was high; I didn't even try to hide it. Gary finally told my mother I had to go as I was also stealing from him to buy the drugs. Mom asked my sister if I could stay with her in Baytown, about 45 minutes from Houston. For all the pain and suffering I put my sister through over the years, she never has turned her back on me to this day.

Amy was staying with an older man named Lawrence and his mother. They were poor. They lived in a 28 ft. trailer that was on its last legs, with two tiny bedrooms. My place again was the couch. Though they were barely scraping by, the fact that they took me in had a powerful influence on my life. Lawrence's main source of money was selling weed and hash. He treated me with kindness and always took me along with him no matter where he went, becoming a role model in my eyes. From Lawrence I learned how to deal drugs, how to shoot a gun, and what to watch out for in people who might be cops. We were always high.

I stayed with them for about nine months until I was caught creeping into a lady's house to steal her purse. That earned me a year in juvenile hall, where I soon learned to fight or be walked on. No matter where you are placed in the system, the juvenile detention centers are the worst, because the young and dumb just don't understand the consequences of their actions, and this makes them dangerous. Most of the kids were Mexicans and Blacks, and being white was a strike against me, making me an easy target. I always had to prove myself no matter where I went because of my skin color and the automatic assumption that I was a chump.

Two months before my release, my sister came to visit and told me that Lawrence's mother had found him dead in the field behind the trailer. I felt confused. The dreams I had of us being together were gone. To me, he was like he father I never had. He had overdosed, and Amy was hitting the road with some other dude. I wouldn't see her again until 1990, eight years later. Amy once wrote in a letter, "We're not normal people."

Not sure where to go upon release, the staff had already contacted my mother and Gary. Two weeks before leaving, I received a letter from my Great Uncle Warren telling me that I would be staying with him. It seems Gary didn't want me around. My mother came to visit and explained to me that she wasn't able to afford the things I needed since I was getting ready to start ninth grade. So off I went back to Milwaukee and Great Uncle Warren, the official leader of our so-called family. He communicated with a combination of sign language and verbal skills. Now, with advanced emphysema, he was unable to leave the house. He was a curious looking man, appearing much older than sixty-two, with an indented hole right next to the middle of his forehead from an accident years ago. He was never without oxygen and his bedside table was filled with every medication known to mankind. Warren had money; he had a fabulous gun collection and a coin and stamp collection I was already scheming to steal. From the moment I arrived, I was given everything I needed and much of what I wanted. I was soon to learn a harsh lesson that few things in the world are free.

To this day I still feel twinges of shame when I remember it. My bed, a twin, was in the same room as my uncle's and the first time it happened, I was shocked and confused. One night around 10:00 p.m., I noticed Warren was still awake, which was unusual. When he asked me to come and lie next to him so we could talk, I felt uncomfortable but not alarmed. He told me how lonely he was and he started fondling me. I just froze up, unable to move. I told him I was tired and wanted to go to sleep, but I was burning with shame and vowed to take this dark secret to my grave. It happened several more times during my stay and I never once said no; I guess I didn't have it in me to reject him. Actually, I had an odd feeling of love toward him.

Another guy and I skipped 9th grade one day and we got an older guy to buy us a bottle of cognac with money I stole from Warren. I also took two matching pearl-handled 38 revolvers. We were going to find a victim to rob. We picked out an older guy just coming from a bank. He ran when he saw us following him and we caught him and wrestled with him in the snow. I remembered the gun when it started to slip from my belt, and I took it out and waved it at the terrified man. The liquor had me feeling mean and uncaring. My finger was on the trigger and I remember thinking what would it be like if I shot this person. You know what saved the man's life? He pissed his pants and when my partner pointed it out, we ended up laughing so hard the man just ran away. We got another bottle and we both got so smashed that my friend passed out on the street and ended up in the hospital with pneumonia.

I never did get my hands on that coin and stamp collection. Soon after the gun scene, my uncle had a major attack and was admitted to the hospital. His son Wally hated my guts and used my uncle's absence to get rid of me. He put me on a Greyhound bus to Houston with no money or food. It took me three days to get there, and another two days to contact my mother, during which I lived in the bus station.

One of the worst places to be in a large city is the bus station, a haven for all types of predators. After three days without food and no money in my pocket, I was an easy target. I kept calling collect the number I had for Gary, but got no answer. I had no choice but to wait at the terminal, and I was desperate. I slept on a bench, and I think it was only my young age and my obvious poor condition that kept them from running me off or arresting me.

By the next evening I contemplated leaving the terminal and taking my chances. An older man with a beer belly who was pulling a dolly of packages asked me if I was o.k. and I almost broke down and cried. After hearing my story, he explained that he and his son were couriers, delivering packages to the bus station and airport. He offered to let me come with him until I could contact my mother. I accepted his offer, not seeing any other possibilities. As we got into his van, his son, a man in his early twenties, did not acknowledge my presence. When the man asked me if I was tired and I said yes, he reached into the glove compartment and took out some pills, telling me it was speed and it would help me stay awake. I swallowed one, and an hour later felt a prickly sensation in my scalp. We had dinner at McDonald's before going to his two-bedroom apartment. His son never said a word to me or made eye contact; soon I'd know why.

The man offered me his couch for as long as it took for me to find my mother. The son went into his bedroom and shut the door. I made myself comfortable in front of the television and the man went into his room, I thought to sleep. After half an hour, he came out butt ass naked, carrying porno magazines. I kept staring at the television when he sat down next to me and asked me if I wanted to look at some magazines with him. I said no, feeling very afraid and not sure what was going to happen. After a few minutes I heard his heavy breathing as he flipped the pages of the magazines. He soon groaned then and sat motionless. I can't describe the feelings and thoughts that went through me as I sat with my eyes fixed on tv. I only knew I wished I was anyplace else. Without saying anything, the man got up and went back into his room. Between the speed and the fear, I barely slept. I knew I was out of there the next day no matter what. In the morning, he gave me $10 to run to the store for cereal and milk. On my way out, I peeked through the kitchen door to see him putting his wallet in the sugar jar. My spirits soared because whether or not I was able to contact my mother, I knew I wouldn't be broke. By 10:00 o'clock that morning, Gary answered the phone, surprised to hear my voice. After explaining to him what had happened, he said he and my mother would come and pick me up.

Before they arrived, the man went into the bathroom and I stole his wallet. I justified it by telling myself he was a pervert, but had none of that happened and the old man only showed me kindness, I still would have taken it. The wallet yielded $80 and some credit cards that I threw out the window.

The first thing Gary told me was that we were moving to a small town called Palestine about three hours away, where he had a job. His parents lived there and he had a two bedroom cottage where we'd live

Palestine was a hick town of about 10,000 people, with two movie theaters, a bowling alley, mall and pharmacy where the old-timers gathered to gossip. This is where I met my two best friends, Johnny Salmon and Roger Hilton. We did everything together no matter what it was. It was quickly established that I was the leader because of my vast life experiences and balls of steel. Weekends we'd scrape our money together and get a bottle of Jim Beam and some weed from the projects. Occasionally Johnny would steal some Valium or Dalmane from his mother's stash and we'd pop those for good measure. We'd always end up down at the river, bombed out of our minds, sitting around a huge fire and thinking of ways we could get rich.

I came up with the bright idea of robbing the pharmacy at gunpoint. The next day, after we chased our massive hangovers away with beer and a joint or two, we waited in a field behind the store and staked the place out. In reality, I was trying to work up the nerve when suddenly the door opened and the employees came out. The store was closing. Secretly, we were all relieved. Deciding instead to break in, we waited until nightfall and, with burglary tools- a crowbar, a pair of bolt cutters and gloves- I volunteered to be the one to climb onto the roof and cut the power to the alarm. Dumb ass me had no idea how much juice was running through this line, and when I put the cutters around the wire and clamped down, I was thrown off the roof and landed on my side, breaking my leg and fracturing my arm. The head of the cutter was completely melted; the only thing that saved my life that night was the rubber grips.

When Johnny and Roger got me to the hospital, I lied and said I'd fallen from a tree. After eight weeks, things were heating up between me and Gary, for not only was I stealing money from him, but I also took some of the pain medication he took for an earlier shoulder injury. We ended up in a fighting match when he confronted me, and when his gun-toting father intervened and the neighbors called the police, I knew I was in trouble. Gary had the police evict me and my mother, and we had no money or place to live. The police ended up taking us to a woman's house where she took in single mothers and their children. It was one thing for me to be thrown out, but I felt bad about dragging my mother down with me. I believe my mother knew it was going to happen anyway, so she stoically accepted our fate. She was a real trooper.

The woman who owned the house was kind. At fifteen, I was still a virgin, and the woman's daughter, Debbie, started plotting to get me in bed before I realized it. She was 26, had two children, and was married to a big shot lawyer. A real estate manager, Debbie got me alone one day and started kissing and fondling me, and telling me she wanted me. I was unsure of what to do; I was definitely aroused. She told me nothing would happen until she moved me and my mother into an apartment that she'd set up for us. It was in a three-story art deco building in the middle of Palestine. I have fond memories of the countless hours I spent alone and pondering my life from the rooftop of that building. I had my own bedroom for the first time in my life.

Debbie came over at 5:00 a.m. three or four times a week with a cheap bottle of wine. My mother knew what was going on, but never objected. I was having a good time. I dropped out of school and got a job at the Bonanza Steak House. Roger, Johnny and I started messing with coke and Quaaludes when we could get them. If we didn't have the money we would case a place out and rob it, it was that simple. The cops began snooping around Johnny and Roger's houses asking questions about me, and it looked like Debbie's daughter, who didn't like me, was going to rat to her old man.

I was sixteen years old going on seventeen now and I knew I was going to have to make a move. My mother had accepted a printing job in Houston. I'd heard some old timers talking about the benefits of the military on their own sons and how good the experience was for young men. I was thinking this was my ticket out. I had to wait until I was seventeen and I would still need a note from my mother. Debbie moved me across the hall to an empty apartment and said she'd cover the expenses until I left for the Navy, but we wouldn't be spending any more time with each other. I wasn't surprised.

My mind was on the future and I was on my own.

I did well at boot camp and was training to be a yeoman, a glorified secretary. The last weekend of our stay, I dated a woman from New York, Marie, who was sixteen years older than me. This thing with older women was getting to be a habit and this was my pattern for many years to come. At least older women didn't play games.

After my training in Meridian, Mississippi, I was assigned to the Willow Grove Naval Base in Pennsylvania. Every weekend the place was full of reservists from all the service branches; I was one of 300 full-time military personnel that lived and worked on the base.

Philadelphia was about 30 minutes away and this is where I would score my drugs. My first taste of free-basing cocaine came through another active duty person. From the moment I took that first hit I knew that I was going to take a much different approach to everything I did. The intensity of free basing has no equal. You can never get enough, so you're constantly looking for sources of money. I never had enough money in my pocket for drugs so I started back on my old ways.

I got a job at Christmas in the on-base liquor store, figuring an opportunity would come up for me to make a few extra bucks. I hadn't been able to steal much, just a few cases here and there, but my luck would soon change.

One night, while sitting in my car and waiting for it to warm up, I saw the manager through the plate glass window as he dropped what looked like paper bags into a mail slot that was hidden behind a picture. I knew he was dropping the days receipts, and I started scheming. I stole a crowbar from maintenance and the next night waited in a bathroom until the building closed. The mail slot emptied into a 600 pound iron safe in a small closet. I didn't have a cutting torch, so I decided to let gravity work for me. If I could get the safe upside down the bags would slip to the bottom and I could reach in and pick them out. If someone had been watching me trying to wrestle this 600 pound safe they'd still be laughing today. I started rocking the behemoth back and forth until it crashed to the floor. I waited about twenty minutes to see if anyone had heard the crash, but no one came. By 3:00 a.m. I'd gotten all I'd come for and left through a fire exit, which set off an alarm but I was by then safely back in my room before the base police responded.

There was more money than I'd ever seen, $16,000 and several thousands more in checks, which I promptly threw away. I panicked and decided to go AWOL the next day, which immediately caused suspicion. I took a plane to Houston and my mother, and hooked up again with my old buddy Roger Hilton from East Texas, who was living there with his family. We got an apartment together, and by that time we were full-blown druggies. I sold drugs while he worked and every night was a party. I managed to stay high for six months until my mother warned me that U.S. marshals were asking about me. I was just about out of money since the drug business went bust because Roger and I were our best customers. To save Mom from the trauma, I decided to turn myself in.

When they took me back to Willow Grove, I was immediately questioned about the missing money. I denied it, and since they had no evidence they had to release me. I was given a Captain's Mast for the AWOL, a lesser form of punishment than a court martial, but I never made it to the mast because two days later I tried to sneak some stereo equipment off base and the authorities were waiting. I was sent to the brig to wait to be court martialed. I was by now eighteen, and I knew I was in serious trouble because the military courts were supposedly much harsher than civilian courts. I got the first of many breaks I would get from the system when I made a deal for two years. They could only prove I'd stolen the stereo equipment though they knew I'd also robbed the safe.

The minimum security brig was small by prison standards with only 300 prisoners, and it was run like boot camp. There was also a female barracks, and once or twice a week a girl I worked next to and I would sneak into a storeroom and have sex.

One day I got a visit from Janet, a local girl I'd dated from time to time when she visited the base. She was swollen like a beach ball and I was the father. Our daughter was born while I was still in the brig, but I had no intention of being a father. When I was released, I'd accumulated several thousand dollars in back pay, and planned to go back to Texas. Before I left, I wanted to score some coke, see Janet and the baby, maybe getting a piece of ass and then leave. Janet convinced me to stay with her and the baby. In retrospect, I wish I hadn't stayed. Not that it would have changed my ways, because I was still going to do the things I did no matter where I went, but because it would have saved a lot of grief for a woman who practically worshipped me, and it would have saved the children from a lot of pain and confusion.

For the next 18 months I managed to hold a job as a groundskeeper at a nursing home, but I was still getting high and there were many nights when I didn't come home. I'd spend many nights in North Philly, smoking crack and screwing anything in the vicinity. To date, that year and a half is the longest period I've stayed out of jail.

In 1990, Janet and I had a major blowout and I left for Houston and tractor trailer school. Though I was heavily involved with crack, I managed somehow to complete the ten-week course. I planned to hook up with one of the big carriers and travel. It wasn't to be, for two weeks after completing the course I was caught burglarizing a warehouse and sentenced to a year in the county jail. I began to notice that every jail I'd been in had mostly black prisoners, and when I compared my experiences with theirs, it was obvious that something was very wrong with the system.

During the year Janet and I started writing, and we agreed I'd return to Philly when my time was up. I tried being a family man, but my old habits continued. Janet was working as a stripper and she justified it by saying she had to support herself and our daughter somehow. I used it as an excuse, and there were times when I wouldn't come home for weeks and months, running the streets, staying high, living with whores and committing robberies. For several years, the few times I did show up at home I only brought problems. I was in and out of jail and got my first state sentence after my 12th burglary and was to serve a 2 ½ to 6 year term.

By some miracle, Janet was still hanging on and we had another child, this time a boy. I decided I had to do something about my full-blown addiction and I got into every drug treatment and self-help program I could, hoping to gain insight into who I am. By the time I was paroled, my mother had died of cancer without me at her side, and Janet had found another man and had a third child with him.

For the first time in my life it seemed I was truly alone and had to rely on myself. I got into a drug rehab halfway house; I had great intentions and honestly believed I had changed. It lasted all of thirty days and I was back at it. The attraction of the streets was too strong and I gave in. I'd had a total of forty days of freedom before I was back in prison with a new felony case for burglary. It was my 13th, and it didn't look good for me. I was expecting the worst, that my line had played out. I'm anticipating something in the neighborhood of 5-15 years, and I was shocked when my public defender got me a deal of 2-4. I couldn't believe my ears. By the time we got to court to accept the plea bargain, the attorney had gotten it down to 1 ½-3 years. I was one lucky fellow. Or was it something else?

There are hundreds of men, most of them black, that I see every day, who have committed far less than me, but are serving my sentence three, four and even five times longer. Is it coincidence? I don't think so. I understand that eventually my rope will play out and I'll be thrown away permanently if I don't stop. But why have I received so many chances when the man next to me has received so few?

Here at Graterford, the overall attitude towards prisoners is one of contempt and lack of concern. You must keep yourself in good physical shape, for the medical department here should really be called the horror ward. In 1999, a friend of mine, Woody, who was serving 1-3 years, died because the medical department didn't treat his asthma properly. The state-employed pathologist, after performing an autopsy, declared that his death was self-imposed because he wasn't taking his medication as prescribed. They are liars. I was there!

In one of my many drug and alcohol treatment programs, the therapist asked what people thought the most powerful motivator out there was. He said it was pain. Although I agree that pain is a powerful force, there is one that is so much stronger, pleasure. A human being will go out of their way to feel good, in many cases risking bodily harm and prolonged misery for a fleeting moment of pleasure.

I can't tell you how many times I've sat in a cell and contemplated my future. The thought of falling prey to my desires is not a pleasant one, but for me it is a very real threat. Don't be quick to judge me because of my history. I have to make some firm decisions in my life, and even though I've grown weary of making plans, I understand the need for support. After experiencing the system for most of my life, I believe the single most important factor in curbing the recidivism rate is meaningful, decent employment. All of the therapy, meetings and good intentions mean absolutely nothing if an ex-convict doesn't remain in MEANINGFUL employment. Even with the support of self-help

organizations, friends and families, so important for addicts like myself, I guarantee a return trip for an ex-convict on parole who remains unemployed for a long enough time. I have good, marketable skills I will use upon my release. As far as the rest, I must play it by ear.
I'm not sure where my children will come into the picture if at all. My son is now nine and my daughter fourteen. Neither really knows me and my daughter only has bad memories. I will just work toward picking myself back up and, if the day comes when I can offer something positive to my children, then I will ask to be let back into their lives. There are many things that have happened that I'd like to change, but cannot. But I am not a quitter; giving up just doesn't fit into my life. In a few years I will be freed and given another chance to do something positive with my life. Will it happen?

I certainly hope so.

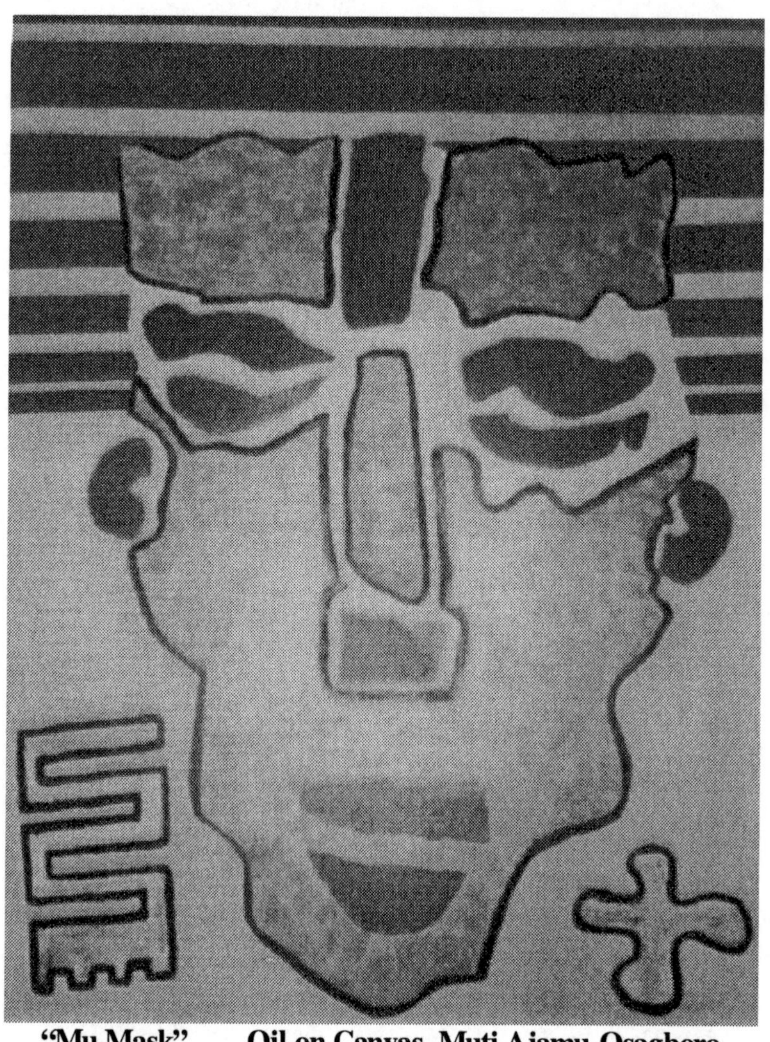

"Mu Mask" Oil on Canvas Muti Ajamu-Osagboro

No problem can be solved by the same consciousness that caused it." Albert Einstein

"Sistah Mother" Oil on Canvas Muti Ajamu-Osagboro

Chapter Four
NOT AS GUILTY AS CHARGED

JAMEEL SALAHUDDIN
($840,000)

SageWriters, Box 215, Swarthmore, PA 19081

Jameel Salahuddin (not his real name) quit school at eleven, his teachers never noticing that he was so bruised and traumatized from the troubles of his young life that he withdrew into himself. By the time he was 18, he was working in a fast food restaurant 60-70 hours a week. He spent his money on fine clothes, even buying tailor-made suits. Living with an older woman who dealt drugs and her eight year old daughter, he found respite in the make-believe family. Wanting to prove his manhood, he agreed to accompany a group of "tough guys" on a supermarket robbery. He says, "I was simply a fool who sought a sense of power and wholeness in the wrong place. Perhaps if there

was someone I could have talked to it would have made a difference. But there was no one."

Convicted of the one robbery he participated in plus another twelve the cops hadn't been able to solve, he was sentenced to 24-75 years instead of 1½-5 years for the crime he actually committed. He will be eligible for parole in 2006 when he'll be 42 years old.

A functional illiterate when arrested, he could barely read and write. When he tried to write a letter to a friend, she could hardly read it. This humiliated him, but also inspired him to improve his skills. While spending much of his first ten years in prison in The Hole, he began reading books and writing letters for the first time in his tortured life. Excited by the worlds that opened to him, he was thrilled at being able to give an articulate voice to his thoughts and feelings. Still resistant to sitting in a classroom, he once stole a G.E.D. preparation textbook and devoured it. Math was his biggest challenge as he had to teach himself algebra, geometry, percentages and long division, topics totally new to him.

When he scored 261 on the test where a passing grade was 225, he was elated. He's completed a 36-credit business management certification program and has an Associate's degree in Human Services from a community college. Over time, encouraged by friends, he took college courses and, by the time he is released he'll have completed his bachelor's degree, paid for by his family, from a correspondence course through a local university.

A man who played a pivotal role in Jameel's' growth and development was Balil, an older Sufi man with an ethereal appearance who'd been at Graterford for years before the younger man arrived. Under Balil's tutelage, the eager student learned about the major religions of the world as well as meditation techniques that enabled him to explore the pain and rage inside him. In Balil, Jameel finally found a father, a teacher, a brother and a friend. Balil was transferred to another prison before he had a chance to know of Jameel's academic and spiritual accomplishments. (Inmates in Pennsylvania are not allowed to correspond with each other.)

After counseling some younger inmates recently, Jameel said with pride, "I'm turning into Balil!"

Optimistic about his future after prison, he dreams of teaching creative writing to at-risk youth back in North Philadelphia. And then there's writing.
He says, "One day I want to become a great Black writer who gives voice to what's going on within the souls of my people. There's so much for me to write about, to let the world know who we are and how we feel. It's time for us to begin defining ourselves. My life experiences, though painful and traumatic, have equipped me not just to fight but to flourish. Recently a guard who's been here as long as I can remember, commented on my change and asked how I was doing. I looked at him and said I'm still in prison, so how well could I be doing? He smiled and reminded me of all the years he had to write me up for not following orders. He said he used to tell his wife about this young, rebellious inmate that was driving him crazy, but whom he respected for his integrity. I smiled, remembering that period of my prison life. Back then I had no idea what integrity was all about, but I knew the value of remaining true to myself. I have changed. Time and struggle have made me wiser. Though in my heart I'm as rebellious as ever, I've learned to channel my energy toward my goals.

"I firmly believe that one day I'm going to be all I long to be. I just have to keep holding on. I will."

JAMEEL

I don't know why I agreed to rob the Acme supermarket in suburban Philadelphia that October night in 1981. I was a pretty boy, and ever since I was 15, I'd been involved with older women. At 18, I guess my need to be part of something caused me to start hanging around with Rick. He was strong, confident and aggressive while I was quiet, naïve and needed a positive role model in my unhappy life. I was involved with Linda, a beautiful woman with an eight year old daughter. I soon learned Linda was a drug dealer. We had a little make-believe family, picnicking in the country, shopping, and even attending teacher's meetings. I guess I agreed to take part in the robbery as a macho thing to prove I was really a man.

The plan was for another guy and me to go into the market while the others stayed in the getaway car. I barely knew the other two. I was supposed to retrieve the money from the safe while the other man held a gun on the manager. We grabbed a cart and walked down an aisle or two like regular shoppers before we approached the manager's booth. The guy with the gun wrapped in newspaper quietly announced a holdup. The manager, cooperating, unlocked the safe and I quickly emptied the contents into a carryall bag. Then we slowly walked out, trying not to call attention to ourselves.

Just as we stepped outside, a police cruiser entered the parking lot. I later learned the manager had triggered a silent alarm just as we approached the booth. The two guys were nervously waiting in the car 30 yards away. Hoping they wouldn't panic and leave without me, I calmly made my way towards them. I don't think at this point the police suspected me, as I was casually dressed like a college kid.

When I was about ten feet from the car, I looked back and was surprised to see my fellow robber still close to the market, waving his arms at the police and pointing to me. As the police drove towards me, I jumped into the back seat of the getaway car and we sped away, leaving the other guy behind. The driver swerved around the cop and a high speed chase followed.

In a few minutes it seemed as though the entire police force was chasing us, and we couldn't shake them. The driver pulled over and the three of us leaped out and ran in separate directions. In a flash, I ran behind a large house and jumped a fence at the rear of the yard. In the darkness I didn't realize that the other side of the fence was a forty-foot drop onto concrete. After being airborne for what seemed like minutes, as my body hit the concrete, the wind was knocked out of me and pain was shooting through my legs. I laid there hurt and paralyzed, but I had to keep moving, for my pursuers were dead on my trail. I heard many police cars and felt them nearby. Above me, several officers who were chasing me looked down, amazed that I'd made such a jump. They couldn't reach me, and, knowing I had to keep moving, I forced myself to my feet and stumbled into the darkness. Thank God none of them shot me. They could have justified murdering me on the spot.

I ran desperately toward the tree line of the woods, hoping for refuge. Suddenly I was flying headfirst down a steep ravine, falling to what surely was my death. I found myself hanging upside down, clinging to some roots and vines. When I looked down, I was terrified, for I was clinging to a steep slope about 30 feet above a shallow, rocky stream. I couldn't let go or I'd fall head first onto the rocks. I could hear police all around, an army of them, with dogs, floodlights, and the sound of walkie-talkies reverberating through the night air. My only option appeared to be staying completely still and praying I wouldn't be discovered.

How had I gotten into this situation? Just that morning, Linda's daughter stayed home from school, excited to spend the day with me and go clothes shopping. Although there were no more than ten years between us, she often called me Daddy. Afterwards we stopped by my mother's and hung out for awhile. On the way home, I picked up some fresh fish for dinner. As Linda prepared the meal, the phone rang and it was Rick, reminding me that I was supposed to meet him half an hour earlier to accompany him and his squad on the robbery. I told him I was chilling and about to eat dinner. Linda, not realizing what was up, overhearing, suggested I go on and handle my business and she'd keep my food warm until I came back. Like a fool, I left, not knowing I'd never be back.

As I hung there, close to an hour must have passed. As the police searched the area, I was drenched in sweat, my arms and muscles burning from the pain of my injuries and the tension of clinging so tightly to the slope. My heart cried out for God's help and mercy.

After a while, the sounds of pursuit began to fade; the dogs were silent and the lights were turned off. Amazingly, it seemed as if they must have thought I'd gotten away. Then a voice above me called out that he'd found some money on the ground, then some more and next thing I knew the police were following a trail of money leading them closer and closer to where I was hanging. In a moment of greed, while trying to escape the police in the getaway car, I'd stuffed some of the stolen money down the front of my pants. I had no idea that while running through the woods, dollar bills were falling from my pants legs, leading the police directly to me. The last thing I remember after being discovered was letting go and falling through the darkness.

I regained consciousness in the hospital, handcuffed to a stretcher. An examination and x-rays miraculously showed nothing was broken. Besides a concussion and a few stitches here and there, I suffered no major physical damage as a result of my fall.

From the hospital I was taken to the police station and arrested on a host of charges stemming from the robbery. The other guys all got away; I was the only one captured. As the detectives questioned me, I remained silent, my body aching and my head so swollen it felt like it would burst. I sat for hours while they drilled me about the identities of the other men. They even smacked me around. I made no statements. This went on for several days, and they threatened that if I didn't give them the information they wanted, they were going to charge me with so many cases I'd never get out of prison. True to their word, within the week I was charged with 12 different armed robberies, all committed within the past six months. Bail was out of the question, so I sat in prison, overwhelmed at the absurdity of my circumstances, keeping my silence, figuring I could beat those extra charges in court since I was innocent of them.

What I didn't learn until later was that these guys had been committing robberies together for months. When I was arrested, the detectives assumed I was Rick, for we looked alike, except Rick had bad acne.

I was in for a rude awakening.

My first court-appointed attorney showed up and asked the judge to be dismissed because he didn't have time to represent me. The new lawyer appointed by the court never once met with me. All he did was write me a letter asking for a list of alibis accounting for my whereabouts at the times of the other robberies. A week before trial, the first lawyer contacted my mother and said he'd represent me for $10,000. She somehow scraped the money together, but I didn't see or talk with him until my first day in court. Considered a top gun of criminal lawyers, he wore tailored suits, silk ties and Gucci shoes. When I tried explaining how I came to be charged with 13 robberies, I could tell by his eyes that he didn't believe a word I was saying about my innocence. I

told him over and over I hadn't committed those other robberies. With an expression of contempt on his face, he said, "You might have convinced your mother that you didn't do those things, but I don't believe you."
The courts refused his request for more time to prepare and the trials began. I knew I was doomed.

While I did my best to come up with alibis for the dates and times when the other robberies were committed, I was uncertain. As a teenager who'd dropped out of school at eleven, I had no job and no structured schedule. Of one thing I was certain—I wasn't with Rick and the others when they did those other robberies.

Through several jury trials, I was found not guilty because there simply was no evidence to convict me. Then, in the next few trials, an amazing thing happened. I sat in the courtroom as a witness who'd never laid eyes on me took the stand and identified me as one of the men who'd robbed a supermarket where she worked. Did she think I was Rick? That was something I definitely didn't expect. I lost that trial. But then the same thing happened over and over again the next few trials (13 in all). When the smoke cleared, I'd lost three trials in a row involving cases I knew absolutely nothing about. It was clear the cards were stacked against me and my innocence meant nothing. I was witnessing the process by which I was legally lynched.

Before the next trial, the District Attorney approached my lawyer with a deal. If I pleaded guilty to the three remaining robberies, he'd get the judge to run the sentences concurrently and I'd get no more time than I was already going to get. It wasn't a good deal but my back was against the wall. Like a fool, I let them play me right out. I took their deal, a deal with the devil. Later, I stood before the devil as he smiled and sentenced me to 24-72 years in prison.

The irony is that the county where I was initially arrested sentenced me to 1 ½ to 5 years in prison for my part in the one robbery I committed.

The horrible smell of Montgomery County Prison caught me by surprise. The air was filled with the awful, musky scent of caged men. Told to strip naked by guards with blackjacks in their hands, I complied. When I asked why I had to bend over and spread my cheeks, the guard snapped, "Nigger, if you don't turn around I'll split your black, motherfuckin' head!" Another guard explained that exposing my ass enabled them to see whether or not I was attempting to smuggle a weapon or other contraband into the prison. How and why I would stick a weapon up my ass was beyond my imagination, but I turned around and complied with their request.

That single act was one of the most humiliating and dehumanizing experiences of my life.

After showering, I was hosed down with a liquid they said was an insecticide or a delouser, given clothing and locked in a cell with three other men. I just stood there in the dark, unsure about what to do.

In the morning, one of the other guys awkwardly introduced himself and I mumbled my name, too tired and beaten down to socialize. I followed him to the chow hall, where whites sat on one side and blacks on the other. After chow, I got on the phone, first calling Linda.

We'd been living together for about a year, and though she was 13 years older, I liked her a lot. She had a special way of loving that calmed and soothed my troubled soul. In her arms, I felt peace, for the first time. At fifteen I'd been involved with a woman twice my age. Beautiful older women just turned me on; I preferred dating them to younger women, who were simply too inexperienced for my taste.

My attraction to older women was not one sided. Linda, who I'd met a couple of other times, showed up one night at the fast food place where I was working, and asked me what time I got off. When midnight came, she was waiting for me in her little car outside the restaurant. As I approached the car, she slid over to let me drive. I felt like a king basking in royal treatment. The neighborhood kids hanging outside smiled and teased me about how I thought I was such a player. When we got to her place, I learned her daughter was away for the week and soon we were naked in her bedroom. This woman did things to my body that had never been done before, and several days later I moved in with her and her little girl. I had a beautiful relationship with her daughter. Though I was a teenager, I quickly adapted to being man of the house and king of the castle.

Being young and totally ignorant of the drug game, I stayed out of Linda's business and asked few questions about the people she dealt with, including several celebrities when they were in town. We got to attend lots of fancy affairs.

Through an acquaintance in the neighborhood, I met Rick and the others who were rumored to be really bad and successful bank robbers. It was these guys I foolishly decided to accompany on their dark deed.

Linda was hysterical when she accepted my collect call. She'd been up all night worrying and wondering what to do. Though I tried to reassure her, she couldn't calm down. I hung up and called my mother just as she was about to leave for work. When I told her I'd been arrested, she had a fit.

My mother and I have always had a great relationship. Besides being the strongest, kindest and most loving person I know, I always knew that as long as I was honest with her, no matter what the problem, I could rely on her to help me sort things out. During the first week of my arrest, as

detectives kept charging me with case after case, my mother visited every day, though we had to talk on telephones behind a plexiglass barrier. Through my tears, she encouraged me to be strong.
(Years later, she and I had a conversation in the visitors' room about her inability to protect me from the sexual abuse. We wept together and our wounds began to heal.)

My father was another story. All my life I've possessed an intense hatred and bitterness toward him, for I had absolutely no respect for him as a man. I never knew him as a child, for my mother left him when I was four. He moved to Detroit, and I didn't see him again until I was about ten. My only early memory of him was a scene where I am standing in the kitchen doorway as my father sat on my mother's chest, repeatedly punching her in the face as she lay screaming.

That single incident made an indelible impression on my young soul.

When I was ten, I asked to be sent to Detroit to live with my father. My mother had remarried, to a white man who abused me. The teachers at school never seemed to notice my bruises and my desperation, and my mother, like so many women at that time, felt she was in no position to risk losing economic support by leaving him.

I thought the move to Michigan would be a good thing, but instead it was like jumping from the frying pan into the fire. I discovered my father wasn't too good at communicating. An extremely quiet man, whenever I acted out to get his attention he responded with violence, beating me with his fists like I was a grown man. After a year and a half, he sent me back to Philly, and I didn't see or hear from him again until I was seventeen. After losing his legs in an industrial accident, he moved back to live with his sister. I visited him often, but the relationship was awkward and strained. I remember at my grandfather's funeral, with the family gathered in my aunt's living room, my father started talking about the special bond we had. I recall at that moment I thought, "This man ain't got a clue as to who I am." But I just sat there in silence. Shortly after that, I came to prison and didn't see him again. That was more than 20 years ago.

About three years ago, I learned my father was sick and dying in a nursing home. I began to consider the hell that his life had been, and when I placed myself in his shoes, suddenly the hate and bitterness in my heart dissolved. It was replaced with love, forgiveness and compassion toward an old and dying man. For the first time in my life, I realized I loved my father, and I was overcome with a desire to let him know. I called my sister and asked if there was any way I could talk to my father. She investigated, but learned it was out of the question, considering where I was.

I felt like a dark cloud had descended upon my heart. All I wanted was an opportunity to reach out beyond these prison walls to tell my father I loved him before he died. But I couldn't, and it hurt like hell.

That night, I had a wonderful dream. I was free and standing in the midst of a reunion with my entire family present. To my surprise, someone told me that my father was there, pointing across the room. He was standing there, tall, handsome, healthy and strong. As I walked slowly towards him, I noticed how much we looked alike, as if we were mirror images of each other. When I reached him, he smiled and simply opened his arms to embrace me. As we hugged, tears streaming from my eyes, I kept telling him how much I loved him. When I woke up suddenly back in my cell, I felt as if a huge burden had been lifted from my heart. Miraculously, from that moment on, all of the emotional issues regarding my father were reconciled.

This healing was accomplished in a single dream.

The first week of my arrest 20 years ago was difficult, as I was led in chains from one cell to another for over a week, as police questioned and charged me with many other robberies. I knew no one in the county prison and I soon realized how out of my element I was. As a young, skinny teenager, I stood out. Back in the eighties, before drugs ravaged the inner cities, most of the Black men in prison were guys who came from poverty-stricken neighborhoods and had resorted to criminal activities as a means of survival. This combined with the racist attitudes of police officers, the courts and society as a whole, was cause for many Blacks to spend their lives in and out of prison.

But I was totally unprepared for prison.

On my first day in the yard, a few guys approached me and asked me if there was anything I needed. I was surprised that they knew my name. It seemed my association with Linda held some weight in such a place. I was embraced almost as a celebrity amidst the subculture of drugs and violence. In no time, I was initiated into their ranks and began smuggling drugs into the prison. Guards met my outside connections and, for cash, would bring in drugs and anything else. On several occasions, they even allowed Linda inside to have sex with me. I was living dangerously in the county jail.

After a fistfight with another inmate, I realized the lifestyle I was involved in went against who and what I was as a man, and I gradually hooked up others to replace me in maintaining the drug connections to the street. My decision to step aside was accepted.

When I heard that the three other men who were with me during the supermarket robbery were arrested and charged with many of the same robberies and had implicated me, I sank into depression. My entire world had caved in and I was slowly being crushed by the weight and pressure of all that had happened.

Perhaps it was their strip searches and false tough guy facades that caused me to hate most prison guards. One in particular, a white sergeant constantly harassed me. His face would get all twisted and he'd say "How you doing, Mr. Prosperity?" One day, I asked him why he called me that, and he responded, "Cause you think you're somebody when all you is a good for nothin' nigger!" His comment took me over the edge, and I spit at him. In an instant, several guards beat me with blackjacks Rodney King style, and then dragged me and handcuffed me in solitary confinement in "The Hole." Somehow I curled into a fetal position and slept, my body aching from head to toe. In the morning, they strip searched me, took my clothes, and left me naked.

It was then I began to notice the wretched conditions in the cell. It was filthy, and the sink and toilet in one corner were completely covered with a thick, brown slime. The smell was awful, and to my astonishment, smeared all over the walls was dried human feces. When the guard slid a carton of milk and a small box of cereal into the cell, I asked if I could be transferred. He responded, "This is what happens when you spit on a guard." I began cussing and banging on the door, but they ignored me. Eventually I got quiet. One can only scream for so long.

After 90 days in The Hole, a guard came to the cell and told me to get ready, I was being transferred to Graterford Prison. I was scared to death. Prior to my arrest, guys used to tell me, "Boy, you are too pretty. You better not ever go to prison. They gonna have a ball with you." Rumor had it that Graterford was the roughest prison in Pennsylvania, a place where young guys were constantly raped and taken advantage of. When I arrived there, the guards asked where did I want my body shipped in case of an emergency. When I asked what kind of an emergency, the guard responded, "In case somebody murders your dumb ass!"

Once inside the cell, I hung a sheet over the door, pulled down my pants and shitted out two fifty-dollar bills which I'd placed up my ass earlier to smuggle into prison. After washing the money off, I went in search of a guy someone told me to contact once I arrived at Graterford. When I found him, he gave me a knife in exchange for one of the fifties. Over the weeks, I carried that knife everywhere, intent on murdering the first man fool enough to say anything out of the way to me.

By the time I was released back into the main population, I had decided that there was no room in my life for sanity or anything associated with it. For the next ten years, I lived a predatory lifestyle, surviving and feeding off of the weaker men around me. Whatever hopes and dreams I had about freedom or a better tomorrow, I completely suppressed. To continue dreaming and hoping seemed a complete waste of time.

My violent response to an attempted rape served as an initiation into the ranks of the strong and aggressive within the prison, and with this came a kind of celebrity status amongst other men. Guys I didn't know, who'd heard about what happened, would walk up to me, shake my hand and say something indicating their respect. It felt good to be admired and respected.

Back in the eighties, most of the inmates at Graterford were either Lifers or those serving long sentences. The place was extremely violent, drug-infested and understaffed, with guards ill-equipped to control such a large institution. The guards smuggled in large quantities of drugs in exchange for money. This, coupled with the fact that everyone walked around with a chip on their shoulder and a knife tucked into their waistbands created a hellish environment. The inmates basically ran the prison, with little or no regard for the weak and innocent. There were few counseling or educational opportunities, but even if there had been, I was too busy trying to survive to consider taking advantage of them.

For me, surviving Graterford entailed more than just struggling against the violence, drugs or predatory rapists. There are many negative forces and elements in a prison that slowly eat away at a man's humanity. Hopelessness is one such force. There were times when my vision was clouded and all I could see was the concrete and steel that encaged me. Sitting in my cell, my soul crying out, I discovered that resistance was the only way to ease the pain. So that's what I did, I resisted! Since prior to coming to prison I was a good man, I resisted any and everything that sought to take me away from who and what I am. Often this resistance was expressed in small things, such as refusing to obey the rules and regulations. There was a guard on the cell block who was frustrated because I showed up late every night when it was time to be locked in. When he'd ask why I was so late, I'd say things like "Only a fool would rush to get locked up in a cage." When I'd refuse to close the door, I'd say, "Living inside this cage is bad enough, but I'll be damned if I'm going to close the door on myself!"
He'd write me up and it was back to The Hole.

For years, all I did was go back and forth to The Hole. I simply refused to obey the rules. Actually, to me, The Hole was the only place where I could get away from the noise, chaos and violence. It was also a place where I did a lot of reflecting and healing. Inside a tiny cell for a long, long time, denied all access to other humans, the mind experiences sensory deprivation, which to me was a state of consciousness more exciting than any drug I'd known. There is nothing to hear but yourself, to see but four walls, to feel but your feelings, to smell but the funk of your own body. While in it, I had a chance to challenge and explore all the fears and insecurities that existed within my mind. At first, they presented themselves as phantoms who sat guarding the thresholds of whatever peace I sought. They kept me from accessing the loftier spaces and places within myself. But it was there, within the solitude of The Hole, that I began the painful process of healing.

While in The Hole, I focused on healing. Out of The Hole, my focus was resisting and rebelling against the negativity all around me. I refused to resort to unnecessary violence. Fist fights are common in prison, because you can't coop men up like animals without their getting agitated and aggressive. A petty argument can escalate in seconds into a vicious stabbing or murder, which I've seen many times. I only used a knife one time, when my life was in danger. You never know when this might happen, so you're in a constant state of dread and defensiveness.

Though I was pretty much a loner, during the first ten years of my incarceration I became close friends with four guys, all about my age, all from different parts of Philly, and all arrested around the same year. I was the only one without a life sentence. Each was serving a life sentence for a murder he didn't actually commit, but each was convicted on charges involving conspiracy, and mandatory sentencing laws put them in prison for the rest of their lives.

As we struggled together just to survive, we'd sit in my cell and talk about how we came to be in this nightmare, tears flowing as we shared. We struggled to give voice to the pain and horror of what it means to be a Black man in America. It was there, sitting in that cell with my friends that I first embraced the challenge of giving language to what we were all experiencing and feeling inside our souls. I made a promise to each of these men that one day I would find a way to tell their stories, even though at the time I was a functional illiterate. There is no doubt in my mind that one day I will become a writer and do it.

"Not by might, not by power but through the spirit of justice and compassion shall our world be transformed."
Zaceriah 4:6

Chapter Five
INNOCENT BUT PROVEN GUILTY

Anton Forde/Trevor Mattis
($455,000)

Anton Forde/Trevor Mattis was born in Jamaica and raised in a single-parent household in the poverty-stricken area of Kingston. At seventeen he attended York College in New York, graduating Cum Laude. In June 1987, he went to Philadelphia to seek enrollment into Temple University's School of Dentistry. Months later, Anton witnessed a murder for which he was wrongly accused and for which, despite testimony pointing to another, he was sentenced to life in prison. As his case is currently under appeal, his one remaining chance to pursue justice and freedom, on the advice of his lawyer, the story of the incident for which he was convicted will not be discussed in these pages.

When he was arrested, the only thing he had on him was a fake video store rental card a friend had loaned him with the name Trevor Mattis on it. The police wouldn't believe that was not his real name, and so it stuck on all court records.
He was tried, convicted and sentenced to life imprisonment on the word of just one man, who later recanted. In Actual Innocence by Barry Scheck, Peter Neufeld and Jim Dwyer, ***"Eyewitness error remains the single most important cause of wrongful imprisonment."***

When first imprisoned, Anton was severely beaten by guards and required surgery and hospitalization for injuries that are permanent. (Estimates on the cost of his treatment are not available.)

Tall, athletic, elegant and well-spoken, in the Creative Writing class Anton always had something intelligent and perceptive to say. When he spontaneously started putting together lists of aphorisms that reflected his impressions of prison life, I told him he should write a book. A year later, Contemplations of a Convict: Aphorisms for the Heart and Mind was published. He is now updating that and working on his second creation, a book of poetry.

Anton/Trevor

In Jamaica, I don't remember much about my early childhood. The times were full of turmoil for people of color, and their frustrations were often passed onto their children. I am the first generation of the single parent phenomenon. I've only seen my father twice in my life, once at age eleven, when he promised to buy me a table tennis board if I passed my high school entrance exams, a promise he never fulfilled, and once when I came to America six years later.
My family basically consists of my mother and grandmother. My mother, Phyllis, is an independent, self-motivated individual. She is the eldest of her siblings and sole sister to

eight brothers. From what I know, she has been a pioneer in almost everything she did. She left her pastoral village on her own to venture into the city. At one time she was the main source of income and inspiration to her younger brothers. She educated herself, attending classes on a wide range of subjects, and to this day is still enrolled in some courses. Today she keeps abreast of the changing technology of the Internet by attending various seminars.

My grandmother, 84 is the matriarch of what's now a large family. She is a 5' 6", wiry, strong woman. She has personally raised over fifteen children and eight grandchildren and is a great-grandmother to twelve. Today she has astounding mental acuity along with an impeccable memory. She can recall minute details from when she was a child. In my life, she's my greatest hero. I am her first grandchild and she actually raised me.

What's hurt me the most about prison is that I cannot see her face to face, to hug her and tell her how much I love her. I cannot even let her know that her favorite grandchild is behind bars; that would definitely kill her. For the past twelve years, a day does not go by without her asking of my whereabouts and how I'm doing. I communicate with her via letters but I'm quickly running out of excuses as to why I can't come to pay her a visit. Personally, my greatest hope is that I get out of prison before she passes on.

I want to be there for her in the same fashion that she was there for me when I was a babe. The earliest childhood memory I have is that of my grandmother bathing me in a bucket. As I write these words, I can feel her strong, loving hands gently rubbing the wash cloth over my skin. The rest of my family consists of numerous uncles, aunts and cousins who I don't really know. They are distantly supportive of me.

As a child, I never lacked necessities. I'd describe us as middle-class poor. My stalwart mother did her best. There was always a roof over our heads and nourishing food. I had a myriad of influences during my formative years. I never lacked father figures. The extended family was the family unit and the entire village still raised the child. I felt free, as a child should, and most of my time was spent having fun and asking questions, lots of questions. I've always been inquisitive and naturally intelligent. According to Jamaican superstition it's because my mother ate lots of fish when she was pregnant with me. Basically self-motivated, I was exposed to all kinds of people, both good and bad. My grandmother instilled educational discipline in me and from age eleven my main desire was to get an education. In spite of the fact that I rarely applied myself 100%, I had the discipline to maintain A's and B's. My mother's mantra was, "I may not be able to leave you any money, but I'm going to make sure you have an education."

From ages eleven to sixteen, I explored the world of my Jamaican culture with its opposite extremes. I lived among the poor and we longingly watched the rich from afar. I was enrolled in one of the best schools on the island-obviously because of merit-where a majority of the upper class sent their children. While I traveled two hours by buses to get to school, the rich children were chauffeured back and forth in limousines. While my 25 cents for lunch was only enough to buy a snack from a street vendor, they got $2 to buy cooked meals from the school canteen. These kids were not the sharing type. In Jamaican society, the road to success is easily paved if you're rich. If you're born poor, the easy way to success is by being the roughest and toughest. Then the rich willingly patronize you when you come into contact with them.

These were also the years of my political education, 1976-1981. Jamaica was split into two parties, the socialist People's National Party (PNP), and the pro-capitalist Jamaica Labor Party (JLP). Politics were taken seriously, splitting up many families, breaking up long-term friendships, and turning neighbors into mortal enemies.

Violence, especially in impoverished neighborhoods, became the ultimate arbitrator, and people were assaulted, beaten, stabbed or even shot to death for their political beliefs. Party affiliation was broken down geographically, so if I knew where you were from, I pretty much knew what political party you supported. What had once been one neighborhood split into two with an invisible borderline which, if you crossed it, you died. Politicians and the wealthy instigated these schisms, started the strife and fanned the flames of conflict.

The violence was so rampant that at times I had to dodge bullets on my way to school or step by a bullet-riddled body from the previous night's political battles.
In a twinkling of the eye, the 13-15 year olds were pulled into the political wars, running errands for the older men, the gateway into the notorious Jamaican gangs.
At night, all roads into and out of these neighborhoods would be blocked with debris and abandoned cars, denying entrance to both foes and police. The boys stayed up all night acting as lookouts. Politicians provided weapons and ammunition with which to defend the neighborhood and intimidate rival gangs.

As long as I didn't venture into a totally strange neighborhood, I remained relatively unaffected by the political winds, for school remained my focus and I was naturally inoculated against peer pressure. While many of my friends jumped at the chance to join the underworld, I was aloof and remained an outsider, which ultimately protected me when the battles escalated. I avoided the hot areas on my way to and from school. Soon afterward, my mother moved us to a neighborhood that was at the periphery of the violence, so I was doubly fortunate.

By the time I was sixteen, more than 70% of my friends from my old neighborhood had lost their lives in the political war.

The state of affairs in the Third World countries is such that the young person's ultimate dream is to come to America. With great expectation and anticipation, I waited six months for the responses to my college applications. Six days a week I would walk a mile to check the post office box. With prayerful anxiety, I would open the mailbox to look for a letter from the States. Finally it came. I was accepted! At that moment, I thought I was the luckiest person in the entire world. But in accordance to my personality, this was contained exuberance. No one in my neighborhood knew that I was about to live their dreams. Only my very best friend knew. The day before I was to go to the airport, I was playing marbles with a group of guys in the neighborhood. In the middle of the game, I casually mentioned that I'd be off to the promised land the following day. Most of them were in disbelief. When we finished that day, I exchanged goodbyes with my friends and vowed to stay in contact and never to forget them.
The first half of the promise was never kept after the first year in the land of Sodom.

When the plane lifted off, I was excited. I felt relieved, like I broken through the Great Wall of Non-Opportunity. I finally escaped the prison of poverty that dwarfs and stifles ambition. Now I was on my way to the land where people pick gold up off the streets. I got to Kennedy and was awestruck by the size of it. The Jamaican airport looked like a bathroom in comparison. The drive to my new home was one of complete wonder. The big streets, the many cars, the sight of highways meandering in circles and figure eights. We got off the highway and drove on the local streets and two images struck me as totally out of context. The streets had potholes and there were high rise buildings made out of red bricks. These things were quite an anomaly to my vision of the land of wealth.

College was one of the greatest experiences of my life. It gave me a chance to express the person I really am. I haven't had a chance to do that since. The academics of college were no real challenge for me; it was the personal development and growth that thrilled me. Academically, I learned a lot but from the door, I questioned the learning process. It was basically rote memorization and regurgitation of information. You were not taught how to think. Only Calculus, Physics, and Philosophy forced the mind to use the thinking processes. Biology was my favorite subject and I've always loved that. I enjoyed the competition. In college, all nationalities and races are mixed on a basically level playing field. Caribbean people have a very proud culture and one of the things a foreigner in this country quickly realizes is that Americans, both Black and White, look down upon them and underestimate their mental abilities. For example if you attended 10th grade in Jamaica, upon coming to the States, they would automatically put you back a grade or two regardless of how you test academically. Nothing could be further from the truth, for academically, Caribbean students are way ahead of the general American student. I was doing college level math in my high school in Jamaica at age 13.

The average 15-year-old Jamaican high school student is academically equivalent to the average American 12th grader. One of my main motivations in college was the competition, especially competing against the white students, who wore their superiority complex around like a badge. I used to sit at the back of the class. Some classes I never showed up for after the first day unless there was a test. I would get the curriculum and that's it. Half the time, I couldn't afford the text book, so I would get my knowledge from a similar book in the library or share with a friend. Most of the times if I got a B or C it was because of failure to turn in home work that came from the text book. My thrill was to ace the test and then watch the white students mill around the posted test results, bewildered as to whose social security number was beside the top grade. Every now and then, a professor would point me out in the class to the hushed astonishment of everyone.

Of my college freshman class of 1982, there were ten Jamaicans. We all bonded immediately, three of us in particular, and we been very good friends ever since. There were about twenty other Jamaican and West Indian students on campus. The men used to play soccer together, then a sport popular only amongst West Indians and the few Greeks who used to stick to themselves

There was a Caribbean Students Club. When immigrants from Jamaica come to America, there is an immediate change in the dichotomy of the socio-economic relationships among the immigrants. America actually levels the playing field. Most legal immigrants from Jamaica are the rich and upper class, but here in America they are just another black foreigner. The few poor who immigrate will mix with upper class Jamaicans who they'd never have a chance to socialize with in Jamaica. The majority of the Jamaicans who immigrate to this country legally end up living a much lower quality of lifestyle in the States than they lived in Jamaica. They may accumulate a few more material luxuries, but back home they lived in houses that you could only find in the rich suburbs of America, something they now can't afford. Back home they had maids and gardeners, something only the very rich can afford in America, and they were held in high respect by the society in general.

The life I observed on campus among the West Indian students was tragically shameful to me. All the Jamaicans and the other Island students tried their best to seem white. Everything was Americanized, caucasianized. I immediately rebelled. Every fiber in me became determined to represent the Jamaican ghetto youth and the Jamaican culture. My two friends felt the same thing I was feeling, and we became the Jamaican trio. We felt we were the only authentic Jamaicans. We found a little corner in a conspicuous place on campus and made that our hangout where we conversed in the typical Jamaican fashion: loud, emotional and vibrant. The area we invaded was in a small student lounge where the cerebral students would pass time between classes. There was a large window through which you could see the students entering our building or the building directly across from us. We'd bang on the window and shout greetings when we saw each other walking by. In less than two weeks the area became little Jamaica; the other students would not even come near there. We'd hang out there all day. It seemed as if we didn't go to classes. The way we dressed to come to school was in the typical flamboyant Jamaican ghetto fashion. Security had a hard time deciding whether we were hoodlums or students. Until they got to know us, we would give a guard the blues. He would approach us as if we don't belong and we would let him have it.

Another peculiar thing about being an immigrant is the effects of racism. In Jamaica, you don't really have overt racism; what we have is more classism. You have white, blue-eyed Jamaicans; they're usually the rich people, but when we interact, it's on the human level. You just don't that cold hearted unfeelingness that hits you at the heart when you interact with white people, especially authority figures here in America. To a foreigner, it's shocking and unacceptable. Nothing in my upbringing taught me to be submissive and afraid to stand up for what's right. So when campus security would approach me with the stereotypical assumption that from the way I looked I must be a criminal, I'd verbally put them in their place.

We always had a lively congregation. We'd spontaneously break out into a rap contest, a party, or playing scrimmage soccer in our little area. I'd wear stuff that advertised the red, green, gold, and black Rasta colors or the Jamaican flag. We had a cassette player and we'd be playing reggae music. We'd eat in the communal fashion of Jamaican ghettoes. Everyone would put whatever monies they could together and then prepare enough for everyone to eat irrespective of whether they'd contributed money or not. The principle was that if you did not have it to give this time around, you might have it to give the next time around and those who could more afford it shared their good fortune. We outright brought Jamaica to the campus. More than a few times, we caused disturbances to nearby classes and a professor had to come and ask us to keep it down. We usually complied for a few minutes. We so infused the campus with the Caribbean flavor that before my freshman semester was over, a lot of the Island students who were previously ashamed of their Caribbean identity found pride in it and began to hang out with us. Our little spot was called the Penthouse. Although we caused such a ruckus, the code amongst our group was that academically you must maintain a C grade or better. Nothing less was acceptable, and that we all did.

In time, the professors came to realize there were a couple of geniuses among our crowd, so though we were noisy, they showed tolerance for the Caribbean flavor. Two of my friends never got less than 95 in any subject. Both are doctors now.

I remember one time we were in the same class four deep and we would tie for first and second in every test getting 99's and 100's. And we never cheated like the white students on campus who either had past tests or the test itself before we got it, or helped each other during the test. Cheating was too much an assault on our pride for the typical West Indian to be comfortable with it.

I attended the Caribbean Students Club a few times, but then it was run by older individuals who were ashamed of their heritage and did everything in their power to act bourgeois. It was here that my true self started to bust out of me. It was just this deep uncontrollable drive that propelled me. I saw that they were stagnant, bereft of ideas, and not doing anything productive. Everything was just the next party. On a few occasion, in their ignorant way, the president insulted the Jamaican culture. Another time, I can't exactly recall what the scenario was, but it must have had something to do with a political issue then in the media, the leadership was just parroting the American viewpoint, which I challenged and lambasted with vociferous argumentation. I think this was the first time they heard me speak in such a context. Everyone was shocked. I was mainly known as one of the rowdies of the penthouse crowd. Bob, Duce and me, the freshman trio, would have debates with the quasi-Jamaicans regularly.

At the next election, I ran for president, with Bob as Vice-President and we won. We then went on to revolutionize the Caribbean Students Clubs throughout the C.U.N.Y system. We were the smallest campus with the smallest Caribbean community, but in my tenure as president we made the most noise. We innovated numerous programs that were way ahead of their time. We took the Caribbean Students club from being just a party club to being a politically conscious entity.

It was non-stop work for Bob and me, but we loved it. It was such pure joy that I neglected my grades and girls for the benefit of the club. I was a very popular person in my community on campus. My popularity was mostly due to my leadership and the values that I stood for. Quite a few girls were in love with me, but they could not compete with the club and the visions I had for it. The few relationships that I got involved with atrophied due to neglect. Plus I had to be very careful, the girls in the club, the backbone of the movement, had this special relationship with me. All of them had equal access and equally shared my time. It was like I was every girl's boyfriend, not sexually but emotionally. There was one girl, one of the hottest on the campus at the time, and she came the closest to being labeled as my girlfriend. She would catch all type of flack anytime she came around. Due to the situation, I consciously kept any close relationships with girls private, and I avoided intimate relationships with club members.

We dedicated club members would spend countless hours plotting, charting, and strategizing how we as young people were going to change the world and make it a better place. We came up with so many good programs that I wish I could remember all of them now, for I am certain they could be useful for many Caribbean Students' Clubs today. I remember one of my concepts was to start at home first. Before we could change the world we had to change ourselves. I realized that America offered the perfect opportunity, if not the only opportunity to make the world a better place. I was starting with the Caribbean, which is made up of many individual small islands. Each has its own culture and that's the way we operate as a people. Though we are from the Caribbean, we are also proud and nationalistic. Each island sees itself as a world better than the next. On campus, I was brought into contact with students from all the different islands. In our Caribbean Students Club, students from the other island wouldn't attend because mostly Jamaicans dominated it. Jamaicans tend to be loud and assertive. They can seem quite intimidating at times. I realized that on campus we'd see each other everyday, but we didn't know a thing about each other's culture. What's it like growing up on each specific island, the food, the traditions etc. To resolve this dilemma I used the club as a vehicle and implemented a program called Each One Teach One. In this program, an individual from each island was selected to present his culture and country to the rest of the club. One by one, we learned about each other and the funny thing about this program is that in the end, we realized we all had the identical experiences, the identical struggles, the identical everything. We found out we were the same regardless of accent and geography. That was a powerful lesson. Our big vision was to unite all the Caribbean Students Clubs across America under one big umbrella organization. We would foster and assist in the development of standardized protocols, curriculum and programs to implement in these clubs. These programs and concepts would be tailored to unite all students from the Caribbean ideologically, socially, and emotionally. Then we as students would take this knowledge of self and each other back home, propagate it and in time be the nucleus around which the Caribbean would be united as one nation.

Our greatest achievement was our fight against apartheid. We marched, protested, disrupted and did everything to force our college to withdraw all it's funds invested in businesses supporting apartheid. Those were our heydays. We raised monies for the ANC and the works. Due to the limitations our club suffered because then we were just a small campus in the CUNY system-we had a very small budget, no club facility, none of the amenities needed for an organization to function effectively. I transferred to Queens College, a more prestigious campus within the CUNY system. I had developed a relationship among quite a few Caribbean Students Clubs on various campuses. When I transferred to Queens College for a few semesters, I was immediately elected president of the club there. I used their club office and campus amenities as a surrogate for York College.

During my stay at Queens, I maintained the title of honorary president for the York campus. I graduated from York College in 1987. After I left college, the ANC sent our York club a thank-you plaque for our support.

I obtained a bachelor of science degree in Bio/Pre-Med at age 20. After graduating magna cum laude, I left New York for Philadelphia, intending to attend Temple University's School of Dentistry. Isn't it strange how fateful events can permanently alter a person's life? The murder, for which I've been sentenced to life in prison, was committed by someone else, and even though the sole witness whose word was the basis of my life sentence has since testified to authorities that he lied, I may never be freed. Based on this false testimony and other evidence, a federal magistrate in October 2000, in an unheard-of 41-page opinion, declared that I should be released from prison in 120 days or given a new trial. The state appealed and won in February 2001, and my appeal before the Third Circuit will probably lose. Most defendants do in that difficult arena. I am hoping my court-appointed lawyer will be competent in representing me in this only possible chance I have to be free. Because my case is currently before the Third Circuit Court of Appeals, my lawyer has advised me not to talk publicly about it.

The transformational processes that I went through due to incarceration are unique. The arrest for the homicide was in essence my first arrest. I was denied bail and held in the Holmesburg facility, a county jail with a notorious reputation. Before I got to Holmesburg, I was housed temporarily at the Detention Center. During that time, I overheard numerous inmates talking in awestruck tones about Holmesburg, which was called "The Terror Dome." While I was on my block and the officer announced the call for all Holmesburg transfers, I observed two petrified inmates scream in fear and they began fighting with the guards as they physically protested their transfer to that house of horrors. This was all brand new territory for me and I looked on as if I was observing myself from a distance going on a dangerous adventure.

When I got there, "The Terror Dome" lived up to its name and some. The moment I walked onto A-Block, I witnessed the violent reality of prison life. With sheets and blanket still in my hands, I saw an individual stumble from within a darkened vestibule pursued by four men who surrounded him after he fell and stomped him into unconsciousness or outright killed him before the guards could arrive. Later I heard that the incident stemmed from his not hanging up the telephone when he was told to by some other inmate.

Holmesburg was a place of palpable tension and hostility. Rival neighborhood gangs came into close proximity with each other constantly and the friction was evident. Hatred was the norm in this environment. You hated the fact that you were locked up, you hated the officers, the officers hated you, you hated the next inmate if he wasn't your homie, you hated each other and some maybe even hated themselves. To exacerbate the situation, I was a foreigner of Jamaican nationality, vilified by the media and hated by all inmates and officers alike.

When I got to Holmesburg, I walked right into the middle of a racial war, Jamaicans vs. the jail and the entire Philadelphia society. The ethnic hatred stemmed from an incident I later found out that happened sometime shortly before I got arrested. Two Jamaicans were involved in a shootout and a five-year- old child was killed in the fray. The incident received major news coverage and the media stereotyped all Jamaican nationals as ruthless murderers who would even kill babies.

The repercussions from this incident were immediately felt statewide within the penal system. Physical assaults on Jamaican inmates by convicts and officers alike were rampant. This was the climate of the prison world into which I was thrown. I went from being indirectly associated with violence (I knew of violence, I knew individuals who were violent, but I was never personally involved with violence) to living directly in violence.

At this point I began a transformation. I went into survival mode. It's strange and I don't know how to explain it, but because I knew I was innocent, I determined that I had to survive this ordeal to expose the truth and a part of me just became a warrior. Another notable point it that this was my first direct social contact with Black Americans; this was basically true for all Jamaicans. On the streets, the relationships back then of Jamaicans and Black Americans was tenuous. They were consumers of drugs and we were suppliers; that was basically the extent of our interactions. We remained foreigners to each other. I could not understand their culture and they could not fathom mine. I could understand them when they spoke but they could not understand me. I saw the results of and heard about the physical assaults on Jamaicans, and it only made me more resolute. I never liked to see a person being taken advantage of and I saw many of my native countrymen being abused, especially the smaller ones, because Jamaicans males in general are small, below six feet in height and slimly built. I saw many of them being afraid, so I became their source of strength and, in many ways their protector. There were individuals who had serious reputations on the streets of Philadelphia and back in Jamaica. In Holmesburg they became fawning cowards. It was only because they were grossly out numbered, physically weak and no match for the wolf-pack, gang-warring mentality of the African Americans, who saw this as a perfect opportunity to even the score against guys whom they feared greatly on the streets where the Jamaicans carried guns.

There were no guns in jail. But there are plenty of knives…

I became real hardened after a time. If you are exposed to constant violence and the threat of violence 24-7- 365 days a year you get hard or you get abused. Every second, every minute of every day I was prepared for violence and I was prepared to defend against violence. I would never initiate violence, but I would defend against it. Every look, every glance, every contact with another convict had to be analyzed for threats or the presence of threats, covert or overt. I was in shark mode, lion mode, and the law of the jungle mode. I was living at the lowest scale of humanity, in the bottom feeder's world. It was really peculiar for me a non-violent person (who'd been basically sheltered in schools most of my life, highly educated, a lover of mental stimulation and logic), now suddenly thrown into this medieval world where brute force was the rule. It's almost impossible for someone on the outside to understand, but internally I was transformed into a gladiator. I am not small in stature, standing some 6’ 4” tall and weighing 205 lbs. I have a physical presence, but it’s the mental transformation that’s indescribable. All I can say is that I was prepared to do violence if and when confronted with violence.

I came to the stark realization that anybody’s capable of violence. I saw first-hand how your environment can dictate a person’s attitude. I understood how a good, non-violent person could be drafted into the marines and trained to be violent and become in essence a trained killer. In prison, the only difference is that the training is not formalized, and you don’t have the moral justifications to hide behind. I guess if self-preservation is the issue, then that’s the supreme moral justification.

Another transformation that occurred was in the area of my relationship with my friends and family on the outside. At the time of my arrest, all my true friends were still in college. I knew that they could not help me and communication was virtually impossible. Plus I’m not the type to place undue burdens on others. I was also ashamed to have anyone know that I was arrested, so I was reluctant to make any contact. Most of my family resided in Jamaica; hence family contact was severely limited. My mom was the only person I made contact with. She was my only connection to the outer world. She stood by me and still stands by me today. I separated myself from the outside world. I compartmentalized my life. That which was beyond the prison gates was just that. All my focus was trying to survive minute to minute. I placed my pre-arrest, outside life securely in its own compartment and tried not to open the door to it very often. I did not think, reflect, nor reminisce, especially after I was convicted and sent upstate, the second leg of my ordeal.

I believe this reaction was a defense mechanism. A collateral result of incarceration is the destruction of your humanity. The entire system is designed to accomplish just that. Feelings and emotions other than hate are taboo in this environment. To express other feelings and emotions usually has to be done in secret. Prison is not conducive to genuine human expressions other than hate, pain and suffering. You actually have to wage a war within yourself to hold on to your humanity. Years of isolation, lack of tactile stimulation, and social deprivation calcifies the heart and results in a coldness that only the long-term incarcerated can understand.

You see, I understood the reality of prison immediately. I witnessed men psychologically fall apart as they desperately tried to hold on to personal relationships that they left on the outside. I saw men commit suicide, get stabbed and killed over access to the telephones, the only direct link to outside relationships. The evidence was overwhelming that once you're in lockdown, to the people in society you're a nobody, a number, a statistic, written off as dead. In prison you're in the land of the forgotten. I chose to bypass what seemed to be the inevitable, the gradual atrophying of friendships into nothing. I did not make contact because I did not want to destroy these friendships. I preferred to leave them as they were so whenever I chose to recall those friendships, I would recall them in their pristine form. This was another compartment into which I had to place my treasured memories.

The other transformation that I went through was not really a transformation but more an evolution. It was the evolution of my inner self, that part of me that remained incorruptible, unaffected, and untarnished by my experiences and surroundings. That is, my true being. Throughout my ordeal, I continued the development of my mind. I wrote poetry, articles, and read and read. I educated myself in the history of my people, the religions of the world, and an eclectic assortment of knowledge. I began an inner journey where I traveled deep within myself. I meditated, contemplated, fasted, and learned to elevate my consciousness. It may sound contradictory, but within the middle of all the chaos, I became super-conscious. I discovered my inner being and touched upon the Holy Grail of spirituality. I was on this path from the day I was born, continued on it right throughout my incarceration, and still walk that path today. I am certain that I'd have gotten here without the experience of prison. Prison at best may've been a catalyst in my evolution. It may have just sped up this part of my inner evolution. At this level, you realize that love is the answer for all social ills, that Love is God.

This is where I'm at in my inner sanctum.

I, along with others, am subjected to what I call low intensity abuse every day in prison. The fact that I'm serving a life sentence for a crime I did not commit is the quintessence of abuse itself.

One of the many physical abuses I somehow survived occurred during my trial. I was held at Holmesburg Prison, a brutal place since closed down. Twelve years ago, the institution had been on lockdown indefinitely because of violence. As I got back to the block from court, I requested a court call from the officer on the block so I could let my family know the defense was starting the next day and they should be there. I didn't trust my obviously incompetent, court-appointed lawyer to make the call. According to policy, during lockdown, inmates were allowed a phone call after returning from court. The officer told me to lock up until after count and that he'd see what he could do. An hour and a half later, twenty minutes after count was completed, I called to the officer to remind him about the court call. He came to my cell and said he was unsure about whether or not we could make calls during lockdown. I said we were allowed and I asked to see the major on duty. He unlocked my cell and then walked off the block. I left the block to go to the next block to speak to the major.

To enter a block, you have to pass through two gates. The outer gate is electronically controlled from a bubble, then there's a small vestibule space and an inner gate that is manually operated by an officer with a key. Due to lockdown, both gates were open.

As I entered the H-block gate, an unfamiliar officer, in an arrogant tone, asked me where I was going. I told him I wanted to speak to the major.

He replied, "You ain't seeing no major, nigga. Go the fuck back to your block."
When I tried to explain why I wanted so see the major, he put his hands on my chest and pushed me backward. My anger began to rise. "Don't put your hands on me," I said with a hard stare. At that moment, my block officer appeared from the inside of the inner gate and I asked him if he'd spoken to the major about my call.

"No, I forgot," he said. I implored him to go back and ask the major. In the middle of a sentence, I was blindsided by a crushing blow to the side of my face, like being hit with a hammer. My head was jarred sideways and I became enveloped in darkness and saw tiny points of light darting in all directions. Instinctively, I went into combat mode. As my hands went up to protect my face from further blows, someone grabbed me from behind, pinning my left arm and slamming me against something iron. Trying to fend off blow after blow, I tried swinging with one hand, but to no avail.

The blows kept coming.

As soon as my optic nerve began to de-scramble the scrambled signals coming from my intelligence, another blow landed to scramble all the signals again. My body switched from combat mode to survival mode. I couldn't see because of the blood streaming down my face, but my thinking was crystal clear. I knew I had to get out of that vestibule into the rotunda where I might have a chance.

While being beaten from every angle, through a Herculean effort and my martial arts training, I dragged myself through the gate. When the blood momentarily cleared from my eyes, I was surprised to see that I was surrounded by at least fifteen officers in a blood frenzy. One sergeant had a two by four in his hand which I didn't realize he'd already used on me. I twisted and turned as the blows continued to rain down on me from everywhere. I refused to be knocked out, fighting unconsciousness three times until they finally subdued me. Still struggling with my attackers, I cursed them as I was dragged to the infirmary through C block, where a few inmates stood at their doors watching the ghastly procession. I remember looking into their eyes and seeing them recoil in shock. One man shouted obscenities at the officers.

When I got to the infirmary, handcuffed, I kept asking to be taken to my cell, that I was alright. A CO named Brock, who had been trading insults with me, punched me twice in the face as hard as he could. The entrance of the nurse kept him from a third blow. When the nurse examined me, there was a strange look on her face and she said I had to get to the hospital right away.

Brock and two others were assigned to take me to the hospital. My blood-soaked clothes were removed and I was given a jumpsuit, a size medium when I told them I wore an extra large. It was supertight, fitting like a g-string in certain places. I glared with hate at Brock, and he tightened the cuffs and then stomped as hard as he could on the toes of my shoes with his steel heels. I laughed at him as he fastened shackles on my feet. I could only stumble to the van, the cuffs and shakles biting into my already broken flesh.
As we neared the hospital, Brock brandished a chrome .38 to my face and threatened to kill me. As the van pulled in, he said, "When we open the door, run, nigga so I can shoot you."

“Shoot me now,” I snapped. “There’s nothing you can do to intimidate me.”

An attendant with a wheelchair interrupted his threats, his face getting a peculiar look when he saw my face. As we got onto the elevator, I saw an elderly Black woman who looked like a nurse’s aide. She gazed on me with such loving tenderness that my seething anger and hatred dissipated immediately. It was like cold water was thrown onto a fire. Tears began to run down the lady’s face as she looked at me. I thought, “I must really be fucked up.”

I was.

My trial was postponed while I underwent reconstructive surgery to repair a broken nose, broken right cheek, fractured left cheek, lacerated cornea and broken elbow.
I have never fully recovered from this incident. Every time I flex my elbow, I experience severe pain; the doctor tells me it will only get worse as I get older. My left eye has blurred vision beyond eight feet. I have recurring nightmares and suffer from some type of paranoia. The slightest jingle of keys puts me in a heightened state of alertness. I cannot tolerate another inmate living in the cell with me. Sometimes I don’t sleep for days. If I’m asleep and someone bangs on the door or attempts to open it, I jump up in full combat mode, and will have a pounding headache for hours afterward.

It should be noted that the officers who assaulted me were among those responsible for the murders of at least two other inmates, crippling another, and assaulting numerous other inmates in the two years I was at Holmesburg.
On one occasion, over 100 inmates were brutally beaten by being forced to run a gauntlet of over 50 officers armed with night sticks. This happened after a minor uprising on one of the blocks.

After about four years into my journey, I began to realize that the people who inhabit this world can be categorized into certain personality types and I saw certain trends. This is my Galapagos.
I began to write down my observations, and I shared them with other inmates to see their reactions. I learned that what I was writing were aphorisms, short, concise statements of principles, maxims or adages. When the collection grew large enough for a book, I hoped they would stimulate thought and discourse in others as they had with the imprisoned.

Contemplations of a Convict* : *Aphorisms for the Heart and Mind (Infinity Publishing, 2001) is a collection of aphorisms written spontaneously in response to twelve years of observation from inside prison where, unless justice is served, I will be spending the rest of my years. Now that Contemplations of a Convict is finally published, I feel differently about it. The book has evolved from the abstract to snapshots of events at times tinged with humor. I now feel the book has universal appeal regarding the human condition. It is for anyone who likes to ponder life, to introspect. An expanded second printing is in the works.

What I've done educationally since then is what I'll continue to do till I die: study and respect life in all it's manifestations. I am a student of life and life is my school and teacher. That's the only other degree I want, the one that Life has to offer.

Now I'm working on a book of poetry.

The vision I have for myself post-incarceration is basically an improvement on the one I had while I was in college. I see myself expressing all my natural talents and trying to reach the maximum of my potential. I imagine myself producing and directing one of my screenplays. I plan to write twelve; I've written three so far. I want to write and produce two theatrical plays that would capture the prison experience and educate the public about the reality of the justice system. I'll publish an anthology of my poems. I want to be a speaker on behalf of prison reform and the alternatives to punishment. I want to do the college circuit, enlighten, inform, and educate college students about the realities behind bars. I would like to speak to high school students, especially those from the Caribbean, about the allure and pitfalls of a life of crime. I want to produce at least two reggae albums from the 150 songs that I've written. I would like to make manifest the 100 business plans and business ideas that I've detailed in my book of goals. Each idea in this book is innovative and could be a highly profitable business on it's own. The common thread throughout these plans is the empowerment of poor people and people from the Caribbean countries. I would set up a network of these mostly homespun micro-industries and be the link between them and the world market.

The greatest damage incarceration has done to me personally is the stagnation of my ambitions. I've never lived just for myself. To this day, I cannot fathom the culture of selfishness socially accepted here in America. Everything I do, believe it or not, is motivated by the desire to give to others or to help others. Those who really know me would verify that. I never had fancy cars or jewelry etc. I never used any type of drugs; I only drank alcohol maybe three times in my life. The only reason I started to sell drugs was because I was coerced into it. After that I was under the misguided impression that I could accrue the $40,000 I needed to start my first business, a West Indian night club in Philadelphia. The goal was easily attainable; what I failed to take into account was the corrupt nature of the people in the underworld that I'd become associated with. Here's another unbelievable fact: I removed myself from the drug gang without any financial gain, because I could not bring myself to compromise a higher moral principle. I voluntarily walked away four weeks before I was to receive a major financial reward. I know it all sounds contradictory; don't puzzle yourself you will never understand.

(*Contemplations of a Convict: aphorisms for the heart and mind* is available fromInfinitypublishing.com, 519 W. Lancaster Avenue, Haverford, PA 19041-1413, 877-BUY BOOK or buybooksontheweb.com $19.95 ISBN 0-7414-1000-1)

Self portrait from an exhibit at Eastern Penitentiary, Anton Forde/Trevor Mattis

"The incredible state of mental breakdown in the nation's prisons is a testament to our efforts to kill not only the bodies but the spirits of our unwanted populations...Even if prison building created no Keynesian stimulus, and there were no private prisons to profit from locking up the poor, and if prison labor were abolished...American capitalism would still have to manage and contain its surplus populations and poorest classes with paramilitary forms of segregation, containment and repression. At the heart of the matter lies this contradiction: capitalism needs the poor and creates poverty, intentionally through policy and organically through crisis. Yet capitalism is directly and indirectly threatened by the poor...Prison and criminal justice are about managing these irreconcilable contradictions." Christian Parenti from ***Lockdown America: Police and Prisons in the Age of Crisis*** *Verso '99*

Anton Forde/Trevor Mattis

Review of Anton Forde/Trevor Mattis's *Contemplations of a Convict*

By Joan Gauker

The American criminal justice system - in its use of primitive crime prevention tactics – works to destroy the well being of its charges, to take away their sensitivities and their ability to think for themselves.

However, Anton Forde/Trevor Mattis, the author of this book, denied the system his heart and mind. Instead, he gave his feelings and intellect to his writings by disciplining himself to journal his thoughts before they passed from his mind. The habit became a lifeline for this young Black man serving a life sentence for a crime he didn't commit. During more than a decade, Forde/Mattis refined his journaling as he improved his skills at recording what he contemplated, saw, heard, felt and learned.

Even though he is confined in a 6' x 9' cell in a stark, ugly, noisy, large, cinderblock and cement building, he escapes the mundane with his ponderings, which he skillfully crafts into profound understandings for all of society. While he gives us a window into his mind, he also opens windows in our own minds, and gives us new insights into life around us wherever we are. In the best of environments, few can contemplate life as well as Forde/Mattis has observed it in his book. So it is especially compelling when one experiences such profound, insightful writings emanating from a prison's depraved environment. Contemplations of a Convict is a clear statement from one of the millions of people in America's unredemptive and degrading punishment system that while the body can be imprisoned, the mind and heart remain free. Forde/Mattis shows us that in his wide range of aphorisms - which are for all people- and which are sad, happy, angry, sensitive and compassionate, but most of all thoughtful.

"To what extent do we remain obligated to the world even when we are expelled from it or have withdrawn from it? We humanize the world through incessant and continual discourse; a world without discourse is inhuman in the literal sense." Hannah Arendt

Chapter Six
WILL DNA TESTING SET HIM FREE?

Robert Muhkam Hagood
($1,085,000)

"A thing of beauty may be consciously realized as a result of distinguishing one's self from the perceived ugly within the environment of one's captivity and isolation."
Muhkam

Robert "Muhkam" Hagood has also been convicted of a crime for which he claims innocence, saying he never had any physical contact with the victim, who was a stranger to him. As with Muti and Anton, who were sentenced to life based on the word of just one person, it was only the testimony of a prostitute who may have been the real murderer that put him in prison for life. In his more than thirty years behind bars, he has become a poet, considered by some one of the best poets in Pennsylvania. A quiet, deeply religious man, he has had little contact with the outside world since his beloved wife died five years ago.
His is a love story.

Papering his cell walls with photographs of flowers and nature, he says he has "the most beautiful garden at Graterford." His is a tale of deprivation and the power of love to transform. With help from Muti, he is waiting for the Pennsylvania legislature to pass a law paying for inmates to get DNA testing and to file a petition to secure the test which could prove his innocence. If the evidence is still available. According to the New York-based INNOCENCE PROJECT, DNA *testing has so far proven 115 people were sent to prison for crimes they did not commit. In almost half of the exonerations, local prosecutors refused to release crime evidence for* DNA *testing until litigation was threatened or filed. For an innocent person like Muhkam, the hope of getting access to the evidence for testing is a crap shoot, dependent on the whims of the state, the county, the judge or a clerk.*

In our class exercise to find beauty behind prison walls, Muhkam wrote about a picture of school children in Ghana he'd been given by Queen Nana Ama Akoffo, co-founder of the Pan African Studies Community Education Program at Temple University in Philadelphia and one of two elderly women who are now his only visitors. "Beauty" is from a class exercise.

BEAUTY

"There were fifty ivory smiles
One hundred sparkling brown eyes,
Faces not unlike any I've seen before,
In fact, quite alike.
There was nothing unlike the starched white shirts
And navy blue trousers of any parochial school in the states.
Perhaps it was all imagery, imagination, illusion or delusion.
Still, I found the photo Queen Nana sent me
Of her adopted children of Akyim Hemang village
In Ghana, West Africa, to be the most beautiful…
Beautiful African boys and girls thirsting for knowledge.
Beautiful Children of the Future…
Precious jewels of my eyes.

He wrote to me the following week.
After you typed it, I looked it over in my cell and decided that with some light touches it was worthwhile. I sent a copy to Queen Nana and, to my surprise, a joyous thing happened. At the time, the chief of her tribe, Dr. Apori, was in Philadelphia, participating in the Pan African Studies Community Education Project. She read him my poem and he loved it so much he asked to take it back to Africa to be read to the children that were in the picture that had reminded me of beauty.

****

"Hope if the thing with feathers
that perches in the soul
and sings the tune without the words
and never stops-at all."
Emily Dickinson

****

Muhkam

I remember as if it was yesterday the judge, saying, "I sentence you to a state correctional institution for the rest of your life." In that moment back in April 1973, I remember thinking, this is unreal. I can't believe someone is taking my life away for something I didn't do. I knew that I hadn't killed anyone, but no one else seemed to realize it. I had come up on the streets and had been involved with a lot of petty criminal activity. Still, I was naïve enough to believe that when it came down to a life sentence, if you didn't do it, you wouldn't be convicted. I felt that this couldn't be happening.

I grew up in Passaic, New Jersey. My earliest childhood memory is that darn table that I was always trying to get away from. Mom tells me that I can't remember that far back, but I do. Mom considered me to be a wanderer. She had a little harness that she placed around me that connected to the leg of the kitchen table. She'd hook me up whenever she had work to do. I seemed to be in a constant struggle with that table, trying to get away from the weight. Looking back, that seemed to be some kind of a sign that as I struggled through life, I was going to have to carry a lot of weight on my back.

There's not a lot I can tell you about Pop, Lemmie John Haygood. He was in and out of our lives until Mom made her final decision that enough is enough!

My father was an orphan from Barbados who had been adopted by an American woman who wanted a companion for her son. Mom and Pop met at a dance when he was working for the Civilian Conservation Corps. When I was in third grade, I convinced everyone in the family to drop the "y" from our name because I thought it looked better. I remember Pop looking across the table at me with his large, very dark face. His teeth were as white as the keys on a new piano. He parted his wavy hair in the center and he was clean shaven except for a thin moustache. Short and wide, he had the muscles and forearms of a bodybuilder, and his stomach was flat even after he was fifty.

As I waited for his reaction to my wanting the name change, he suddenly smiled and looked over at my mother and said, "You teach my son to read and write before he can wipe his ass, and now he thinks he's a genius." He used to brag to his friends about how well I could read and write, and sometimes in the morning his friends would come by and I'd read the help wanted ads for them, marking places that needed their skills. As a child, I thought they did this for luck, but years later I realized that Pop and his "no good friends," as Mom called them, hadn't learned to read.

Once a promising student, my teachers wouldn't tolerate my errant behavior, and until I finished my education at

Graterford, I was almost as ignorant as my father and his friends.

Looking back, I see he was never abusive to me and my sisters, but he and Mom just couldn't get along. I don't know why. Pop died on New Year's Eve in 1974. He'd slipped on ice and was injured, and he later had a stroke. I was already incarcerated when this occurred; I got the message from the chaplain. I was not allowed to attend his funeral. I recall sitting in my cell just saying over and over, "Damn, Pop, Damn!"

As an adult, I lived in Harlem. I was traveling through Pennsylvania when I was arrested. I'm still trying to get through Pennsylvania…

In reflecting on my life, I feel shame for the man I was then. I was the oldest of five children of a single mother who was hard-working and would do any honest work with dignity and pride, encouraging her children to do the same. Still, I had no dreams or aspirations other than what could satisfy my immediate selfish desires. I had no bonds with anyone, male or female, that were not connected to my needs or personal gain. I took advice from no one and only punishment deterred me. I had no goals. I remember in grade school, teachers would ask the class what we wanted to be when we grew up. I didn't think I was going to be anything. I had no vision of anything good coming out of my environment or my life, so I never had any plans or false dreams.

Some of the children would say they wanted to be firemen, or doctors, or cops. I just wanted to be. If I existed today and survived, then maybe I'll exist tomorrow. Every day was survival time. No one put me on TV, but I was a survivor and that was it.

I couldn't point to a single person as a role model and I didn't want to. My environment suggested that if I wanted to survive, I had to be a certain way despite evidence around me that people were doing a lot more than surviving. Because of the limitations I'd placed on myself by not daring to have a dream beyond that microcosmic world, I became what I was.

I was a criminal in my mind and in my deeds. I felt that any action (other than hard work) that led to my survival or enjoyment showed my courage and intelligence, and that made me worthy of respect. The fact is that I had never experienced love or respect until I met and married Doris Dean Hagood, my first and only love, the woman I married sixteen years after my arrest and conviction. I'll talk about that in a minute.

The reason I could be accused and convicted of a crime I did not commit was because of my criminal mentality and actions. Because of my brutish behavior, my academic and social ignorance, it was not unlikely that someone could eventually be killed by me. It wasn't beyond me, and most people on the street considered me quite capable of just that. But I have never killed; I never wanted to kill anyone. Yet I've been falsely accused and literally lynched for the murder of a white man I'd never known.

I've been in prison now more than 30 years, costing the state more than $1 million. I spent the first ten years bouncing my head off the concrete wall, thinking my rebelliousness was going to alter my situation. I thought that by striking out, kicking, screaming, growling and putting myself in more unwholesome situations, things would change.

My cries of innocence fell on deaf ears, my countless attempts at appeals failed, and for years I wallowed in disappointment and self-pity.

During the years of my imprisonment certain events that occurred or facts that were made evident at my trial have come to mind. Some of these occurrences may seem unbelievable to those outside of my experience, however, one truth should be evident, and that is, I am innocent and the activities of all involved denied me the right to a fair trial.

THE KNIFE:

During the trial, the detective told the court that the alleged murder weapon was given to him by his captain. Also, that the captain told him that a forensic check was not necessary because the weapon had been handled too much. Question: BY WHOM? Unanswered.

The detective continued to say that the captain told him that he had been directed to the weapon by an anonymous caller.

QUESTIONS:

(A) Why did the captain go alone to a secluded area to pick up this weapon that he was directed to by the anonymous caller?

(B) Who else did the captain know had handled the weapon besides himself and perpetrator?

(C) Why were there not photographers and a forensic team present when the captain retrieved this weapon that he believed was the cause of a homicide?

(D) Who was the anonymous caller?

(E) Was there a caller at all? If there was not an anonymous caller, did I receive a fair trial? Linda Lane, an admitted prostitute and drug addict, and the state's star witness, testified that she pulled the knife out of the victim's body and threw the weapon into an abandoned building. Also, that she did not recall which building. She denied making the anonymous call or that she had told anyone where she had thrown the knife. However, Linda Lane identified the knife as the murder weapon for the state.

The captain was never called to the court by the prosecutor or trial counsel to explain his behavior, unusual in a homicide case. The trial judge, the prosecutor and trial attorney each acted in a concerted manner to deny me a fair trial. By not forcing the captain to take the witness stand, my conviction was the result of conjecture rather than one proven by evidence.

Since others have been found innocent based upon DNA evidence that did not exist at the time of their trial, and both the state and the state's star witness alleged that I was in an altercation (physical fight) with the victim and stabbed him with a knife, that testimony is at least suspect if not tainted. I know that DNA evidence from the clothing and person of the victim as well as DNA evidence from myself will prove that I am innocent of the crime for which the trial judge, prosecutor and trial attorney have caused me to spend thirty years of my life in prison.

I need people to help raise funds and to represent me in the courts and to demand that I be given an opportunity to prove my innocence through DNA testing.

In and out of The Hole, I was fortunate enough one day to sit down and for the first time begin to reflect on my situation. The process of change started then. I decided the way I was wasn't working for me, and I started thinking seriously about my wasted life and why I thought that was the only way to be. As I pondered God and Satan, life and death, good and evil, heaven and hell, I decided to change, I'd rather serve in heaven than rule in hell. That is still my choice today.

Sometimes a seed of transformation has been planted in the soil of the mind that you're not aware of until it manifests in the future. In December 1984, after spending a year in The Hole at Huntingdon for "leading a protest" against the beatings and horrible food, I was transferred to Graterford and attended a Kwaanza celebration. The program concluded with men and women guests greeting each other. I was still a little paranoid about crowds of people, so when I saw the crowd of large men standing like trees around a small, cute brown woman, I watched from a chair while my heart tried to leap out of my chest. She had a pleasant smile for all who greeted her and an occasional dimple would appear on soft cheeks. As I watched her slowly walk out the door, I promised myself that the next year I was going to meet this wonderful lady.

By the next year, as a result of my involvement with cultural activities in the institution, I was the host for the Kwaanza program. I also read with drama one of my poems about the 1985 Move tragedy in Philadelphia. The inmates and outside visitors roared their approval.

I sat behind the podium after introducing the next performer and heard this sweet voice sing into my ears, "That was a beautiful poem, brother." I responded, "But not as beautiful as the lady in my presence." It was Doris, the woman of my dreams. We smiled and chatted easily, and I was taken aback when she declined my invitation to write, something she'd already said to others with the same proposal. As we walked down the corridor after the celebration, her hand brushed mine and, without a word, we walked with our hands linked, unaware of the stares of visitors and prisoners. When we reached the security bubble, she turned and told me she was going to give me a chance to write to her. "I'll write tonight, pretty lady." And I did.

I don't remember what I wrote, but I remember vowing that I would never lie to her about who I'd been or what I'd done. I answered her questions with an honesty of which I didn't know I was capable. She came to visit often, arriving at 9 am and not leaving until the mandatory 3 pm. When I told her about my case, she trembled in my arms and tears streamed down her face. My heart quickened and I stopped talking and just held her gently, her cheek on my chest. This was during the time when men and women could still embrace each other in the visitors' room; now there is no touching or the guards can terminate the visit. Doris looked up at me, told me she believed in my innocence that she would do whatever she could to help me. I didn't know a happier day except for the day she told me she loved me and would be pleased to be my wife.

We were married in the visitors' room in 1990 in the presence of her son, two of her three daughters, her granddaughter and her two closest friends, Annie Hyman and Queen Nana, co-founders of the Pan African Studies Community Education Project. Both of these wonderful women have remained close friends to me even though Doris died of a brain aneurysm on June 28,1997. Because of their age, they don't visit often, but were it not for these occasional visits I would probably have none at all.

My mother is also elderly, residing in Shelby, NC. I'll never forget the wonderful surprise that Doris and my mother gave me back in the summer of '93. My mother flew alone for the first time from NC and spent a week with Doris. We're only allowed four visits a month, so Mom visited me three days in a row and saved the last visit so Doris and I could have time alone. When I went to the visitors' room that morning and saw the two women I loved with all my heart and soul walking down those steps, I released all the energies of love, joy and excitement that could flow from what my wife called my 'romantic soul." No, I never loved a woman with the depth of integrity, with the commitment, trust and caring that I reserved for Doris.

After our marriage, it seemed that my attitudes, my way of thinking and my behavior changed. I became much more tolerant of others and I was suddenly participating in every possible program in the prison. I got my associates degree and helped others learn.

I've never known a greater love than that which flowed so freely and abundantly from the heart of this magnificent lady, the wonderful woman and my wife, Doris Bridges Dean Hagood.

I haven't seen my mother since then.

I've transformed myself from a 34-year-old man with an eighth grade education capable of doing only third grade math to one who got a "C" in Algebra from Northampton Community College. I have 86 college credits and an Associate degree in business management. I have more than five years experience teaching or tutoring other prisoners wanting to pass their G.E.D. tests. I've been President of the Pennsylvania Lifers Association at Huntingdon Prison, the first President of the Board of the Graterford branch of the NAACP, the founder of a group called "Students of Cultural Arts," chairman of the Lifers Cultural Affairs Committee, a team leader with the "End Violence" program, and a facilitator for the People Against Recidivism program (PAR), which helps young prisoners stay out of prison once they're released. As a poet and artist, I've been involved with making a documentary in conjunction with Kevin O'Neill and the Painted Bride Arts Center in Philadelphia. Presently I'm a peer assistant for the Institution's Community Orientation/Reintegration Program (COR) where I teach resume' writing, cover letters etc. for prisoners going out on parole

Equally important is that I have become a man of faith. I think a lot about what it means to be human on this planet. My faith is a major factor in my daily life. While I've forgiven myself for being the man I was, I pray seriously to be forgiven by any people I've harmed, hoping that if they are in a state of prayer, they will forgive me.

There are trillions of incidents and accidents that occur in life that you don't have anything to do with, but they impact on your life nonetheless. I may be in my cell maybe eight or nine hours, studying the Qu'ran or trying to work out the rhythm of a poem. If I decide I want to go down the block to talk with a friend, I'm awakened to another reality because maybe my cell is double-locked. The block of 500 men is shut down, maybe the whole prison. Something has happened that has impacted on me that I had nothing to do with. This can happen at any time, day or night. In this environment by the time you walk out of your cell to shower you will meet at least fifty dudes who will get you more time, any time, whether you like it or not. Because these incidents have a way of forcing themselves on you, there are limited alternatives: you deal with it or you run away from it. Running away can have greater disadvantages in a prison situation; whoever you run from, you will eventually have to face them. If you're a man like me, struggling to be free, you must deal with what's in front of you, like it or not. Even though you've changed as a human being, your guilt or innocence doesn't matter. What matters is surviving what is right in your face. Because someone has gone crazy and is on a mission to destroy themselves, they bring their misery into my life and I'm compelled to restrain them. Meanwhile guards are watching to see how I deal with whatever I'm faced with. This can happen at any time. I pray every day that I can avoid this kind of situation. I don't want to test that!

Aside from my writing and reciting my poems, when I'm free I envision myself telling people about the disparities in the criminal justice system and what can occur when police officers and prosecutors abuse their offices in order to gain political power. I want to talk about how cultural biases and prejudices of both judges and juries impact on verdicts despite evidence or lack of evidence. Close to my heart is the vision of speaking to children in the poorest neighborhoods and public schools about not only the importance of education, but the greater importance of not allowing the violence and corruption in their environment to become entrapped their minds and hearts. Also, I'd tell them that as they struggle against crime, violence and corruption with their minds and hearts, they will be empowered to rise above it and create a better life for themselves.

THE CIRCLE OF OPPRESSION

By Robert Muhkam Hagood

The circle of oppression is wide and we are all inside
being screwed in the same vise
lest anyone misunderstand.

I am aware of the Arab marauders and the European pirate exploiters who kidnapped and murdered millions of African men, women and children and distorted the pure beauty of Kemetic civilization while they pillaged and occupied the land...

Still, if the issue was as non-complex as skins being black or white, Mother Earth would have long ago cleared and freed herself of the pale savage blight.

The circle of oppression is wide and we are all inside... The injustice that touches me touches you...

The injustice that touches you... touches me!

Through a video lens, the "best" observe the shanty towns of the downtrodden.

Their night crawling prostitutes, drug abusers, street sleepers; alley creepers and long lines of unemployed standing in front of overcrowded prison houses...

He sees what he alludes to be "The white man's burden." A sarcasm! A lie that he imagines to be a subtlety.

The injustice that touches me touches you...

The injustice that touches you touches me!

In the catacombs of society, prison houses captives made wise by the experience of being gnawed in the crunching iron jaws of the beast, and who have seen with minds of crystal light, the beast's giant claws dripping, dripping, with the blood of the slaughtered oppressed who cry out their admonishment with pleas for solidarity — their voices unheard — in the blowing of the wind.

The circle of oppression is wide and we are all inside... The injustice that touches me touches you...

The injustice that touches you touches me!

Within the circle of oppression minds attracted to the glare of computer windows believe that their new house in town has made them separate, different from those who stare at conveyor belts where they twist once and tap twice, but we are all being screwed in the same vise. The circle of oppression is wide and we are all inside..."

DNA EVIDENCE EXPOSES SYSTEMS FLAWS

By William DiMascio,
Executive Director, Pennsylvania Prison Society.

Prosecutors' quests to win disregard the damage done to innocent individuals. New evidence by DNA testing has fueled a watershed development in forensic science. Its certainty in identifying people makes fingerprinting look like guesswork. The odds against DNA mismatches are said to be in the realm of a quadrillion to one.

In recognition of this powerful tool, Pennsylvania is one of many states to pass laws regulating its use in the criminal justice system. Despite some early squabbles, the law as finally passed has been roundly applauded by defense attorneys and people they represent, as well as prosecutors and tough-on-crime politicians.

Ironically, however, the most profound benefit of DNA technology may have less to do with making sure the "right" people get convicted and more to do with highlighting the substantial flaws in our current system.

Police and prosecutorial misconduct are among the most frequent factors in wrongful convictions, according to the Innocence Project, which has championed the use of DNA evidence. These acts - not accidents or errors of judgment - include suppression and destruction of evidence that might be helpful to defendants, fabrication of evidence, coercion of witnesses and confessions, and other deliberate misdeeds.
The quest of courtroom "wins" has cut a putrid path littered with 115 wrongful convictions that have been overturned by DNA evidence so far. Each of these incidents represented a tremendous waste of public funds, as well as the far more costly erosion of human lives. Prosecutors and others are fond of currying favor among the masses by bold talk of making criminals take responsibility for their actions. Who now will take responsibility for the loss of years suffered by the 115 we know about?

These wrongfully convicted individuals served an average of more than 10 years for each of them. (Cost to taxpayers: approximately $40,250,000)

Montgomery County's District Attorney is Bruce Castor, who did his best to deny DNA testing for inmate Bruce Godschalk, who served 15 years on a double-rape conviction. (Cost to taxpayers: $525,000) His attorneys had to get a federal court order before Castor would provide access to DNA evidence. After two independent comparisons of the evidence, Godschalk was released. Castor was still unwilling to accept the facts and only grudgingly conceded to the news media that he didn't believe Godschalk was innocent, just that he couldn't be proved guilty.

"Prosecutors don't want to admit to any mistakes - past, present or future," said Ray Krone, who spent three years on death row, then seven more under a life sentence in Arizona ($350,000) before DNA analysis showed he was innocent of the murder, kidnapping and sexual assault of which he was convicted.

"DNA is going to be the undoing of them if they don't start doing a better job in the courtroom. It's a good sign that some prosecutors are willing to act in good faith."

In a way, DNA is laying bare the sins of a system that is often too adversarial, with reckless disregard for the damage done to innocent individuals. Now it is time for an informed citizenry to demand a higher level of accountability from the people who are paid to see that true justice is being served.

****

"There is nothing training cannot do. Nothing is above its reach. It can turn bad morals to good; it can destroy bad principles and recreate good ones; it can lift men to angelship." Mark Twain

****

"When the policy of an entire country is predicated both covertly and overtly on the systematic destruction of a people by refusing to give them basic human rights, the racist acts of any of their citizens in the furtherance of such policies, like in the assassination of Martin Luther King Jr., are the result and responsibility of that country."

John W. Griffin, A Letter To My Father

Chapter Seven
DID HE EVER HAVE A CHANCE?

TONY HARPER
($875,000)

Tony Harper was born with his feet on backwards. His early life was one surgery after another. Like several of the other prisoners, he's been in prison for over 25 years, since he was a sixteen, for a crime he did not commit. Tony dropped out of high school at sixteen because he was so far behind due to illness. Most of his childhood and early teenage years were spent in hospitals and rehab centers for a disease that "made his bones soft." He was once in a body cast for four months as a young child.

When he was interrogated by the police for a robbery-homicide apparently committed by his almost-identical looking brother, Tony was beaten so badly that his injuries put him in the hospital for three weeks. His brother was later killed in a drive-by shooting.

One of the beginning writers in the class, Tony, who could only write his name when he was first sentenced, shows promise. He is intelligent, has an excellent eye for detail and is a curious and sensitive soul. Once while waiting to be escorted out by guards after class, I noticed him sitting alone in a corner. When I sat down on the floor next to him to discuss his work, he seemed surprised. And pleased.
A strong connection was made.

His work was confiscated by guards during one of my interrogations that led to my resignation, and he became afraid to write, saying in a letter:
"I was disappointed to learn you resigned as our writing teacher, though as I looked at the situation and the way the guards treated you, I can understand why you had to step away from this place. The people who run this place are not nice. You are awesome because you came into these conditions to spread some much-needed light. I congratulate you for staying as long as you've done without doing emotional harm to yourself. I do understand.

Since this happened to us, I have not written a word. I felt violated to the point of being scared. I just wanted to thank you for the encouragement. You have allowed me to shine."

A year later, after steady correspondence, he spirit was again strong as he wrote, "The only thing I have left in this life is my voice, and I won't allow anybody to stop it no matter what. The state only has my body; my mind is my own. The way things stand, I may never get out of prison. Do you really think I will let them take any more than they already have from me? I fight for whatever rights I have based on my values, not theirs."

Tony suffers from Hepatitis C, diabetes, a weakness in his bones and a strange lung disease that interferes with his breathing. He is harassed by guards when his feet swell so badly he can't put on shoes and instead wears sandals, which they claim is against regulations.

During a recent trip outside for medical treatment, his first time outside prison walls in 25 years, Tony was so sick he slept most of the trip there and back, barely noticing all of the changes.

Tony's aging father, a World War 11 hero, and his family are his constant supporters. His father, 88, says he knows his son is not guilty because the police know who did the killing. "My son is innocent and I'll spend my whole life trying to get him free!"

****

"The mind, once enlightened, cannot again become dark."
Thomas Paine

****

TONY

I was born Tony Ricardo Harper on October 31, 1958. My parents had ten children, four girls and six boys. Most of them have passed away since I've been incarcerated, the biggest blows of my life. My grief was low-key, for people in here who can't keep their emotions in check aren't looked at kindly. My younger years were full of nothing but turmoil. For me, every sight and sound was a source of wonder, and I had a thirst for learning what this world was about, even its underbelly.

I'll never forget a church trip to Canada when I was thirteen, my first exposure to people of all colors. I recall being amazed at the streets uncluttered with trash and the way the people related to each other. I promised myself I'd one day revisit this land. My father, who'd seen the world during WW11, wanted his children to see and experience the true beauty of different places and different people.

When my sister, Jerry, died during childbirth, it seemed to do something to my parents. It was like something dark was hanging over the house; it was so bad I went to live with my sister.

I remember once coming home from middle school and finding my mother with her head down, sobbing, at the kitchen table. Unhappiness filled her daily. When I asked her what was wrong, she told me I knew about my father having a relationship with another woman and I owed it to her to tell her who it was. I told her I knew nothing, that the trips we went on were to collect rents from some of my father's tenants or to attend sporting events. She hollered at me that I knew what was going on and she'd fix me along with him. From out of the blue, she slapped me in the face because I wouldn't tell her who the woman was. I told her to talk with my father.

That evening, she tried to end her life by taking an overdose of pills. She'd been badly abused in her first marriage, which my father knew. A few months later, when my mother got out of the hospital, she told us she'd be moving in with my brother-in-law to help take care of the motherless baby. She abandoned her own children to look after her grandchild and the family broke up without resolving any of their issues.

In retrospect, I think if my mother had stayed around to raise us, we would have turned out better. I've never held her abandonment against her, because only she knew what she was dealing with. I keep in touch with her once or twice a month, but she never visits me.

I left school at sixteen and was working when I was arrested.

On September 12, 1975, I had the day off from my job at a Philadelphia hospital and I slept until about 9:00 am. After making myself breakfast, I rode my bike around to 71st St. and stopped to talk with some friends. It was around 10 am. My brother Robin came up and asked me if he could borrow my bike; I gave it to him and told him I'd be waiting on the corner. Frances Wilson lived in an apartment on the corner, and she asked me to come up and see her, and I told her I'd be by later.

After a while, Robin came back with the bike and I rode it to Frank's gas station where I talked with Frank and my father for about half an hour. A police car pulled in and the cop told Frank there's been a homicide a few blocks away. We stood and talked for awhile, then the cop drove off. My brother, Marcel, asked that I wait at his house for his son to be dropped off by his mother.

I left the bike in front of his door when I got to his house. I was there for about twenty minutes when Robin and another guy, Gator, knocked at the door and asked me if I wanted to get high. I was using drugs, all kinds of drugs, every day. We went up to my brother's bedroom and got high. Later, when my brother came home, he asked me if I wanted to ride with him to see my mother. We went downstairs and played with his son while he took a bath, saying we'd go about 6 pm.

Marcel hollered at me that the police were outside and to dump the drugs. I thought he was joking. I was at the top of the stairs when the police, who'd forced their way in (though they later claimed the door was open), were at the bottom of the stairs and told me to come down with my hands behind my head. The cop slammed me against the wall, hitting my face. I thought it had to do with drugs, but I soon learned this was not the case.

They asked me if I had a gray sweatshirt. I asked why? They searched the house and all three of us were taken to the Roundhouse, the police administration building. Robin, Gator and I were taken to separate interrogation rooms. I was handcuffed to a stool and left alone for an hour. Two detectives came into the room and asked me my name. I said I wanted a lawyer. He said the guy I shot didn't ask for a lawyer and the other detective punched me in the neck. I had trouble breathing for awhile and they walked out. Two more detectives came into the room and I again asked for a lawyer, saying that I didn't understand what was going on. One of them kept punching me in the ribs and the other kept saying I'd robbed and killed a man at the corner store. After an hour of beating and questioning, they walked out. Another officer came to the doorway and stood there with a police dog, which I thought for sure he was going to command to attack me. He just stared at me, then walked away and closed the door.

With blood pouring out of my nose, I was alone in the room for about half an hour.

Another guy came in and asked me if I needed anything and I told him I needed a doctor and a lawyer. He said they'd make sure I saw a doctor after I answered the detectives' questions. I told him I wanted a lawyer, that I knew my rights. He responded, "You have no rights."

The two detectives came into the room, one holding a thick phone book, and said Robin said I did the crime. An old guy came into the room and sat at a desk, writing something. While one of the cops kept saying I'd done this crime, the other kept hitting me with the phone book, over and over until I almost passed out. The old guy got up and asked if I had anything to say. I again asked for a doctor. He hit me on the side of my face and told me to sign a paper. I told him I wasn't signing anything. He finally left the room where I stayed alone for two or three hours. During the beatings the detectives used all kinds of racist statements, saying several times, "We could kill you and you would not be missed, nigger."

The two detectives returned, cuffed me and as we walked out of the room, a woman and her children looked at me and one of them said, "They beat him up!"

I was pushed past them real fast.

When I was placed in a cell, I told the sergeant I needed a doctor and he sent me across the street to the police hospital. The doctor looked at my eye, felt my side and gave me a pain killer, telling me to see my family doctor the next day. I was returned to my cell. After many complaints, I was taken to the prison hospital for observation. From there I went to an outside hospital where I spent three weeks healing from internal injuries.

Once back in jail I was placed in a unit with people with drug problems and I was told I'd have to continue taking a drug that would "put my system back to normal."

A few months later I was taken to a hearing to see if I could stand trial for the homicide. My court-appointed lawyer, Ralph Swartz, said he'd take care of the fact that I'd asked for a lawyer during my interrogation and had been denied. He never did anything about it or many other miscarriages of justice.

After the hearing, I was transferred to Holmesburg Prison, where I was placed in some kind of a mental unit and given drugs. I stayed medicated all through my hearings and at my trial. I realized this is what those racist crackers wanted, for me to be doped up. Before this happened, I did not use words like racist crackers towards white people. But what happened to me has taught me to hate, and I do it with passion. I was wronged by those detectives and the whole system. So I started taking the drugs every other day until I was eased off them. I asked my lawyer to postpone things until I could get off the mind-numbing drugs, but he said to just relax. I couldn't formulate my thoughts and everything came out jumbled.

My attorney didn't object to an all-white jury, for some reason. The court found me guilty. I really had no idea what was going on through my arrest and trial; the judge acted like I wasn't even in the room. I was sentenced to life without the possibility of parole. The judge was Paul J. Silverstein.

When first in prison, I was unable to deal with what had happened. Behind these walls we are subjected to the harsh realities of what one man with the keys does to another when no one is looking. My jailers inflict pain with so much ease, hurting us in the name of some perverted justice. They think they can do whatever they want to us in the name of whatever they perceive to be the wrongs we've inflicted on society.

I became cold emotionally. When I fell into the old pattern of getting high, the warden did me a great service by shipping me to another jail. That's when I started to get myself together, enrolling in a GED program. I owe all that I am to God and having my family stand by me.

Over the years I've been involved in many groups, programs and therapy classes. I became willing to change and offer the community my efforts and talents. All this has contributed to my growth.

Once I was found guilty of murder, I called my girlfriend Marge and tried to break things off with her. I didn't think she had the staying power. She claimed she'd be there for me as long as I needed her. She lasted two years. I knew in the back of my mind that not many people on the outside could endure the pain and suffering heaped on the people who care about those of us behind these walls.

My family and their love and support helped me change my life without becoming bitter with the conditions of prison. My oldest brother, James, is one of my greatest fans. He learned at my father's feet that we are indeed our brothers' keepers. The whole family suffers from my incarceration. I've acknowledged my drug problem. That first night at Graterford, I tried to overdose.

While spending a few months in the mental health unit, I found a copy of the Bible. Trying my best to read it despite my inability to read, I was inspired to enroll in basic education classes, and my hunger to learn continues to this day. Though my case is now in federal court, I have to not let myself hope that I might someday be freed from this house of insanity.

At this time I am going through something horrible. It all started when the prison painted my cell. When I moved back in, I smelled shit, like someone had taken a dump in my cell. So I went about cleaning the cell again. But the smell still prevailed so I chalked it up to bad paint. Then I discovered that someone had taken the light fixture casing off and stuffed shit up into the holes of the light, and it started to fall down on the casing.

I came in from work a few weeks ago, and learned that someone had thrown pee on my cell door. This has been going on for a while. One day, during count, I went to get my insulin from the medical department. When I came back to my cell, someone had thrown water on my floor. Each time something happens, I get the impression that a few of the guards are allowing these abuses. I have every emotion running through my body from rage to pure anger about this indecency to my life. I even thought that this young boy in the cell next to me had something to do with it, but could never prove anything. So I have started to limit the number of people I have around me. As they say, "what doesn't kill me will make me stronger."

If I was freed, the first thing I'd do is get out of this backward state. I have a sense of who I am, and what I've learned is that parole officers send people back to prison for the flimsiest of reasons. I'm not sure I want to risk it.

But my father is getting older and I know he needs someone to be there for him. Some of the things my Dad taught me about love and loyalty to family have stayed with me in spite of the pain and suffering that prison heaps on me daily. My love has grown even stronger. My father wiped my butt when I could not do so out of his love for me. When age becomes too great for my father, I want to be there to insure him that what he taught was not lost on me.

Of course I'll need a job, and I know whatever society states they will not be kind to an ex-convict. I'll have to keep in mind the most important thing I'd have to deal with is the parole people.

My family needs me, and as I've had the strength to survive the prison experience, I can do anything I want to as long as I stay focused.

I've always yearned for the love of a woman, which I've only had a taste of. But I have become a more aware person and because I have medical concerns (Hepatitis C and diabetes), I don't want to harm anyone else. I will most likely stay single so I won't infect anyone else.

Life has thrown me a fast ball with these illnesses, but I will learn to find other things which I can devote myself to.
I will look after my father when he needs me, and will find interests to keep me strong.

I might even start the vending business which I spent a lot of time preparing for in prison.

Who knows what the future holds. Right now I'm struggling just to breathe. All I hope is that whatever comes my way will bring beauty to this man who yearns to be free.

****

"Justice delayed is justice denied.
Freedom's road's so narrow, while incarceration's wide.
Once you've been entangled in this web,
Escape is like swimming upstream with lead."

Anton Forde/Trevor Mattis

"A human being is part of the whole that we call the universe, a part limited in time and space. He experiences himself, his thoughts and feelings, as something separated from the rest-a kind of optical illusion of his consciousness. This illusion is a prison for us, restricting us to our personal desires and to affection for only the few people nearest us. Our task must be to free ourselves from this prison by widening our circle of compassion to embrace all living things and all of nature." Albert Einstein

Chapter Eight
RAPES, MURDERS AND ABUSES

This chapter was the hardest for the men to write, and not all were able to participate, as if these horrors were just too much to dig up and revisit. One said, "Please don't ask me about that!"
For obvious reasons, the identities of most of the writers in this chapter will not be revealed.

Last year an inmate at Graterford died of a "heart attack" after a confrontation with guards when he demanded overdue medication. The word among prisoners is he was stomped to death. One writes, ***"The guy who died in here a few months ago is coming back to bite this jail in the rear end. From what I learned, his family has filed a formal complaint against the guards who attacked him. They said he died from heart failure, but the family learned he had a crushed windpipe. I hope those guards get jail time for what they did."***

****

Inmate

Rapes, murders and abuse? I've been around so much of this shit in the past seventeen years, I don't know where to start. I've seen quite a few people get stabbed. In here, death is not such a significant event. I've heard screams of rape in the night, but the guards never come. I've listened as one convict beat another to death two cells down. I've heard the blood-curdling screams of a man being bludgeoned. I never knew humans could make such a sound. You can actually hear the soul depart in those ghastly screams. I hope never to hear it again.

One night I was awakened in the middle of the night by desperate screams coming from the young man in the cell opposite mine, "Rape! Rape! He's trying to rape me!"
He banged and kicked the cell door, the noise and his screams echoing throughout the 500-man cell block. He was a nice kid; we'd played cards together. I knew his cellmate, a guy named Ice in his early forties who looked like the stereotypical hardened convict—6'2", 200 pounds of chiseled muscle, bald, and with his front teeth missing and a growl for a voice. Ice and the kid were from the same neighborhood; I thought they were friends. Ice was a penitentiary boxer from back in the day and had a reputation in his community. Never smiling, his face mean, you knew this was a guy life hadn't treated kindly. If you came face to face with him, he would look you dead in the eye until you lowered your eyes in submission. I remember laughing to myself when I first met him that he was a caricature of a man. He taught fundamentals of boxing in the yard, and the young men who surrounded him when he shadowboxed were in awe.

I jumped to the door and peered through the 4" x 12" slit of a window and glimpsed two wide eyes looking back at me, terrified, pleading for me to do something. That look burned into my consciousness as I held his gaze in what I hoped was support. I was enraged by my helplessness and my inability to protect the kid.

I silently told him I wouldn't leave him, and continued reaching out to him with my eyes.

Around us the cellblock broke into a cacophony of banging and shouts of both threat to Ice and reassurance to the kid, who was well-liked. The outburst seemed to deter Ice, and it gave the kid confidence when he realized he wasn't alone.

I stayed at the door with him until dawn broke and it was time for us all to be counted.

****

"I am of the opinion that my life belongs to the community, and as long as I live, it is my privilege to do for it whatever I can. I want to be thoroughly used up when I die, for the harder I work, the more I live. Life is no 'brief candle' to me. It is a sort of splendid torch which I have got hold of for a moment, and I want to make it burn as brightly as possible before handing it on to future generations."
George Bernard Shaw

Created more than fifteen years ago, Graterfriends is a monthly newspaper devoted to prisoners' issues and justice. Now published by the Pennsylvania Prison Society, it is circulated around the country. Joan Gauker, the founder and editorial writer, is Coordinator of Volunteers at Graterford Prison.

GRATERFRIENDS, NOVEMBER 2001

"STATE'S MEANNES SHAMEFUL"

by Joan Gauker

To encourage family visits for prisoners in England, the government reimburses family members for transportation costs between their home and the prison—usually within a 25-mile radius of the offender's home. Keep prisoners close to home in our country? Encourage family visits? We don't think so!

And there's more! Prisoners in England can buy phone cards—they don't do collect calls. In visiting rooms, there are snack bars manned by volunteers where prisoners and visitors may buy food. Those in minimum-security prisons may have four visits a week, go home on weekends, have their own dishes, bedding (pillows, blankets) and clothing from home— even their own stereo. Women prisoners are treated with respect. When a pregnant woman delivers her baby in prison, she and the baby stay in a Mother & Baby Unit for six months.

Other Western civilized nations recognize separation from society itself as the punishment and don't try to make that time even more miserable. They see imprisonment as the perfect time to encourage such noble undertakings as continuing education, getting job training, honing social skills or strengthening family ties. But not us.

For us, prison time is "mean time" for prisoners and their families. We in the U.S. would never think of having volunteer-manned snack bars in prison visiting rooms; allowing minimum security prisoners to go home for the weekend and have their own bedding—for heaven's sake! Instead, we feel we must belittle, demean and punish our prisoners— and their families—at every turn—even in little ways.

For instance, the mail. Mail sent by Pennsylvania prisoners is unnecessarily demeaning and embarrassing for family and friends who receive it. Across the front of the envelope is stamped. **INMATE MAIL, PA DEPARTMENT OF CORRECTIONS**. Other states—some considered oppressive for prisoners—don't embarrass their citizens on the outside in such a way. Prisoners' mail from Florida, Georgia, Texas and Utah, to name a few states, arrives with no indication on the envelope front that the mail is from a prison. Texas mailroom people drop a small note into the envelope before it is sealed saying it is from a prisoner, some other states mark the back of the envelope, and others do nothing. Cannot Pennsylvania, at least, put its offensive stamp on the back of envelopes—if they must be stamped?

And there are the drab or striped uniforms, expensive phone calls, restricted visits, lost family days, reduced education support, diminished commutation opportunities, etc. Is it just plain meanness?

Consider the rules for Pennsylvania capital cases and their visitors. For some Draconian reason, our officials believe these people must be isolated—from each other and from family and friends. Pennsylvania confines death-row prisoners to their cells 23 hours a day and allows them outside (weather permitting) for one hour in a dog-run-type yard, and then only at a time when no one is in either run next to them. While people who have killed are in the general population, those who have killed and received a death sentence must be isolated from human touch. What is the logic?

We learned of more state meanness from a member of an anti-death-penalty organization in England who recently visited a Graterford death row prisoner. She also had visited in Texas and Georgia, and was surprised by Graterford's crude visiting arrangements. For instance, in Texas, where no prisoner receives contact visits, death row prisoners share the same glass-divided visiting room as the general population. But, even with 35 booths, the acoustics are good for conversation. The visitor-side of the booths is large enough for two people and has two phones to speak in normal tones with the prisoner. There are vending machines and microwaves on the visitors' side and toilet facilities on both sides of the glass. Visitors may bring food, and have it delivered by an officer to the prisoner.

At Graterford, the small death-row visiting room is far from conducive to a relaxed visit. The booths are tiny and the narrow room lacks acoustical amenities. There is a small grate in the dividing glass to which folks are supposed to put their lips and ears to speak and listen to each other while leaning uncomfortably forward. Still, they struggle to hear above the noise of other visitors' voices or correctional officers lurking nearby talking on their cell phones or walkie-talkies or to each other with little regard for the visitors' efforts to have a meaningful visit. Nothing may be taken into the securely divided area by the visitor or prisoner—no food, no pictures, nothing of their worlds to share through the separating window partition. No vending machines or toilets are available for either party. If one party must leave to use the toilet, the visit is ended.

Georgia death row prisoners have six-hour contact visits. They may hug family members, play with children, share photos, have their picture taken with visitors, and leave gifts to be given visitors upon leaving. The state gives its death-row prisoners a TV, permits arts and crafts materials, group recreation outside two hours a day, and gathering in a dayroom from 6-9 p.m. to play cards or board games. Often, it's little things that show a mean streak—like not letting capital cases play cards together, or stamping prisoner's mail with the equivalent of a scarlet letter. These things denote a state or nation's humanity.

Our English visitor told us the prisons in her country are more concerned with the process of preparing the prisoners to return to their families and society. "We treat prisoners like human beings," she mused. Should we do less?

"My religion is very simple. My religion is kindness."
The Dalai Lama

****

Inmate

I was in a cell with a 16-year old and an older mentally ill man about thirty. Twice a day, a prison nurse, accompanied by a guard, came to give the older guy medication that kept him like a zombie. All he did was eat, pass gas, sleep and use the toilet. He never washed or showered and his smell was awful. We were confined to that cell 23 hours a day.

The young guy and I became pretty tight. He was from the suburbs and had a family that visited him regularly. Though he wasn't from the inner city like me, we had a lot in common and spent time talking and playing cards, writing letters and basically just trying to keep our sanity while living like caged animals. The stress of such intense confinement was extremely hard to handle and we did the best we could. After awhile, we grew to really appreciate each other, even meeting each other's families in the visitors' room. Because I was a little older (18) I took on the responsibility of looking out for this young guy and making sure no one took advantage of him.

One day, after the mentally ill man was transferred, the guards moved a state prisoner into the cell with us. Right away, I sensed something wasn't right. He'd served 12 years of a life sentence, and had been brought to this prison after stabbing another prisoner. You could tell he was a predator and that he had his sights set on the young guy. I knew he wouldn't try anything while I was there.

Then I went to trial and was gone for a month. When I came back to the same cell, the young guy was alone; he seemed withdrawn and tense. The other guy had been taken upstate.

He told me that one night the older guy made sexual advances towards him and when he resisted, they started fighting. Though he fought as hard as he could, the older, stronger guy beat him up and raped him. He told me there was absolutely nothing he could do about it as the tears streamed down his face. I could feel the depth of the pain and humiliation that some madman had forced upon him. There were no words to ease his suffering.

About a year later a guy stepped into my cell when I was alone, closed the door behind him, pulled out a knife and announced his intention of raping me. I rushed him, catching him by surprise and getting the knife out of his hand. Ignoring his screams, I repeatedly slashed and stabbed at his face, and by the time I stopped there was blood everywhere. Guards arrived and began beating me with blackjacks. I was handcuffed and dragged off to The Hole. The other guy was rushed to the hospital and I was charged with aggravated assault and attempted murder. One week later, the guy showed up at my hearing, his face all bandaged, and testified I'd called him into my cell and started stabbing him for no reason. I was convicted and received a two-and-a-half to five-year sentence. On top of that I was held accountable for the guy's hospital expenses and locked up in The Hole for almost a year.

Inmate

Personally I'm subjected to what I call low-intensity abuse every day in prison. The fact that I'm doing time for a crime I did not commit is the quintessence of abuse itself. In addition to that, I'm tall, Black, muscular, intelligent, sport dreadlocks and maintain my dignity. This makes me a very serious threat to the system, so I'm a favorite target for harassment by many of the correctional officers, especially those with racist tendencies. Their goal is to break me before I infect the already broken, a moot cause, for after you've broken a man's spirit, all the king's horses and all the king's men can never put it back together again.

****

Anton Forde/Trevor Mattis

I expect a visit full of anticipation
My number's called full of elation
As I draw close full of expectation
Bend 'n spread 'em pure humiliation.

I have the kind of sorrow that never shows,
the kind where all seems well and no-one ever knows.
I have the kind of sorrow that grows and grows,
the kind of sorrow that comes from soft and tender blows.

Strange bonds develop between men in peril.
Attachments form against your will,
while the threat lasts, it doesn't matter
whether they be friend, foe, or some other.

Years living with men in close proximity,
the same space shared intimately,
stripped naked of all privacy,
yet still I don't know them and they don't know me.

Two men, strangers not friends,
in an area four by ten,
sixteen hours a day, seven days a week.

I can hear his heart beat and smell his feet.

****

Inmate

Prison is designed to dissolve a man's humanity as well as his sense of individuality. From the moment I entered, I was stripped naked and forced to conform to a system designed to render me powerless. My name was replaced with a number. My clothing was taken and I was issued a uniform.

Separated from everything and everyone I loved, I was forced like an animal to live in a steel and concrete cage. And though no one is capable of totally resisting the many negative influences of the prison, those who attempt to find it difficult to maintain such resistance for a long period of time, for there is a constant bombardment of madness on all sides. To resist in one area often means succumbing in another. Total resistance is impossible.

Just the other day while walking in the yard and talking to a younger prisoner, he said to me, "Someone told me you'd been in here for twenty years." When I said that was true, a pained look came over his face as he said, "But you don't look like you've been in here that long!" I asked him how is a man whose been here that long supposed to act? He thought for a minute and then responded, "He's supposed to act crazy!" This young guy, like many people, was judging me by what he imagined the impact on his mind would be after twenty years. I don't claim to be the sanest man on the planet, but I am far from crazy. The level of sanity I've been able to maintain is a direct result of my ability to resist those forces that seek to diminish me. I am a human being! Not an animal!

****

Inmate

Racism in its blatant and more subtle forms is a daily experience for incarcerated black men at Graterford. Remember when Blacks had to ride in the back of the bus until Rosa Parks stood up against it? That same cold-hearted attitude of privilege in white employees favors white inmates with better treatment than Blacks or Hispanics. The most treacherous form of subtle racism experienced by Black prisoners is the superior, self-righteous air of dominance whites hold toward Blacks. Add to that all of the negative stereotypes they carry about blacks and you have preexisting psychological conditions that support the systematic abuse of Black and Hispanic inmates.

With 28 state prisons in Pennsylvania holding approximately 60,000 citizens, some are considered better than others. In the language of inmates you have "black jails" and "white jails." The difference can be compared to the treatment inner-city children receive in the public school system to that received by white children in suburban schools. From this perspective, considering Graterford as a "black" prison, it becomes a term synonymous with abuse. The reality is that the prison experience of Blacks and Hispanics is based on a foundation of systematic, institutionalized racism.
The following are just some of the major forms this subtle racism takes, impacting on the lives of Blacks and Hispanics:

1) Whites at Graterford go to "honor" blocks sooner than Blacks, where living conditions are better; white prisoners tend to qualify more for living and working outside the wall, and they don't suffer as many of the frustrating parole denials common to Blacks and Hispanics.
2) On certain trade work details inside the prison, the crews are all white.
3) Requests and complaints by whites are treated more seriously by staff.
4) The attitudes of the guards are softer and more humane towards whites.
5) White prisoners receive more medical attention and better care.
6) Black and white guards do not ask white inmates to show their I.D. cards when leaving the cell block as they require of Black inmates.
7) Upon completion of Islamic religious services which are attended mostly by Blacks, a guard force is always posted outside the chapel area to pat Muslims down. This is not the case with Jewish or Christian services.

These differences are so routine that no serious challenges are ever made against them. Yet these racial slights are like a weight over the lives of Black and Hispanic prisoners, affecting our freedom through parole, medical care and equal educational and employment opportunities.

What makes it subtle racism? It is the fact that although these practices occur consistently, they are not so glaring as to rise to the level of mass protest and rebellion.

****

Inmate

I had to pee in a bottle. The urinalysis scenario is always a trip. The devils actually like looking at your dick. Their fascination with the Black man's dick is the real basis of Freud's penis envy theory. When you see their blue eyes transfixed on your phallus, especially when you shake it, there is no doubt that they possess some type of built in homoerotic fantasy. They start to blush and lick their lips like I do when looking at a gorgeous woman. They always ask, "Why is your dick so big?" I laugh because it ain't that big, they're just into some perverted lust and see what doesn't exist.

I wonder what they go home and tell their wives and girlfriends after watching scores of Black dicks all day?"

****

Inmate

Let me tell you about the Camp Hill (PA) prison riots in 1989. The prison population was very high at the time, with double-celling in every block. Half the population had no jobs as they were all filled, and showers were regimented to a total of ten minutes. The abuse of prisoners was so high that the Hole was so full they were double-celling there too. There were many occasions when prisoners were tossed down a flight of stairs for just talking back to a guard. HIV/ADD was epidemic and the staff housed the sick and suffering with the general population. This caused a lot more tension, and the riot started with two guards who didn't know how to do their jobs.

After the first day of rioting, the guards came into the cell blocks along with the state police to help them lock us down. The guards knew the housing units couldn't be locked down because the panels to the locks were open. They knew before they left that they could not be locked down. So a few hours later, the blocks were opened and all the prisoners were back out of their cells. The state police told us to come out with our hands up. We were handcuffed with our arms behind our backs, and then were taken to the big yard where for four days and nights we were forced to sleep in our own urine. The nights were so cold many people became ill. What amazed me was that the guards said we'd destroyed our own property, which was a lie, and the press consumed their lies like they were cotton candy.

After the fourth day in the yard, we were escorted, still in handcuffs, back to our cells where we were forced to strip naked in front of men and women to see if we had any illegal items on us. Then eight of us were each placed in a 12'x6' cell, where we remained for another week. Some cells had ten prisoners in them. When the guards wanted to beat someone, we were forced to face the wall so we couldn't see what was happening. I was taken to the prison hospital with an eye injury from a guard beating me while I was handcuffed. I let the guard know my anger, and the next day I was transferred to another prison where I spent two years of my life in The Hole.

My life behind these walls was forever changed to the point where trust comes hard for me. The abuse that's allowed to happen in prisons is well beyond my understanding, because human beings are not supposed to subject another person to this kind of abuse. But they get away with all the illegal stuff they do to us prisoners.

Inmate

I worked in the library with this guy Billy. He was about thirteen or fourteen years old. We got along well together because I'd come to prison when I was only a couple of years older than him. I always wondered why this state would allow its young offenders to be housed with the adult population. It was as if prison officials knew that something would happen to Billy.

I learned after Billy didn't come to work for a week that he'd been raped by four guys on the block. From what I could piece together, they lured Billy into an empty cell at the back of the block and all five proceeded to get stoned. They gave him all kinds of drugs while they pretended to be his friends. Once Billy was beyond understanding what was going on, the four guys took turns penetrating him in the butt until he passed out. When the officials found Billy later in his cell, bleeding from the four guys' handiwork, he was taken to the hospital where he stayed for a long time.

Yes, there are some people in these environments who take advantage of the young whenever they get a chance. I blame prison officials for what happened to Billy. They knew what would happen to someone Billy's age if left alone for some time.

One good thing came out of it for Billy—he was released from prison a few years later and allowed to renew his life, what was left of it after he experienced such horrible brutality.

****

Inmate

I recently filed a complaint against a guard who wrote me up for violating a dress code. I have several severe medical problems, one of which, diabetes, causes my feet to swell, which makes walking difficult. Not able to get shoes on my feet, I am forced at times to wear open-toed shoes with socks. He said I was wearing shower shoes to the mess hall, which was not true.

When I went to his superior, they acted like I was wrong without even hearing my case. The officer has used policy to subject others to mistreatment. They sometimes just think up rules to justify their behavior. I've seen this officer standing out front of the control office just waiting to stalk whoever comes by. It may be something as simple as a button being undone, yet he blows it all out of context. This attitude is expressed daily, and for some of us, it is what we have to cope with for the rest of our lives, with no signs of relief.

21st Century's Dawn's Early Light

by Leonard C. Jefferson CL-4135
A/A 10745 Rte. 18
Albion PA 16475

My country tis of thee
this is about your reality.
By the 21st Century's dawn's early light
there ain't no justice for you here
if you ain't white.
Sweet land of liberty
bitter was the taste of your slavery
and that putrid taste remains strong
in all of our mouths
as we now see you lynching us
downtown in your courthouse.
The whole world watched
you beat down Rodney King
then we saw white jurors
who couldn't see what we were seeing.
With open eyes their closed minds

saw that the police were right

You know there ain't no justice for you here
if you ain't white.

Today's lynchings are performed
via police state-style trials
perpetuating this injustice American style
highlighting the unstated semantic reality
that lynchings don't require bodies
hanging from trees.
Oh say can you see
strange fruit no longer hangs
in America's trees.
Now in the land of the free
and home of the brave
prisons conceal the lynched children
of America's slaves.
Remember Martin told us
to let freedom ring
so my country tis of thee
that I sing
Now in the land of the free
and home of the brave
prisons conceal the lynched children
of America's slaves.

****

"There is no birthright in the white skin that it shall say that wherever it goes, to any nation, amongst any people, there the people of the country shall give way before it, and those to whom the land belongs shall bow down and become its servants." Annie Wood Besant (1847-1933)

****

SOME THOUGHTS ABOUT GUARDS

Most people working as American prison guards (correctional officers) are decent people just wanting to make a living, a living that with overtime can be as much as $70,000 a year. There's something about the job and the system that brings out cruel power cravings in the keepers of the keys. A study back in the '70's at Stanford University divided students into two groups, prisoners and guards. The study had to be stopped when the "guards" became abusive to the "prisoners." Clearly the education levels, psychological screening procedures and training of COs must be changed so they can become more counselors than keepers.

If psychiatric hospitals can subdue violent patients without beating them, why can't prisons?

Part of the problem is that rural whites who keep the keys have had little or no exposure to urban Blacks and Hispanics, the majority of the kept, fueling racist attitudes and actions. Inmates say the further away prisons are from Philadelphia, the more racist the guards.

In his best-selling <u>Newjack: Guarding Sing Sing,</u> author Ted Conover tells about the year he spent undercover working as a prison guard. He described his colleagues as those who couldn't get into the army or the police force, with little education and brief training focused only on control rather than treatment. Guards at Sing Sing had urine and feces thrown at them by prisoners who felt they'd been abused or treated unfairly.

Conover found himself getting violent with his four year old after a year of the stress of working as a CO.

Graterford has a few female guards, some single mothers seeking security after welfare reform. Like most macho groups, the male guards resent the presence of female guards, for the women tend to be gentler with prisoners and less willing to set them up so guards can score points and advancement by busting them. An example of this misogyny and the mindset of some male guards was illustrated when it was rumored that a white male guard invited a black female guard to his home to have sex. While they were into it, she was unaware that he was secretly videotaping them. Nor did she know that he'd show the video to everyone at work the next day, staff and prisoners, causing her to resign in humiliation.

Homeland security needs to launch an immediate examination of the state of mind and behaviors of prison guards.

When does the healing and rehabilitation begin?

****

A white correctional officer was asked at a party, "What type of work do you do?" He answered, "I keep niggers in check."
A Black correctional officer was asked "And what type of work do you do?"
"I keep niggers in check too," he quipped.

Anton Forde/Trevor Mattis from <u>Contemplations of a Convict: aphorisms for the Heart and Mind</u>

Chapter Nine
SEXUALITY & RELATIONSHIPS

"In here, babies die by the billions"
Anton Forde/Trevor Mattis

This was one of the most difficult topics for the men to address and again, as with the previous chapter's topic, some of them just couldn't do it. Those that could were promised their privacy would be respected by not having their names revealed.

Inmate

Yesterday morning, an intense sadness came over me as I watched two guards, a man and a woman, patrol the yard during the two-hour recreation period. It was a beautiful morning with bright sun and gentle breezes. I noticed the carefree way in which the pair slowly walked around the yard, deep in conversation. Though I couldn't hear what they were saying, their facial expressions and body language clearly conveyed that they were discussing something quite intimate. The special way she smiled at him, tilting her head, listening and looking at him as he spoke, caused a painful stirring deep within my soul. It's been so long since a woman responded to me that way. I envied the male guard, for he was experiencing something I've been denied for most of my adult life. Between them was an openness and intimacy that was simply beautiful to behold. As I stood alone in one corner watching them, I was overcome with a deep sense of desolation. This feeling was so intense it brought me to tears. Yes, dammit, I cried. I cried because something inside me longs to experience that level of closeness with a woman.

It's amazing how the small things that many men take for granted can mean so much to me.
Having been in prison since I was a teenager and thereby denied the opportunity for positive and healthy interactions with women has impacted on me in ways that mere words cannot accurately convey. Sometimes I dream I am free and in the presence of a beautiful woman. We are sitting beside each other, both of us naked. I say to her, "Please just let me hold you." As I hold her in my arms and feel the warmth and sensuality of my flesh against hers, I begin to cry. It is at this point that I always awaken. Lying in the dark cell, my face and the pillow wet with my tears and my senses alive with memory, I feel tortured by the vividness of the recurring dream and the intensity of my desires. And yet, despite the pain, I'm glad for the experience, if only in my dreams.
I know many men who've been in prison so long that they are no longer capable of dreaming. They neither have nocturnal dreams nor thoughts of ever experiencing anything beyond these walls. This is something I find amazing and sad. This inability to dream or see beyond one's present circumstances says a lot about the negative effects of long-term incarceration and the hopelessness and despair that can set in when human beings are locked in cages and treated like animals.

What can a society hope to accomplish through such dehumanizing methods?

****

Inmate

One of the most difficult aspects of my incarceration is the pain I feel as a direct result of being denied access to women. Besides the forced celibacy, having little or no positive interaction with women has had quite an impact on my life and my development as a man. Even with the love and support of my mother, sisters and female friends who visit occasionally, not being able to share and grow in a healthy adult relationship with a woman has created an unnatural void in my life. Because I was only a teenager when I was sent to prison, I've never had a chance to have a real partnership which has really stunted my development. The impact is often quite painful. There are times when I cry for the love and inspiration that only a woman can give to a man; this is what I yearn for the most.

It is a myth that all men in prison are involved in homosexuality; such is not the case. Sure, because most prisons are all male environments, quite naturally there exists a certain level of homosexuality, but the level isn't high. There's also a myth that lifers frequently engage in homosexuality, but this too is untrue. Most of the homosexuals are men serving short sentences or are repeat offenders. Rapes are becoming less frequent as many more men are participating in religion, which is bringing about a remarkable change in the prison sub-culture.

For me, refraining from participating in homosexuality hasn't been that difficult. Having sex with another man isn't something I find at all desirable. Plus the sexual abuse I suffered as a child has left me with so many hang-ups and insecurities that I seldom allow anyone to get too close to me.

Prison has had quite a negative effect on me. In order to survive, I've become withdrawn and I know I have a warped sense of myself and others. As Anton says in his book, Contemplations of a Convict, "Prison irrevocably changes a person. Much in the same way that war does. The experience changes you, but you don't necessarily have to show it. Though you feel normal and may act normal, you're not normal."

I often think of the difficulties I'll encounter upon my release. Readjusting to the world beyond these walls will present me with one of the greatest challenges of my life. Twenty-five years is a long time to be trapped in someone's prison. There are so many things I've lost touch with. How will I adjust? Who will be there to help me? Will I be successful and never return to prison?

These are questions I often ask myself.

****

Inmate

Dealing with issues related to my sexuality during the past twenty years of incarceration has been extremely difficult. From the beginning, I've maintained communication and friendships with women on the other side of the wall. This has always been important because it keeps me in contact with the world. Also, I'm afraid I'll lose touch with my ability to relate to and interact with women. I've tried to stay in contact with women I knew before coming to prison, and though my circumstances dictate the limitations of what level of intimacy I'm able to experience, I've struggled to maintain as meaningful relationships as possible. Trying to maintain outside relationships is difficult; many men simply choose to do their time alone so they don't have to deal with the pain, disappointment and aggravation of trying to stay connected with family and others.

Then there are many family members and loved ones of men in prison who just aren't able to visit or can't afford the exorbitant cost of collect calls, the only kind allowed. I know many men who've been at Graterford for years and have never received a visit or even mail from anyone beyond these walls. It's not that no one out there loves them, but for some people it's easier to close their minds to the pain and struggle of others.

I'll never forget a friend of mine, Mike. He was a lifer, a few years older than me from my old neighborhood. He was well-respected and always had pretty women, nice clothes and fancy cars. His family came regularly and were very supportive. His four children came whenever anyone would bring them, but Mike didn't know how to love from prison. This was a source of great pain for him, because he wanted to be loving but just didn't know how. One day out in the yard I asked him how he coped with the pain of missing his children and family. He looked at me and said what he felt was the most humiliating powerlessness a man could ever feel.

Soon after our conversation, they found Mike dead in his cell of a drug overdose. I often think of Mike and how important it is for people, especially men in prison serving extensive sentences, to learn how to love in the face of extreme difficulty.

****

Inmate

There are no conjugal visiting rights in Pennsylvania like there are in more progressive states. Prisoners are not allowed to have sex with visitors. As a heterosexual man, this has been very difficult for me. To make matters worse, inmates are only allowed to briefly embrace or kiss visitors as they enter or exit the visitors' room. This embrace must be simple and brief, otherwise a guard will be quick to approach you and demand that you separate from your visitor. If caught kissing or hugging during the visit, an inmate is subject to receive a misconduct, which could result in his being sent to The Hole for a 60-day period as well as losing his visiting privileges for up to a year. Some men do engage in homosexuality and in many instances the institution promotes such activity as many guards just look the other way when they encounter such acts. It's accepted as normal behavior here. I've always been afraid of being caught up in homosexuality, fearing that besides it not being attractive to me, it would damage my self image and take me too far away from who and what I am. I refuse to risk so much. Plus I have enough personal troubles and hang-ups without adding that shit to it. Therefore I have not had sex of any sort, except for a few encounters with a former girlfriend while in the county jail awaiting trial. Even that was against the rules, but guards were paid and rules broken.

My desire for sexual intimacy is as strong as ever.

During the early years in prison, not having access to women was the cause of a great deal of stress and tension. I sought release through strenuous exercise and sometimes fighting with other inmates.

The long nights are the most difficult.

Sometimes I lie awake as my whole body and soul come alive with a longing that masturbation can't quench. There's a crippling impact caused by the loneliness I often feel at the lack of access to a woman. Sometimes it's so bad that throughout the day I move around as though caught in a dark cloud of depression. I feel incomplete and stunted in my growth. Years ago, while on a visit from my mother, I shared with her my longing for a meaningful relationship with a woman and how at night I pray for God to send me someone to love. My mother told me to just hold on because one day I'll find the proper woman and all will be well. She also told me that out there somewhere is a special woman who's praying the same prayer as I am, and God has already decided that the two of us will come together, but we have to wait until the time is right. So I wait, remembering what Mom told me. One day, when this nightmare is over, I'll be free to experience all that being in prison has denied me for so long. Sometimes I wonder how I will adjust after being alone for so long. I'll just have to go slow and give myself

time. It is said that time heals all wounds. Perhaps it will heal mine as well.
One day I'll get my chance to be all that I can be. I just have to keep holding on. I will.

Inmate

I can state for the record that I am NOT homophobic. I like all kinds of people in my life, and that includes homosexuals.

Things happen sometimes which are out of our control and one has to come clean. Just because I am not sexually attracted to another man doesn't mean I have hang-ups. It's just that the same sex doesn't do it for me regardless of the circumstances.

Yes, being incarcerated in a men's prison for many years brings on some desires one wishes could be tightly locked away.

When I'd only been in prison for five years, I recall a guy I got friendly with. Gay before he came to prison, he was very comfortable with who he was. The sexual dance started off very easily. In my mind, I will always see him as a nice person. He came to my cell every day early in the morning. We talked about everything under the sun, from sports to relationships. I'd never had any open sexual feelings toward another man; I was fresh meat for him.

That summer, my sexual yearnings hit an all-time high, though my feelings weren't about him. He took advantage of all occasions to touch me in a non-sexual way. I enjoyed the attention he showered on me. After awhile, he asked me if I'd like to have sexual relations with him. I told him I enjoyed our friendship but didn't want it to reach that point. He really wanted to have a sexual experience with me to endear him to me, but I just couldn't get into the moment with him. So he backed away, and sat on the edge of the bed and we just talked the morning away, neither of us referring to what had almost happened. Instead of fighting over this, we became the best of friends. I think what he really did for me was to make me see that people who are gay are in a light that is all their own. To this day, I'm comfortable around all kinds of people.

****

"Agape is understanding, creative, redemptive goodwill towards all men. Agape is an overflowing love, which seeks nothing in return. Theologians would say that it is the love of God operating in the human heart. When you rise to love on this level, you love all men not just because you like them, not because their ways appeal to you, but you love them because God loves them." Martin Luther King, Jr.

****

OPEN SPACE

By Anton Forde/Trevor Mattis

Open space, open space,
oh how I'd love me some open space.
No boundaries, no walls, no doors, no gates,
space to breathe, space to see, space to feel
ninety percent of the universe,
yet can't find any in this wretched place.

It is fully known they carry a deadly disease,
yet still they engage in procreative activities.
Caged men seem to lack the ability
to choose between life and sodomy.

Cure hate with hate? That makes no sense.
How do you rehabilitate with punishment?
You ignored me until I bit you.
Now you feed me hate when I need "I love you."

Dehumanized for an act I've never done,
now murder's forever part of my legacy.
Though I have the proof, I lack the money.

Twelve years and it still hasn't sunk in
that I'll be here till I die.
Because I'm innocent, I keep believing
the next appeal will rectify.

To those whom I've left behind,
don't think that I'm unkind.
Out there means out of mind.
I can't bear memories too sublime.

Confined together three thousand strong,
Every step I take, I take amongst a throng.
Everywhere I turn, I see a brother I've known
despite that fact I am all alone.

If I can see beauty in this world,
if I can find love in this world,

then there's hope
If I can believe,
if I can have faith,
then there's hope.

****

NO DREAMS

By Anton Forde/Trevor Mattis

I never, never want to dream, so I never sleep.
I just get shuteyes.
My brain is re-wired to recognize rest but no REM.
My subconscious suppresses any indulgence in fantasies.
My consciousness is hardwired to reality.
My brain has adapted to cope
and survive in an environment without hope.
So I no longer dream
and I no longer have to wake up.

****

"It is ironic that politicians candidly admit to making mistakes in their lives and learning from them. Then these very same politicians make laws by arguing the incorrigibility of convicts." Anton Forde

****

"It would take a miracle for someone to learn to love others in this environment of hate." David Mandeville DN7632

****

Chapter Ten
THOSE WHO LOVE PRISONERS AND THOSE PRISONERS LOVE

"A mother's love for her children, even her ability to let them be, is because she is under a painful law that the life passed through her must be brought to fruition. Even when she swallows it whole she is only acting like any frightened mother cat eating its young to keep it safe. It is not easy to give closeness and freedom, safety plus danger. No matter how old a mother is she watches her middle-aged children for signs of improvement. It could not be otherwise, for she is impelled to know that the seeds of value sown in her have winnowed. She never outgrows the burden of love, and to the end she carries the weight of hope for those she bore. Oddly, very oddly, she is forever surprised and even faintly wronged that her sons and daughters are just people, for many mothers hope and half expect that their newborn child will make the world better, will somehow be a redeemer."
Florida Scott-Maxwell from The Measure of My Days

THE VISITING ROOM
by Judith Trustone

The wall of waiting women silently wails and weeps
as Daddyless children wander, their energies restless
in such a place where Daddy's treated like a thing.
Each woman holds a number, like a piece of deli meat.
Hearts broken over and over; cruel guards treating them
like the human garbage their loved ones have become.

How did they come to be in such a place?

Recorded by cameras, the women and children
have just a few cherished moments with him.
Secret talk and silent touches under scrutiny,
trapped and guarded like wild animals in a cage.

Soon they must leave him again, going alone, shivering
into the cloudy dusk, a half-moon peeking
from behind dark shadows, a reminder of the Light
as the sun sets on yet another day in Shadow America.

****

"One day I'll make it home, baby, one day I'll be free
Then I can thank you for all the times you've loved me.
I'm doing life without parole, but I'm still hoping
To get out of this hole and find you waiting..."
Anton Forde/Trevor Mattis

****

No one more eloquently articulates the agonies of loving a prisoner than Asha Bandele, whose **<u>The Prisoner's Wife</u>** *has become a best-seller. Going into a New York prison to teach poetry workshops, she is seduced by the words of one of her students, words that inside men must cultivate if they want to communicate, words that all women hunger for that so many free men seem to lack. She says, "You haven't lived until*

you get a love letter from a prisoner!" Eventually they marry in prison, and, because New York is a state that humanely allows conjugal visits, they are able to spend a few nights together in privacy and intimacy every couple of years, though their lovemaking is interrupted when it's time for her husband to be counted.
After eight years, Bandele stops visiting him because she can no longer tolerate the abuse by the guards.

The stereotype of a woman in love with a prisoner is of someone with low self-esteem who is unable to find a man on the outside. This picture demeans the thousands of women (and unfortunately too few men) with the courage to care about prisoners. Connie DeLano certainly fits no such category by marrying a much younger man of another culture and color in Graterford's visitors' room.

****

"Our goal is to create a beloved community, and this will require a qualitative change in our souls as well as a quantitative change in our lives." Martin Luther King, Jr.

****

"Making the choice to love can heal our wounded spirits and our body politic. It is the deepest revolution, the turning away from the world as we know it, toward the world we must make if we are to be one with the planet-one healing heart giving and sustaining life. Love is our hope and our salvation." bell hooks

****

"Salvation is being on the right road, not having reached a destination." Martin Luther King, Jr.

CONNIE DELANO

Connie's heart lives full time in Shadow America. Bright, gentle and articulate, her clear blue eyes sparkle with love as she talks about her husband, Jose' Hernandez, ($595,000), twenty-one years her junior and from another culture.

Connie's late father, a minister who volunteered at Graterford, introduced them twelve years ago, so taken was he with Jose', a young lifer. She was in an unhappy marriage and working in the corporate world when they met, and the connection they both felt immediately was puzzling. Under these unlikely circumstances, a relationship never crossed her mind.

As the attraction between them grew stronger, she was increasingly impressed with who he is despite the horrendous experiences of his young life. She says, "His spirit is mind-boggling. His thirst for knowledge and understanding constantly amazes me."

Her son and daughter, both in their thirties, aren't happy about their mother's commitment to Jose'. Her closest friends are supportive; some have even been to the prison to meet him.

Their wedding took place in the Graterford visiting room on New Year's Day, 2000. She wanted the ceremony in order to reaffirm her commitment to Jose'. She visits him once a week, though sometimes they cut back because the environment of the visiting room is "hard to handle." Because of DOC rules, they may hug, kiss briefly and hold hands, all under the constant scrutiny of video cameras and guards. Their phone calls, always collect, are monitored and recorded. Imagine some invisible stranger listening in on every phone conversation, often a prisoner's only link to the outside world, to family and loved ones. For the rest of your life.

Connie says, "The guards are either polite or disapproving of our age and color differences. One time we were sitting together, and Jose' put his hand on my knee. The guard shot out of his chair, screaming, and grabbed Jose' and took him away. When he returned, trembling, he told me the guard had threatened to write him up for making sexual advances to me."

Jose' calls her two or three times a week, and their attempts at verbal intimacy always include a third, anonymous person. From his 41 cents an hour job, he sends her frequent gifts, and, at times, money, according to the values of his Hispanic culture. In networking with other women married to prisoners, Connie has found them to be intelligent, caring, concerned about racism and social issues.

"If I had it to do over, I would without hesitation. I have no regrets. I've become a much stronger person. I pray a lot, and have conversations with God. I stand by Jose' and my belief in his innocence and his right to live a free life."

****

"The moral duty of man consists of imitating the moral goodness and beneficence of God, manifested in the creation toward all His creatures. That seeing, as we daily do, the goodness of God to all men, it is an example calling upon all men to practice the same toward each other; and consequently, that everything of persecution and revenge between man and man, and everything of cruelty to animals, is a violation of moral duty." Thomas Paine,
The Age of Reason

****

"Love takes off the masks that we fear we cannot live without and know we cannot live within. I use the word love here not merely in the personal sense but as a state of being, or a state of grace-not in the infantile American sense of being made happy but in the tough and universal sense of quest and daring and growth." James Baldwin

****

"Ancestral Rhythms" Oil on Canvas Muti Ajamu-Osagboro

Inmate

The scene is the visiting room at the Pittsburgh prison. An elderly woman is weeping as a young man tries to comfort her. She'd traveled a great distance to see her incarcerated son for the first time in years. She'd been through cancer and chemotherapy, and when she went through the rigorous search by guards, one of them snatched her wig from her head to see if she had any contraband. Weakened by the humiliation, the weary woman had to sit and try to regroup to regain the strength any mother needs to visit with her imprisoned child.

****

Inmate

One Saturday morning the guard came and told me I had a visitor. I walked to the visitors' area, pulled down my pants and bent over before being allowed into the room. Once there, I waited an hour and a half for my visitor to be admitted. Then a guard told me my visit had been canceled. At that point I had no idea who'd come to see me. When I asked the guard why the visit had been cancelled, he arrogantly responded, "They left." Not wanting to give him the pleasure of humiliating me even more, I left the room to return to my cell, once again baring my butt to the guards. As I walked back, a silent rage bubbled in me. But I knew if I exploded it would only make things worse. To react emotionally by throwing a tempter tantrum or demanding the guards provide me with more reason for the cancelled visit would accomplish nothing except for maybe a trip to The Hole and possibly a brand new case of "assaulting an officer." I kept my emotions in check and laid down on my bed, comforting myself with the knowledge that if the visitor who'd left was my mother, she wouldn't have left without a legitimate reason. Two hours later, the same guard showed up at my cell to tell me again I had a visitor. Once more I made my way to the visitors' room, once again bending over and showing my ass to the guards.

Forty-five minutes later, my mother and seven-year-old niece appeared. Once my niece spotted me through the crowd, she ran straight for me and flung her little arms around me in a warm embrace. I picked her up and held her in my arms and for several minutes I stood there oblivious to everyone and everything. Eventually my mother, my niece and I moved through the noisy, crowded room, searching for a place to sit.

Mom explained that she'd arrived at the prison at 9 am and after sitting in the waiting room for several hours the guards called her up to the desk and said she needed more extensive identification for my seven year old niece. They claimed that the two pieces of identification she'd shown them wasn't enough. And even though my mother produced a copy of the parental visiting approval form that my sister was required to fill out and send back to the prison ensuring that she had given my mother permission to bring her to see me, that wasn't enough. They still claimed more identification was needed. How much identification can a seven year old have? The parental forms are required before any child below eighteen can visit. Without the forms, adults are not allowed to bring children into the institution. Despite the fact that my mother had the form and several pieces of identification for her, my niece was denied access. So my mother and my niece drove the 45 minutes back to Philly in order to get my niece's birth certificate, then all the way back to Graterford. By the time I saw them they were tired and stressed out, but we still managed to have a good visit.

What my mother experienced was typical of the way visitors are treated when attempting to visit their loved ones here. It's as if the guards go out of their way to harass and discourage visitors. This treatment has been inflicted on my family for the past twenty years. I can understand why some of the guys in here never get visits.

One time, the guards at the front desk denied an elderly aunt of mine a visit because she refused to strip naked and submit to a complete body search. She was 79 years old at the time. They claimed to suspect her, an old woman, of attempting to smuggle drugs into the prison. My aunt said they talked to her as if she was a criminal, taking her off to a side room and totally disrespecting her with all sorts of crazy accusations. But as I said, such treatment is typical in Pennsylvania prisons. Visitors are constantly harassed and discouraged from visiting. Some swear never to come back after experiencing Graterford's visiting room practices.

I've always wondered what it is that causes prison guards to treat inmates and their loved ones with such contempt and disrespect. This negative treatment and attitude isn't just in relation to white guards and black inmates. In some instances, black guards treat black inmates worse than white guards do. And most of the time, this ill treatment isn't expressed in the form of physical violence, for rarely do the guards actually brutalize inmates. The brutality is more psychological. They play head games and constantly nag and harass inmates over the most petty things. It's as if many of the guards possess a deep-rooted hatred and resentment toward black inmates. Most of the time, when an inmate assaults a guard it's because he's been pushed so far he just couldn't take any more abuse. The guards know if an inmate pushes or strikes them, it will result in a new case and a new sentence, adding to time to be served. The guards know this and use it as a psychological blackjack to beat inmates over the head with. For me, a new case and sentence of any sort added to what I'm already serving would place me in a position where I'd never get out of here. This is why I can't afford to allow my emotions to dictate how I respond in any situation, be it with another inmate or with guards. Because of this I've grown into an expert at finding viable alternatives to violence. I simply can't afford not to.
My future freedom depends on it.

****

Thousand Pound Visits

By Wendy Pellinore

I weigh 1000 pounds. I barely tip the scales at 120, but I am carrying the weight of years of accumulated stress. The weight is invisible, but it casts its shadow on every sunny day, taints every bite of food, and turns the earth to quicksand. It drags down every thought, tugs at every word. I have become scatter-brained, forgetful, routinely confused, distracted and disconnected.

It is my first visit to my son in jail at Chester County Prison. My husband and I visit separately in order to break up his weekly routine. My son has not yet been sentenced for his drug offenses. I am angry with him and resent having to take a place among the dregs of society that I expect I will find in the prison visiting room. I decide to put all 1000 lbs of myself into a bubble in order to avoid contamination. I try to attain a zen-like calm.

My picture taken, I wait in the outer visitors' room. I notice random things: the guards' tattoos and pot bellies, how many people are speaking Spanish, the number of babies and toddlers, the absence of older kids. My name is called. I go to the double-doors. It reminds me of the birdhouse at the Philadelphia Zoo. One door must close before the other opens in order not to let the birds escape. I mention as much to the woman waiting between the doors with me. She does not respond. I think perhaps she has never been to the Philadelphia Zoo. Maybe she doesn't speak English. I curse myself for leaving my bubble. I get back in it.

I sit at a table and wait. The room could pass for any corporate cafeteria without the food. I stare straight ahead, but I can see through my bubble. I notice the overwhelming number of young prisoners, but my attention is drawn to the older couple waiting at a table in front of me. I think they are there to visit their son or grandson, but I am mistaken. An older prisoner approaches. The gray-haired lady jumps up and exclaims, "How are you?!" They embrace and he replies, "Better, now that you are here." I turn away. I try to swallow.

My son enters the room. Our visit is strained. It does not go well. I look about the room. And then I see her: a middle-aged woman presumably visiting her spouse. The visit is over and she is hurrying to the door. She is trying not to cry before she can escape. She does not look back as her husband disappears with the guard wearing the bright blue gloves. Her mouth is set, breath held, eyes brimming. The bird door just can't open fast enough to let her out before she loses her dignity. I realize I am looking at myself.

Several months later I visit my son at SCI-Camp Hill, a two-hour trip. I am still angry, but not with my son. My non-violent, drug-offending 21-year old has been sentenced to 4-10 years with innumerable years of probation attached at the end. ($140,000-$350,000) He is at Camp Hill to be 'classified'. We find out he has been exposed to and/or has tuberculosis. He has also contracted a skin fungus. He is being treated for both in addition to another medication he takes. I am now worried that he could contract hepatitis. I send him newspaper clippings about the hepatitis epidemic in the prison system. I sign each letter, "Be Aware- Don't Share!" He pays for the nurse's visits out of the commissary money we send him. We are appalled to find out Montgomery County takes 20% of every cent we send him to cover 'court costs.'

I enter the outer visitors' area. The guard barks at me to get behind the red line. I look everywhere and can't find it. Another visitor points it out to me- it is on the wall, not the floor. I wait and wait. I notice random things: the girth of the guard at the desk where he sits, eating; the plastic bags that people bring their money in for the vending machines; the number of babies and toddlers, the lack of older kids. I note the racial makeup: I am the only white visitor in the room. My name is called and I go through the bird doors that lead inside/outside. I find the correct building and visitors' room. My son awaits. I hardly recognize him. He is 40 lbs heavier. He no longer does drugs so he has attained his proper weight for his height. Our visit flies by. He asks me for a TV, but I can't afford the $180 plus 20%. I tell him he has to wait. He understands the meaning of the word "wait."

It is eleven months since my son was first incarcerated. He is now in SCI Cresson, a four-hour trip. My husband and I go together now because the visit requires an overnight stay. It has turned into a costly and time-consuming event. We try to make the best of it. We pretend it is the long weekend that we had been planning to take to see the change of leaves in New England. We note that this trip will be hazardous and impractical during the winter.

The next morning we drag our unspeakable sadness, our collective 2000 lbs, to SCI Cresson. We enter the outer waiting room. There is not much to notice here. There are only a few people waiting. They all speak Spanish. At this moment I cannot remember one word of Spanish. I play peek-a-boo with the toddler. Another young mother enters with her baby. She tells me it is 5 weeks old.

We enter the inner visitors' room through the bird doors. Our son awaits. Now he has a beard and we joke and tell him he looks like a Dutch boy. He tells us his cellmates thought he was Muslim. I look at my beautiful, tubercular, fungified, ADHD-addled son and feel the weight of my 1000 lbs pressing me into my seat. He has his TV now. He shares it with 3 other TV-less cellmates. He has completed his citizenship course. He works in the kitchen. The visit flies. My eyes wander. I notice the father of the 5-week old baby. He is holding the baby on his lap and his eyes do not leave her. He stares at her in awe the entire time. I turn away. I try to swallow.

I discarded my bubble a while ago. I realized after the first few visits that I would not be 'contaminated' by the people around me. There are only regular folks here in the visiting room: they are our neighbors, business companions, teammates, fellow taxpayers- all carrying their 1000 lbs of sadness. But I am still angry and confused.

When did we, as Americans, become comfortable making laws based on sound bites and clichés? **3 Strikes?** We must be satisfied with sentencing repeat offenders according to the rules of baseball. It does give new meaning to "The Great American Pastime." **Zero tolerance?** We must be content to absolve our leaders from looking at individual circumstances and taking responsibility for making decisions. **Mandatory minimums?** We must be endorsing the power of the district attorney to decide the case instead of trusting our judges to exercise their powers of discernment. **Trying juveniles as adults?** Is this not an oxymoron?

One of the basic laws of science states that matter cannot be created or destroyed, only transformed. I add my 1000 lbs of sorrow to the 1000 lbs that each prisoner's loved-ones carry. I come to my unscientific conclusion that there must be a way to transform this tonnage of sadness into the critical mass of energy needed fix our broken system of justice. And I marvel that God forgives, but our astoundingly self-righteous society does not.

****

Inmate

My visits have been limited these past three years. However, prior to that I was receiving regular visits from my then wife and two small children. Perhaps for the children there are drawbacks to the experience of seeing their father in prison. But this must be weighed against not seeing their father at all during the long years of incarceration. Even though I haven't seen them for the past three years, I believe the knowledge and constant reminders from exposure to media, prison literature, and their mother that their father is in jail has already caused irreversible damage.

I'm not sure how to describe the effects of visiting me here had upon my wife. Certainly it wasn't all positive. Of course, it helped to continue our turbulent connection, but overall, I think the visits created more problems than they actually helped to save. On many occasions, we would argue or I would poke or badger her about any possible extramarital affairs. Unfortunately, the reality of a wife or girlfriend having a relationship with another during the time of incarceration is a very bitter pill to swallow. The end result of a visit was usually a mixture of hope, denial, desperation and anger. It has always been exhausting for me and others.

****

Inmate

In August, I got a visit from a couple of friends. Anthony and Elizabeth. I have known both of them since childhood. Elizabeth, who goes by the name of Bitty, came to see me because she would be going away for some time, working to help prevent alcoholism and drug abuse on Native American reservations.

Bitty came in with a white outfit with the top coming down to her knees to match the shorts. The guard pulled the top up without her consent to see if the panty line could be seen through the shorts. A female guard told her that she would not be allowed to visit me because she could see her panty line through her shorts. Luckily Anthony keeps his workout clothes in the trunk of his car, and just had them laundered.

I could see the pain and hurt on her face and I implored her to write or make an appointment to see the superintendent about the assault on her physically and mentally by this corrections officer. But she was afraid of what the guard would do to me later on. I told her I will be glad to have her report this guard so it will not happen to the next person. But as the visit went on, I could see that this would be the last time I would see her behind these prison walls. As they were leaving, Bitty pressed herself against me like it would be the last time I would see her in this setting again. Sure, she made a promise that she would see me when she got back, but I knew I'd never see her again unless a miracle occurs and I am released. Anthony promised he would come back to see me when he got another weekend free. As they left, I had felt it would definitely be the last time I would ever see Bitty.

The moral to this story is that the prison system claims it promotes the building of relationships with family and friends, but they seem to do all they can to break these ties down every chance they get by making women visitors feel so uncomfortable that some will have doubts about ever returning again to prison to visit friends.

****

Inmate

One evening recently, guards entered the cell in which I was housed and ordered me to strip search - get naked- to prove I wasn't concealing any weapons or contraband. After putting my clothes back on, I was handcuffed and taken directly to the Hole with no explanations. Several hours later, a written incident report was dropped into the cell simply stating that I was being placed under "Administrative Custody," stating "inmate is a danger to some person(s) in the institution who cannot be protected by alternate measures." Now what this meant I still don't know.

On my third day of being held incommunicado in the Hole (unable to write a letter or make a phone call to anyone), a guard informed me that I was scheduled to be transferred to another prison. An hour later I was told I had a visit and was escorted in handcuffs to a small room separated in half by a thick Plexiglas partition. On each side of the partition was a row of stools and telephone receivers through which a visitor and prisoner could speak. Already seated on one side was my mother. Still handcuffed, I picked up the phone on my side and sat down.

My mother's first question to me was, "Are you okay?" I told her I was fine and asked how she found out I was in The Hole. One of my friends had called and told her what happened. I shared how I had absolutely no idea what was going on, and that I was to be transferred. Where to I didn't know. With those few details out of the way, I went on to assure my mother that I was okay. I hadn't been charged with breaking or violating any institutional rules or regulations. We were allowed only a one hour visit. And despite the handcuffs and thick partition separating us, I reassured my her that all would be well and I'd call her when I reached whatever prison they transferred me to. It was important that my outlook on the situation was positive because I knew my mother needed to draw from my strength and leave the prison knowing I was okay.

The next morning, around four o'clock, I was awakened by guards, handcuffed, shackled in leg irons and tossed into a van with no idea where I was headed. Looking out into the semi-darkness through the van's window, I was mesmerized by what I saw. As the small van exited Graterford's property and began to snake its way through the early morning traffic, I was filled with an incredible sense of fear and excitement. Sprawled out before me was the world beyond the prison's huge walls, a world I had been locked away from for the past 21 years. The trees, the roads, the houses, the people, their cars, everything had an eerie look about it. I felt as if I was seeing these things for the very first time. Yet I was afraid because I didn't know where they were taking me. I was so emotionally overwhelmed by the experience, I didn't notice I was crying until I felt the wetness of the tears rolling down my face. I laughed when I went to wipe them and couldn't because the chains wrapped around my wrists and body prevented me from even the slightest movements.

For twelve hours I sat chained in that hot ass van as it traveled all over Pennsylvania, stopping at prison after prison, finally reaching my new home. My entire body was aching from sitting chained in the same position for so many hours. Once inside the prison, I was fed and then placed in a temporary holding cell to await an official hearing scheduled for the next day.

At the hearing I was asked whether I knew why I was transferred. I told them that I had no idea. One of the hearing examiners, who had what I assumed was my folder in front of him, snapped "You were transferred here because you were suspected of being involved in a major drug ring." I responded that this was the first time I had heard such an accusation. Another of the hearing examiners then stated, "There's no report of any misconduct charges against you involving drugs. So they probably made such a claim to justify transferring you. They do it all the time. Apparently someone wanted you out of there, and quickly."

So here I am, all the way at the other end of the state. I've been placed directly in the prison's main population. And although I hate all prisons I hear this one isn't that bad. Some say it's better than Graterford. I guess we'll see, huh? One thing for certain is that I know damn near half the other inmates here. Having been in Graterford so long, I've mingled with some of the roughest prisoners in the state. And, since I've always been a man amongst men, I get a lot of respect from other prisoners. It matters not whether it's here, Graterford or any other prison.

So far, I kind of like it here. My younger brother from California and his wife came to visit me here last week. The visiting room here is a lot better than at Graterford, a much less oppressive environment. They've actually got beautiful trees and flowers in their visiting room yard. It felt so wonderful sitting under the shade of a tree with those I love. And the guards weren't walking around harassing us.

As far as visits go, my family will visit me even if I were to suddenly be transferred to China. My squad is tight like that. We've successfully survived 21 years of Graterford. Surviving anywhere else is a piece of cake. Plus, as Black folks we're experts at surviving.

****

Chaka Turner BW6610
Box 1000
Houtzdale, PA 16698
($350,000)

People by nature are social creatures. Thus, it is necessary to have relationships anywhere we find ourselves in life, including incarceration. However, caution and discretion must be exercised in the prison environment when entering into a relationship. Trust often times is conditional since many times an individual that you thought you could trust turns out to have had a different agenda and maybe only wanted something from you. Despite that, there are many good people in prison who have simply made bad choices in their lives at one point or another; these people more often than not turn out to be some of the strongest, most trusted relationships in your life. For example, convicts often stick together and support one another after release because of the stigma that attaches to the status of felon placed on us by society. Many times a prisoner is released and finds employment or starts self-employment and keeps in touch with a buddy who, when released, is given or assisted in obtaining gainful employment, in addition to friendship, etc.

Regardless, whether within the walls or on the outside, relationships are built on trust, honesty, and understanding.

Without these qualities a relationship cannot be considered good, can it? Relationships are a very important part of human existence and good ones are to be treasured and maintained at all costs.

****

DISENCHANTED

by Chaka Turner

For Susan

I woke up this morning
feeling kind of blue
dreamed of drowning in the pain…
my sea from loving you.
I drifted to an island
of once again loneliness
searching for lost treasure
the beautiful you I miss.
Instead I landed atop a mountain
miles from love's distant shore
and fell upon a bed of rocks
eroding, like your love, no more.

****

A MOTHER'S TALE

by Betty Jean Thompson

My only son is an inmate. ($350,000) He has been in prison since 1992. One day in May of '92, an awful thing happened. A man was killed. My son was convicted of Third Degree Murder in the man's death. I am sorry for the sorrow caused by my son's actions. I know that my sympathy will never relieve the family's pain. I still agonize over this terrible situation. My family was traumatized too!

Many people forget that as a mother of an inmate, I am sometimes made to feel like I committed the crime. I am not a horrible person. I am simply a mother who loves her son. I do not love my son any less because he is in prison. I can feel his pain and frustration, his fear, his guilt, his humiliation. He tries to hide it but a mother knows. I guess it's what we call "Mother's Intuition."

I have been grieving over and over with no reprieve. I try very hard not to show how scared and grief-stricken I really feel. You see there are times when I see my son fading away from life, wanting to slip away, just give up. I can't let that happen. He looks to me for strength, support and hope. There is no way I can allow myself to break down in front of him. I know he could not take it. I don't want him to give up on himself. He is talented and intelligent. I know most people don't care what happens to him, and fewer care what happens to me. I often feel that I am held accountable for the crime too! I am not ashamed of my son. I am saddened by the choices that he made as a very young man. Soon after my son's conviction, he was brutally beaten by some correctional officers at Holmesburg Prison. He was beaten so badly that when he came out for a visit, I did not recognize my own son. It was that beating that catapaulted me into becoming an activist.

****

For most of the SageWriters, their feelings about their loving and loyal mothers (and occasionally fathers) reach almost mythical proportions. Here are just a few testimonials.

TEARS IN PARADISE
by Muti Ajamu- Osagboro

If the souls of the righteous are
allowed to grieve once they physically leave…
I know my Moms is cryin' at this very moment cause
She's missin' me just a sure as I breathe.

****

"Ms Majestic" **Oil on Canvas** **Muti Ajamu-Osagboro**

Mother

by Salvador Scuderi EJ-5857

***God took the fragrance of a flower,
The majesty of a tree,
The gentleness of morning dew,
The calm of a quiet sea,
The beauty of the twilight hour,
The soul of a starry night,
The laughter of the rippling brook,
The grace of a bird in flight.
The tender care of an angel,
The faith of the mustard seed,
The patience of eternity,
The depth of a family's need,
Then God fashioned from these things,
A creation like no other.
And when His masterpiece was through,
He called it simply - Mother.***

****

MOTHER

by Anton Forde/Trevor Mattis

***Upon whose shoulders does the responsibility for the continuation of mankind rest?
On a mother,
for the arduous task of incubating the miracle of life,
for the maintaining and propagating of that single act of God, creation.
Only a mother was chosen to bear the burden.
What a task. Can there be any other like it? Never!
In throes of excruciating pain, in bewailing travail,
in anguish and torment, she produces joy,
a joy only a mother can understand.***

Oh, how complex a person must a mother be
to experience joy in pain and happiness in tears.
And then the task has only just begun,
because that which just entered the world is nothing
without love and nurture.
It is nothing without the care and protection of a mother.
Oh, how much must it cost to forget one's self and devote
all to another, only a mother can understand,
attached for life by that umbilical cord of love,
for good or bad, better or worse, not even death
spares a mother.
Oh, my God, I know that it is too much for one person to bear,
so my mother, I am indebted to you forever.
Forgive me, for I can never repay.

Only my mother can understand.

****

MOTHER

By Michael King

When I think of my mother, it is often with sadness and appreciation for her undying years of love. She is no longer with me, but I can now look back and know that she gave to me what I can never have again. Unconditional love. Although I didn't understand the hardships she faced throughout her life as a single mother and deaf mute, I now can see how much she sacrificed for her only son. She always gave without question. Even though I didn't have the best clothing or the latest sneakers, as least I had them. No matter the poor decisions I made in life, she never turned her back. She made sure I went to school and showed her love the best way she knew how. She was always there for me. In the end, I wasn't there for her. This is a cross I must bear for my life and would change if I could. We are only given one mother in this lifetime and I shall always miss mine.

****

"Truth is the nursing mother of genius." Margaret Fuller (1819-1850

****

MAMMA I NEVER TOLD YOU SORRY

by Anton Forde/Trevor Mattis

It's been twelve years since they found me guilty and took my life from me. Mamma, I know how much you cry and stress yourself with worry about your only child, the apple of your eye, in whom you vested your future, wasting away your dreams in a prison cell. When friends ask you where's your son, you're too ashamed to tell. You know you brought someone great into this world, a lawyer, a doctor or a world leader, only to see him become nothing but a common prisoner. I know you fell because I let you down - Mama I never told you sorry. You did everything for me, sacrificed your own self, only child - single parent, you went hungry to see me eat properly. You went poor to make sure that I had all that I needed. Many times you gave up a vacation to ensure I got an education. You delayed your life until I became an adult, but look at the result, in your eyes it must be an insult. Mama, I never told you sorry, I know you had aspirations and dreams to live through me. I had the ability but lacked the opportunity; it's a sad reality, but life brings with it no guarantees. You did good, did all you could, made me into a good person, don't be ashamed of me for any reason, my situation being locked up in prison, in no way reflects upon you as a person. Don't cry; hold your head high, what was meant to be must be. Mama, I never told you sorry. I promise that one day I'll make you proud; as long as I have life, you'll live to see a day when the world recognizes me. The day will come, when you'll be proud that I'm your son for what I achieve, because you always believed you brought someone special into this world, believe me - Mama now's the time to say it "I'm sorry"

****

MY FATHER

by Tony Harper

My father has been there for me for most of my time in prison. He's been with me through the good times and bad, when everybody else in my life couldn't stand the test of time. Yes, it takes a very strong person to stand by someone you love who's incarcerated. Because time, as well as some of the staff, will do everything imaginable to turn them away from you. But my dad is a strong person because he laughs in their faces, because our love for one another is stronger than the evil that dwells in the people who have me locked away.

****

MEMORIES

By John Griffin
AM 8535
1111 Altamont Blvd.
Frackville, PA 17931
($1,050,000)

*John's eloquent memoir, **A Letter To My Father**, was published in 2001 by Xlibris.com. Written just before his* *brother died, it captures what it was like growing up in North Philadelphia in the tumultuous sixties, his relationships with his children, and also his involvement with the Nation of Islam. In his book, he documents the events that have affected his family since his father's death as a soldier when John was four years old.*

My mother raised my brother James and me to be respectful to everyone, especially women. We never heard a curse word, or the dreaded 'N' word in our house. She was an exceptional woman. From the day my father died -- he was killed on my fourth birthday -- she became both mother and father to us. She exemplified love, confidence, and courage, and taught us about our father's love for us.

My love for my father, my respect for him and all that I know about him came from her. She saved all his pictures for us; little mementos and letters he had written to her while he was serving in the army during WW11. It was because of her efforts that my brother and I learned the true value of family.

From ***A LETTER TO MY FATHER***

A collection of past events
Coexisting as images.
Some are mine,
Others are borrowed
From those who knew you better than I.
Sometimes I confuse the two. Their memories
Become mine. Their time with you
Became my precious moments. My personal
Glimpses into a mirror, shattered,
Each piece reflecting a different view,
A separate part of the same puzzle
In the mind of a three-year-old. Fragmented
Images of a tall, dark man
With a white, toothy grin,
His outstretched arms

Reaching down over a vast distance,
Lifting me, picking me up,
Rubbing his cheek against my skin. And,
Through another shattered piece,
I see his large hands,
Rope-like veins pushing up
From beneath black, leathery skin,
Wiggling like fat worms as I
Play with them, pushing them
This way and that way.
But it wasn't just the memories
Though we cloaked ourselves in them.
As if they were a shroud rendering us safe,
we anchored them around our necks so that
no other man would have our love.
It was her devotion to you, a display
Of loving that never changed
Even after her life had been tragically altered.
Like a poetic griot, she gave you life in death.
She excited our young minds with accounts of you;
Like an artist, her words the brush,
our minds the canvas, she brought you into our world.
With a voice more enchanting as she spoke,
Sometimes pausing, an intense hush adorning her
As she seems to relish and appreciate the taste
of her thoughts. Like the food a mothering eagle feeds
to her young, her words rolled around in her mouth
before she'd drop them, unselfishly,
into our minds. No, it wasn't just
the memories, Dad, it was her love.

****

"History is like a clock that tells a people their political and cultural time of day. It is a compass that locates a people on the map of human geography. History tells a people where they have been and what they have been. What they are and where they are. Most significantly, history tells a people where they still must go and what they still must be."

John Henrik Clarke

****

"The future of humanity lies in the hands of those who are strong enough to provide coming generations with reasons for living and working." Sister Iva Haliber, OJF

Nathan Oil on Canvas Muti Ajamu-Osagboro

Chapter Eleven
WOMEN IN PRISON

As horrible as the men's stories are, in comparison they sadly pale to what happens to women in prison. In Pennsylvania, the maximum security prison for women is at Muncy, five hours away from Philadelphia, home of most of the inmates. While women continue to visit men in prison, only 2% of women who are imprisoned ever receive visitors. A recent study showed that prior to incarceration, the average income of the women was less than $5,000 a year. The following is taken from a paper presented by the Co-

Director of the AFSC Prison Project at the conference "From Cell Blocks To City Blocks: a movement in search of freedom" at SUNY Binghamton, March 16,2002

Bonnie Kerness, American Friends Service Committee, Criminal Justice Program, 972 Broad St., Newark, NJ 07102 Co-author, Torture in U.S. Prisons: Evidence of U.S. Human Rights Violations

The relationship between women living in poverty and women being incarcerated is indisputable. There are currently 950,000 women in criminal justice custody in the U.S. with thousands more living under other forms of social control such as parole or probation. Since 1980, the number of women entering US prisons has risen almost 400%, double the rate for men. Women of color are imprisoned at rates between ten and thirty-five times greater than rates of white women in fifteen states. Nearly a quarter of these women are mentally ill, with untold numbers being infected with AIDS. 40% held no jobs prior to imprisonment, two thirds of them are women of color and 60% of them are mothers of an estimated 1.3 million minor children. Their average age is 29 and 58% of them haven't finished high school. Without any fanfare, the "war on drugs" has become a war on women and it has clearly contributed to the explosion in the women's prison population.

I'd like to share with you some of the voices of the women in prison that I hear during my day:

From New Jersey: "We are forced to sleep on the floor in the middle of winter with bad backs and aching bodies, cold air still blowing from the vents no matter what the temperature outside. At two o'clock in the morning they wake you up and tell you to clear the room. They go through your personal belongings and then put them in the trash…"

From Texas: “The guard sprayed me with pepper spray because I wouldn’t take my clothes off in front of five male guards. Then they carried me to a cell, laid me down on a steel bed and took my clothes off. They left me there in that cell with the pepper spray in my face and nothing to wash it away. They did that to me just because I didn’t want to take off my clothes in front of them…”

From Arizona: “…If you want a drink here, you have to drink toilet water…”

From Missouri: “When I refused to move to a double cell, they came and dragged me out and threw me on my back. I was beaten about my face and head. One of the guards deliberately stuck his finger in my eye. I was rolled on my stomach and cuffed and put in leg irons. Then I was put in a device called a “restraint chair” where your hands are cuffed beneath you. They stripped me naked and kept me there nine hours until I fouled myself on my hands which were tucked beneath me through a hole in the chair.”

The increasingly disturbing complaints I’m hearing from women in prison describe conditions of torture. They suffer from sexual abuse by staff with one woman saying, “I am tired of being gynecologically examined every time I’m searched.” Another prisoner put it, “That was not part of my sentence, to…perform oral sex with officers.” In one current New Jersey case, the woman who filed charges of rape has been in solitary confinement since the day she filed her complaint. This incredible woman actually held the semen in her mouth, spitting it into a plastic bag when she returned to her cell. She called me to tell me the guard who forced her to have sex was still working in the prison.

Reports of giving birth while handcuffed and shackled are horrible. One woman’s baby was coming at the same time the guard who shackled her was on a break somewhere else in the hospital.

Other abuses include medical care which is often so callous that it is life threatening...Coupled with the increasing use of long-term isolation, lack of treatment for substance abuse, lack of counseling services, concerns about the inappropriate use of psychotropic medications, inappropriate use of restraints and you have a clear picture of what life is like for our sisters in prison...yet there are far fewer advocates focused on women in prison than men. Part of the reason is that women are used to being the helpers, not the helped.

Each of the practices that the women testified about are in violation of dozens of international Treaties and Covenants that the U.S. has signed: The United Nations Convention Against Torture, the UN Convention on the Elimination of All Forms of Discrimination Against Women, UN Minimum Rules for the Treatment of Prisoners, the UN Convention on the Rights of the Child and a dozen other international and regional laws and standards.

****

"What you deny to others will be denied to you, for the plain reason that you are always legislating for yourself; all your words and actions define the world you want to live in."

Thaddeus Golas

****

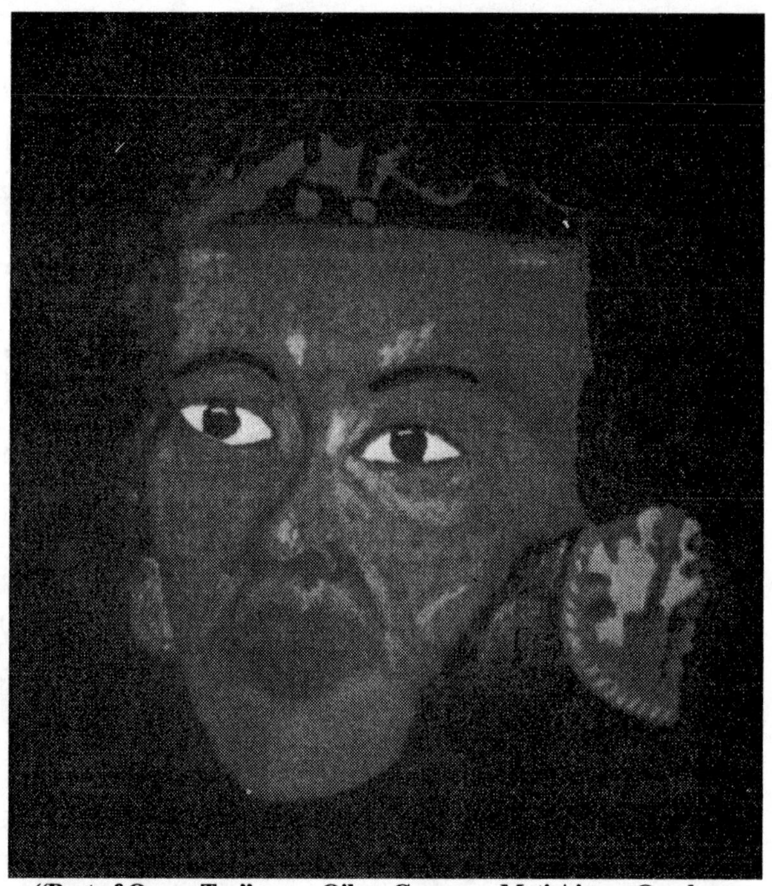

"Bust of Queen Tye" **Oil on Canvas** **Muti Ajamu-Osagboro**

The conditions of women in prison and on Pennsylvania's death row are dramatically described in a four-part series that began June 5, 2002 in the Philadelphia New Observer by Carol Williams. The focus of the series is on Donetta Hill, a death row inmate.

Muncy Horrors
Revealed by Death Row Inmate

Donetta Hill, a Philadelphia native has been on Death Row for ten years for a crime she insists she did not commit. She has already won one appeal. Her prison experience has been filled with cruelty, betrayal and inhumanity. Calling for the end of torture of prisoners, she describes life at Muncy:
"It's horrible. We are subjected to strip searches every time they take us out of our cells. You have to be strip searched before you shower, after you shower, when you go into the yard, to the library, to a visit, before and after everything you do. It can happen fifteen times a week depending upon how active you want to be. I feel raped every time they do it. They hold a mirror between your legs…"

While she says there are many good guards at Muncy, some of them play "mind games," part of the conditioning process meant to "break you."

"It's all about power," she said as she described a recent incident when she was brought to another facility for an appeals hearing: "They told me that the police van was coming at 1 pm. I was told to strip, lift (raise the breasts) spread my legs and cough. I was on my monthly and it was particularly humiliating. I complied anyway. They told me that they saw something in me."
She was asked to repeat the procedure two more times. Then she was told to "wipe from front to back and show them. They said that maybe there was some tissue in me" The experience, she says, left her feeling frustrated, humiliated and demeaned. "I almost cried."

Rather then continue the torture, Donetta Hill says that she initially decided not to go to her hearing. I said, "Then I guess I won't go, but my lawyer and the judge will know and there better be a good excuse. After a while they told me that the van left anyway."

After being returned to her room, she experienced a severe anxiety attack. Then she was told to get dressed, that the van was back and she would receive a misconduct charge for resisting the trip upon her return to Muncy.

She says that when she got to the Sheriff's gate, correctional officers asked her why she was refusing to come to court, that they had received a call from Muncy to that effect. Ms. Hill says that she explained that she was told that the van had left. They told her the van had never left the institution.

She went on to talk about the mysterious deaths of two prisoners at Muncy. In April 1992 a transsexual named "Jennifer" arrived at Muncy. The prisoner was in transition and still had his testicles. Ms. Hill says that this was the reason why he was at Muncy, a female institution, rather than a male facility like Graterford.

To complicate matters, Ms. Hill says that he was so emotionally tortured, taunted and harassed by the guards because of his difference that he committed suicide.

The death of "Denise Wallace" especially troubles Ms. Hill, who was in the room next to hers. Ms. Wallace was a "mental case," Ms. Hill said who used to swallow pens, spoons and forks.

"The guards and the staff would not help her. She kept throwing herself against the big steel door in there and you could just hear it all night long. I asked them to please take her out of there before she hurt herself. One night, around 11:30 pm, they took her out and she had a huge knot on her head from banging it against the door. They laughed at her.

They still did not take that little girl out of that cell. I asked if they could tie her down but they refused. I would like to find out who her family is. I want to tell them that they killed that little girl. They said that she hung herself, but she was just a little thing. White folks go to the state hospital or a mental facility, but they put that baby in here. They might as well have their own cemetery up here," she said sadly.

"There is a blue code of silence. My lawyer said that he is worried that something will happen to me for exposing this to the public, but I'm not worried about that right now. For me, the important thing is to bust this thing open.

She complained about green mold on the bread, mice droppings and mice nibble marks on the trays. She said that in January, she contracted food poisoning from the food. She complained about huge bugs and rats in the bathrooms and food unfit for human consumption.

"You're looked down on, judged. They make it so hard for you. The loneliness is the worst part. I need somebody that I can trust, to go to with these problems. I need somebody that I can talk to about what is going on here. This is why I am giving this interview, so that people will know on the outside. No matter what they say, all of this is true."

Ms. Hill stated that it is a known fact among the inmates that every day the women prisoners engage in sexual activity "behind the books." "And they get no misconducts for it. It's horrible up here."

Bob Esking, the Public Information Officer for the Philadelphia Prison System, had this to say about her claims of brutality: "Upon investigation, we found Donetta Hill's allegations to be unfounded."

****

"The person who doesn't fit in with our notions of who is worthy of love-the bag lady at the corner, the strange old man who rides through town on a three-wheel bike all strung up with flags- is just the person who, by not fitting into our patterns, insists that we expand not only our views but our capacity to love. Today, see if you can stretch your heart and expand your love so that it touches not only those to whom you can give it easily, but also to those who need it so much."

Daphne Rose Kingma

Chapter Twelve
FREEDOM AIN'T EASY

William Jameel Whitaker
($525,000)

SageWriters, Box 215, Swarthmore, PA 19081

Jameel is the first one of the imprisoned SageWriters to be freed after serving fifteen years for bank robbery fueled by drug use. His middle-class family has been incredibly supportive, yet he has had trouble finding employment that would enable him to live even modestly because of his record. He was given NO training or preparation for returning to the outside world where he had to learn all over how to do simple things like safely crossing the street.
He called me often after his release for advice on jobs, housing and relationships. When he'd feel sorry for himself, I'd remind him that the other six SageWriters, still locked up, would give anything to be in his shoes.

His re-entry has been difficult, and he is fortunate that he has so much loving support.

One wonders what would happen to him if he didn't.

JAMEEL

It is 5:30 a.m. on a Monday morning inside the fortress walls of Graterford Prison. There is a dim piercing light that permeates downward just above my bed. I'm usually up by this time of day; however this particular morning I can only lie in bed deeply pondering the many challenges ahead of me. Tomorrow I will be finally released after serving close to fifteen years in both federal and state institutions for the conviction of three counts of bank robbery.

As I lay in deeper contemplation on my bed, the lights on B-Block suddenly come on along with an all-too-familiar rattling sound of multiple keys being inserted in the doors of prison block-workers before the breakfast meal is served. I then see two images move quickly by my cell in military fashion; they're no doubt C.O.'s (Correctional Officers) who are about to man their stations while the other prison guards head towards the prisoners' dining room that is adjacent to the rear of B-Block. I then hear the lever pulled by an officer, which opens the tier I am housed on for the morning meal. As I prepare myself to take a shower, I always hold my towel, washcloth and shower shoes in my left hand; and my soap dish is kept in my pocket; my boots are laced up tightly without any socks on my feet.

I always keep one hand empty in case of any violent situation I may encounter while walking anywhere in prison. A friend of mine, for no reason, was bashed in the head with a brick by another inmate. This safety ritual was taught to me many years ago by an elite group of men called 'THE FRUIT OF ISLAM' that flourishes inside virtually every prison in the United States. The training I received from this body of men ultimately kept me alive while I served out my prison sentence inside the belly of the beast.

Just as I turn to enter the shower, a senior Corrections Officer summons me to the guards' station and hands me my discharge papers. As I retrieve this paper, a surge of energy rushes throughout my entire body, because I have waited 15 years for this glorious day. As I turn to walk out of the office, the C.O. says, "Good luck, Jameel," I nod my head in acknowledgement and enter the shower. I wash-off and then return to my cell, thinking that tomorrow I can have a long, luxurious bath without interruption or observation. I study my release papers carefully. I had to endure pure hell, as well as undergo some of the worst treatment humanly possible to get to this point. Now it has become certain to me that I am about to cross this River Jordan from Graterford Prison into the welcoming arms of a family that stood resolutely by my side for fifteen years.

I emerged from the bowels of prison, February 27, 2001 on a Tuesday morning. The C.O. took one final look at my prison I.D. that showed my picture and my institutional number: DQ-5653, and lifted the gate that separated me from 3,300 other prisoners.

Within minutes my beloved mother, Joanne E. Whitaker, a well-educated, strong Black woman who recently retired as a social worker for the city, pulled up in her black Plymouth into the prison parking lot. She emerged from her car and gave me a long hug, then opened the trunk of her car so that I could place a few personal items I chose to keep throughout my incarceration.
As we drove away – it is often said to never look back once you have left the precincts of prison for it said it is bad luck- I just had to take one long, last stare at the walls that literally held me hostage and a captive political prisoner for so many years.
I knew that many of my closest associates wouldn't be as fortunate as I was—at least by exiting by the front door.

While my mother and I drove towards Philadelphia, we talked about various things; what we actually spoke about during this hour drive I really don't remember. What I do recall is my constant thanks for granting me a place to stay until such time I could provide for myself. Even to this day, it's difficult for me to fathom the unyielding love a mother has for her children. I later found out just how degrading and emotionally stressful it was for my mother to have to enter a prison environment to visit me.

When we arrived at my mother's six bedroom home in the Mt. Airy section of Philadelphia, all I could think of was taking my first bath, eating my first home-cooked meal, and seeing my brother and sister, who shared this luxurious home with my mother.

And of course---getting laid!

In prison for fifteen years, now I'm entering back into a society that kept evolving while my prison environment virtually stood still. I soon found out that all of the years of running the yard, exercising in the gym, working in the prison industries, and reading about numerous subjects while incarcerated, did little to prepare me for the harsh and often brutal psychological treatment I was about to encounter in this free society. I can honestly say that while I was incarcerated, I never fell victim to any of the inequities that tend to flourish in prison like drugs, savage beatings and homosexuality.

Men that I drew inspiration from were brothers like Jo Jo Barnes, Clifford "Lumumba" Futch, Ra'u, Min. Joshua Asadi, Min. Derrick X. Jones, Muti Ajamu Osagboro and Mumia Abul Jamal. These uncompromising soldiers, whose examples while in the Pennsylvania prison system displayed a strong posture and fearlessness to prison officials that has served as a meaningful model for any Black man while in the belly of the beast.

One of the turning points for me while I was in Graterford came when my friend, Muti, suggested that I sign up for an upcoming creative writing class. Muti and I shared views on an array of topics, and he is one of the few Brothers I've crossed paths with while in prison that spoke with a burning passion about social change and who has a profound love for Black people just as I do.

When our writing class began, I remember entering in a room with fifteen other men who shared the same interests as I did. Although I've walked the prison walls with these men for years, I had virtually no social contact with any of them, because prison essentially is the type of environment where one chooses not to become overly acquainted with other prisoners because of the distrust that seems to permeate the very air we breathe.

An attractive, middle aged white woman entered the classroom, and her warm demeanor and radiant smile helped dispel the negative energy in the room. As she walked modestly but confidently towards her chair, she introduced herself as Judith Trustone and insisted we form a circle. She then sat in her seat, crossed her legs in the large cushioned chair in a meditative stance and asked us to introduce ourselves.

This broke the ice amongst the other men in our class, and an air of excitement replaced the ordinary cynicism. Because of years of daily tension and constant threats of violence in Graterford Prison, class exercises showed me the deep-seated anger I needed to focus on uprooting if my creative side were to be tapped into before my eventual release. I also had dreams of success as a writer when back in society as well.

After one writing session, I pulled Judith to the side and expressed to her how much I really enjoyed her class and that I was scheduled to be released soon. I told her I would like to continue learning ways to improve my writing skills along with a desire to be pro-active in society. She assured me there wouldn't be a problem with my request and then told me how I might remain in touch with her. And although neither one of us is any longer at Graterford Prison, she has demonstrated on numerous occasions just how dedicated and caring she is as a teacher, a counselor and a friend.

One of the greatest misconceptions we former prisoners tend to be misled by is in thinking all one must do is to remain drug free and not succumb to the immediate pressures of economic instability and we will reap our reward within a few trying months.

Nothing could be further from the truth.

After receiving a warm welcome from my immediate family, my mother told me that she didn't want me to feel pressured to look for a job right away and told me in a very kind and loving way not to seek employment the first thirty days of my freedom. Instead, she wanted me to gradually become reacquainted with the unseen pressures this society would eventually unleash on me, read the paper every day and to basically brace myself for what was about to befall me. My mother is a very strong-willed Black woman who has always been available to her children. She holds a Masters degree in Clinical Social Work.

My family members all had cars and took me everywhere I needed to go. My first few weeks, I literally was driven everywhere. Between my mother, sister and brother, they invested thousands of dollars for clothing, food and other necessary expenses.

After I'd been home a couple of weeks, my Mother sent me out to the Germantown branch of the Philadelphia Free Library unattended. After fifteen years in prison, this was my first time out in the public alone, without the watchful eyes of family members. I remember everything going well until I reached a red light at the intersection at Germantown and Chelten Avenues. When the light turned green, I froze and was afraid to cross the intersection. Everyone else crossed the street with calmness, but I was terrified of the cars that lined up awaiting the green light. I waited for the light to turn; then I summoned every atom of courage I could muster just to cross the street.

This incident only made it more obvious to me that there were imposing side effects of prison I had to overcome if I were to have any measure of success in free society.

My first week in the so-called "real world," a good friend of mine named "New York" picked me up in his spanking, brand new Infinity with two beautiful young women in his car. One was his girlfriend and the other was a lovely, well-endowed woman with a pecan complexion named Sonja. As we drove around Philly, Sonja asked me if I found her attractive. Need I expound on what my response was? We immediately hit it off on a positive note and everything seemed to just flow from that point. As the night ended, we went back to New York's apartment. She told me that I had a certain glow about myself and commented about how nice my physique was. I was just as attracted to her. Then something extraordinary happened--- I couldn't keep an erection. "DAMN!" I thought to myself, how could this be happening to a healthy soldier like me? Sonja then told me that my homie had informed her of my plight and that I was "thorough" and that she would be my first lay in fifteen years. This one of the many unforeseen problems I would encounter with women. It's one thing to masturbate while in prison to ease the tensions and loneliness of prison life. There were many times I'd fantasize just how I was going to exhibit my sexual prowess on the right sister upon my release. However, it took me about two months before I could actually get my groove back. It took practice, practice, practice.

When first released, I had a series of under-the-table jobs, for I found out most people don't want to risk hiring an ex-felon. My first legitimate job in society was when I acquired a sales position working for a large firm in sales and marketing. I was so happy getting this job primarily because I used what computer skills my dear sister, Susan, had recently taught me. The job required sales and marketing skills as well as the ability to deal effectively with the public. This was a huge accomplishment for me considering I had no real marketing skills prior to this job. What worked in my favor was the fact that I was hungry for gainful employment and the manager that interviewed me saw that I had a good work ethic.

Then I made a serious mistake. When an executive from a larger corporation came by to have her Lexus serviced, I managed to save her a few hundred dollars in repairs. While we were talking, she told me she worked for UPS as a senior manager and she implied that she could secure me a position with this company making approximately $50,000 a year if I were to leave my present company. Not doing my homework thoroughly, I left a secure job with the company that I was already with on the false promise of something more lucrative. When I went in front of the UPS corporate board, I disclosed that I was an ex-felon and, after a long time, I was offered a part time position which they said would eventually lead to a full-time job. It didn't.

This was the beginning of a downward employment spiral. A friend of mine was able to help me get a security job with a major hospital in Philadelphia. I held this job for about two months, but after my background check came back, I was released. After I lost this job, I went into greater depression and seclusion. I finally called Judith and sought her opinion regarding these encounters. She informed me that all of these trials I was undergoing were stepping stones, and that I shouldn't lose sight of where I came from and that I was the only one in her writing class that made it back into society. She said I had to remain strong and that these were things I had to experience in order to rise above these adversities.

With each failed attempt to find a job that would pay well enough for me to live however modestly, I knew I had to hold on to what I had because I didn't want to return to prison, mainly because so many people had invested their votes of confidence in me, and I couldn't fail them.

Judith eventually invited me accompany her to a play produced and directed by Paula Sepinuk of TOVA, theater of witness, that was being held at S.C.I. Chester, one of Pennsylvania's newer prisons. I was uneasy about going back into a prison, any prison.

What I found really extraordinary about this event was upon arriving there and seeing the performance, "Living with Life," I had actually served time at different institutions with four of the prisoners who were performing. One was my cousin; I had no idea he was there. While watching the players enact their stories, many for the first time, I felt myself blinking back tears from witnessing how all these brothers really wanted was an opportunity to return to society. And here I was crying about how difficult it was after serving a long prison term.

All these brothers wanted was a chance to be where I was.

Judith eventually drafted a job support letter along with those of State Senator Shirley Kitchen, Paula Sepinuk and a few other individuals who had faith in me.

After nights of driving a cab, with the support of so many professionals, I've finally landed a job as a youth counselor at a well-known juvenile justice facility. This position enables me to give back to the community and to use my life experiences to prevent young people from ending up in prison like I did.

However, it literally has taken me eighteen months to reach this point.

Being out in society has posed many obstacles, and in no way has it been easy. However, one of my greatest joys was when I met my first lady friend and love. While I was working at UPS, I met a very lovely, older Latina woman named Angelita. For awhile, I watched her from afar. Eventually I discovered she was a great conversationalist and she spoke from her heart. (Plus she had a great body.)

We hit it off immediately. She not only accepted me for who I was and where I'd been, but she was brutally honest and trustworthy. Angelita introduced me to a whole new world, a new expression of life. Through her, I became more willing to expose my feelings and take chances that helped me to grow. Having a strong, virtuous woman in my corner to aid and assist me through all the trials and tribulations has really been a blessing.

Angelita used to always put me first, my first experience with this kind of love. This affection so overwhelmed and scared me that I started rebelling from so much closeness as our relationship deepened.

Eventually, the romantic part of our friendship stopped, for I wasn't ready for the commitment she wanted. We both focused on our careers, but we stayed in touch and still hang out together as friends. In fact, it seems we're better friends now than when we were a couple.
To this day I feel immense love for this woman, and she says she feels the same about me. Hopefully, if it's meant to be, we will someday rekindle the fire of romance, but on a higher level.

There is nothing easy about re-entering back into society after serving a lengthy prison sentence. The prison did nothing to prepare me; if I hadn't had the emotional and financial support of my family and friends, I can say emphatically that I would have eventually returned back to prison with a much longer sentence.

If there is one piece of advice I could pass on to the Brothers in Judith's Creative Writing class it would be to discipline your body, mind and spirit, because you're in for a rude awakening once you've emerged from the lion's den.

****

"We who lived in the concentration camps can remember the men who walked through the huts comforting others, giving away their last piece of bread. They may have been few in number, but they offer sufficient proof that everything can be taken away from a man but one thing: the last of human freedoms-to choose one's attitude in any given set of circumstances, to choose one's own way."

Victor Frankl

****

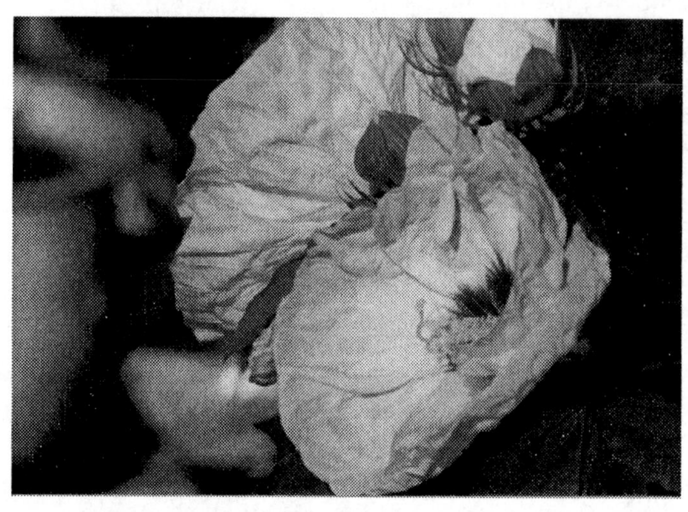

Part Two: TRANSFORMATION: VISIONS OF WHAT COULD BE

This section includes comments from a wide range of prisoners, activists, teachers, and families who responded to two questions:

First, what do you think of the current criminal justice system?

And second, if you had no political, legal or budgetary restraints, what kind of a new system would you build from the ground up?

While dozens of people said they wanted to write something, not all who promised did. A couple of guards decided it was too risky. Many of those I interviewed or who wrote are not included in this printing due to space limitations.

Anton Forde/Trevor Mattis

BH-3126
Box 244
Graterford, PA 19426 ($455,000)

Before taking on the gargantuan problem of changing it, we have to define the justice system, which is comprised of three parts: 1) Law enforcement 2) the judicial system and 3) the penal system. Each part must be changed if we are to effect change in the system. Each of these arms, though independent, work in concert, and the problems at the entrance wing, law enforcement, are only compounded as we go from one arm to the next. I will tackle this evil system one arm at a time. One common theme running through all arms of this system is racial discrimination. Racism unites this system into a cohesive body.

Law Enforcement

First and foremost, law enforcement has to change its attitude to the community it serves, particularly the Black community. Police are the first prong of the justice system, making arrests, investigating and gathering information to substantiate guilt or innocence. However, with Black suspects, the latter doesn't apply. The problems with the police are two-fold: 1) Racism in historically and inherently ingrained within the police force, and 2) the unwritten code of the police is that Black suspects are guilty until proven innocent. This institutional racism is behind the prevalent practice of stereotyping done by every police department across this nation; they try to make every suspect a criminal, criminalizing African Americans by making arrrests in the Black community that would be warnings in white communities. Because of the presumption of guilt, they slant their investigations to try to obtain the most serious charges possible and overzealously look for evidence with the highest probability of obtaining a conviction. Here's a common scenario. Two people are apprehended. One possesses a small amount of narcotics. The police run a check on their backgrounds and find that the person without the narcotics is a parole violator or is on probation. What they do is charge the innocent person with the narcotics because they know that with his record, the probability of a sentence being imposed is higher for the repeat offender. Other common, unethical practices by police include hiding exculpatory evidence, not investigating exculpatory evidence, coercing confessions and, most common of all, lying on the witness stand. I'm certain that no less than 99% of all police officers have lied on the stand at one time or another. This was illustrated most graphically in a recent PBS documentary about public defenders, "Presumed Guilty."

The main villain in law enforcement is the unseen and rarely spoken about prosecutor, the person most responsible for setting the tone of the police force. They are the ones with the final say on who will be charged, what charges will be brought to trial, and who will be released. Here is where the institutional racism flourishes virtually unseen and unchecked. It's the prosecutor who decides in a murder case if the charge will be 1st, 2nd or 3rd degree or manslaughter. In cases where the suspect is Black, the probability that the charge will be 1st degree is very high. If the suspect is Black and the victim is white, the death penalty where allowed is almost guaranteed. If the suspect is white and the victim black, the possibility is high of 3rd degree or manslaughter. The circumstances of justifiable homicide like self-defense is almost never applicable to a black suspect. These discriminatory practices of prosecutors are well documented but rarely discussed. The Philadelphia District Attorney's office, under the pro-death penalty leadership of Lynn Abraham, according to the PA Defender Association, is known nationally as one of the most racist in the nation.

To change law enforcement, I would implement a system of neighborhood policing where only people who grew up in or live in the neighborhood would be hired to police those districts. Town meetings would be held monthly to get information about inmates' progress as well as concerns of the officers and their superiors. I believe the most effective policing is where individuals with ties to the community are in service. Individuals in this position would have a better feel for who has committed a crime and who to arrest. I would give these police officers wide latitude as to when to make an arrest, when to reprimand or warn, and when to turn a suspect over to parents, counselors or a treatment program.

I would set a high standard in the area of investigations. The police would have to investigate all cases thoroughly before bringing charges. Doing this would eliminate the practice of using confessions, often coerced, and deals with alleged co-conspirators as evidence in criminal trials. If an individual chooses to confess or cooperate, this evidence could only be used as leads to gather independent or corroborating evidence in another person's trial. A suspect charged for a crime could plead guilty for a reduced sentence but could not get a reduced sentence by implicating or testifying against a co-defendant.

I would make illegal the tactic of police officers who coerce confessions from a suspect by promising them leniency. I would make it mandatory that all defendants and suspects get counseling prior to making any statements to the police and that counsel be present during any and all debriefing. I would enforce the selection of grand juries to bring any indictment which exposes a defendant to a sentence of five or more years. At these grand jury trials, counsel for the defense would be present to argue for a lesser charge or the dismissal of the indictment.

THE JUDICIAL SYSTEM

This is the stage where a defendant faces judgment and receives his sentence. The trier of fact, the alleged impartial referee of the adversarial competition between the defendant and the accuser, is usually never that. Many judges were once prosecutors and a statistical analysis of their rulings from the bench reflects that bias. The judge is in a position that can easily determine who will win or lose at trial. He decides the rules of the game and long before the trial starts he makes rulings that can determine who will succeed. For example, the judge determines what will be allowed in as evidence and what will not.

I would change this stage by implementing the following: Judges could not have been prosecutors or lawyers before being on the bench. All judges would have to spend one week in anonymous identity in the following a) county jail b) medium security prison c) maximum security prison d) death row. Juries would be mandatory for all cases where the defendant faces a sentence of five or more years. I would repeal mandatory sentences and return to a discretionary sentencing scheme. All sentences would carry automatic time reduction incentives determined by the convicted person's progress and development while incarcerated. I would allow for more creative sentences like house arrest, banishment, conscription for humanity work in impoverished countries and disaster areas, work on farms, natural reserves and wilderness areas.

I would eliminate conspiracy as a hauling net charge where the state can give ten individuals life sentences for murder when only one person did the actual killing.
Sentencing for conspiracy would be according to individual culpability. I would abolish the death penalty. The maximum time any person could continuously stay in jail would be 25 years. Teenagers could not be tried as adults. I would eliminate the practice of using sentencing factors not

presented to a jury or not proven beyond a reasonable doubt to enhance a person's sentence. For example, today a defendant can be tried and convicted before a jury for the possession of one ounce of cocaine. This would expose the person to a sentence of 2 ½-5 years, but he can get an additional five years because the prosecutor says he used to have a gun, or the person was within 1000 yards from a school (another five years). Neither of these things are brought to a jury, only to the judge at the sentencing phase. These are considered sentencing factors, things used to increase the sentence. The defendant was never charged with possessing a gun and that may never have been mentioned at trial. However, the prosecutor could bring it up at sentencing. I would make any element that can be used to increase a defendant's sentence be proven to a jury beyond a reasonable doubt.

THE PENAL SYSTEM

This is the stage where a person is housed to do the time imposed by the judge at his/her sentencing. This is also the stage where society expects professional personnel to implement programs to rehabilitate the offender. However, the prevailing tendency in the penal system is that of punishment. The political atmosphere saturated with the present political propaganda creates a mentality in the prison guards that it is their duty to punish offenders. Forgotten in this process is the fact that the forfeiture of freedom is the sole punishment legally provided by the law.

The first thing I would change would be the concept of the penal system. I would redefine those who offend society's laws as patients in need of treatment and prisons would be more like hospitals where offenders are treated to curb their anti-social behavior. All incoming inmates would be evaluated to see where best to place them within a variety of programs and institutions. All would be given extensive psychological evaluations and proper treatment. Great emphasis would be placed on the reconstruction of self-esteem and the correction of deep-rooted emotional problems stemming from socio-economic conditions. Aggressive programs for self-development and self expression would be promoted. All these programs would carry various incentives of time reduction and increased personal privileges. When given an unfettered chance to improve themselves, most inmates respond positively.

Within the penal system the emphasis should be on education. The daily routine would be structured around such programs, many of which would be mandatory, thereby reducing time-wasting activities. These programs would also be tied to time reducing and financial incentives. For example, if an inmate went to school, he would be paid the highest wages offered in the institution unlike the present system where wages are at best 60 cents an hour.

I would increase the volunteer programs where people from the community participate with inmates in various rehabilitative programs. All inmates would have to participate in a victim's awareness program where they come face to face with crime victims to fully understand the effects of crime on victims.

I would have many of the educational programs designed and implemented by ethno-centric instructors who would cater to Blacks and Hispanics, the majority of the people now in prison. African and Hispanic-centered curricula would connect directly to the inmate population at the grass roots level. I would have families and loved ones work closely with prison officials in monitoring inmate progress.

Inmates who are parents would be given the opportunity to actively participate in the parenting of their children, and I would develop programs to maintain and strengthen family ties.

These are just a few of the programs I would implement if I had the power to implement changes.

All of these suggestions address the symptoms but not the root causes of crime. To address these causes we would have to radically change the inequities of this capitalistic economic system by changing it into an egalitarian socio-economic system. At the same time, we would have to find a way to address the economic legacy of slavery in concrete terms and determine its effects on African Americans and the wealth of white Americans. We need to find a way to compensate African Americans.

Then we have to eradicate racism and oppression in all its various forms. Finally, we would have to allow all citizens fair and impartial access to good education and good job opportunities.

Only when we have achieved an egalitarian socio-economic society will America truly live up to the words penned by its founding fathers.

****

William Ayers, PhD.
The University of Illinois at Chicago
1040 W. Harrison
Chicago, IL 60607-7133
bayers@uic.edu

William Ayers is a school reform activist, Distinguished Professor of Education, and Senior University Scholar at the University of Illinois at Chicago. A former member of the Weather Underground, he is the founder of the Center for Youth and Society and founder and co-director of the Small Schools Workshop. His books include A Kind and Just Parent: The Children of Juvenile Court (Beacon Press, 1997), To Teach: The Journey of a Teacher, (Teachers

College Press, 1993) which was named Book of the Year in 1993 by Kappa Delta Pi and won the Witten Award for Distinguished Work in Biography and Autobiography in 1995 and (with Rick Ayers and Bernardine Dohrn) Zero Tolerance: Resisting the Drive for Punishment: A handbook for parents, students, educators and citizens, (The New Press, 2001). His latest book is Fugitive Days: A Memoir, (Beacon Press, 2001).

A QUESTIONNAIRE

by Bill Ayers

- What is the average sentence in the US given to a person convicted of stealing $50,000 or less? What is the average sentence give to a person stealing $1,000,000 or more?
- Of the more than two million incarcerated Americans, what percentage are doing time for non-violent offenses? For drugs? What percentage of the prison population never graduated from high school? What percentage is illiterate or low literacy, diagnosed with a learning disability or a mental health problem?
- What is the racial representation in our prisons? How does it compare to the racial representation in society as a whole?
- Of inmates on death row, how many were born into wealthy families? Poor families? How many are African-American, Latino, white?
- How many prisons did California build in the last two decades? How many universities? During the same time how much money did Illinois spend on prison construction? On school construction?
- Besides the Democratic Republic of the Congo, which government permits the execution of juvenile offenders? (Hint: Recently, China, Saudi Arabia, Pakistan, Bengladesh, and Nigeria banned the practice).

- Now that Somalia has signed the UN Convention on the Rights of the Child, what nation stands alone in refusing to sign?
- Which government stands against 74 other nations in opposing the treaty that developed an International Criminal Court whose mission is to prosecute genocide, war crimes, and crimes against humanity?
- With over half the nations of the world committed to the Convention on the Elimination of Discrimination Against Women, which major country has not signed?
- Which nuclear power withdrew from the treaty barring nuclear testing in space? (Hint: The same power recently scuttled a nuclear disarmament agreement, "unsigned" a global warming treaty, and walked away from a world conference on racism?

Rousseau wrote regarding justice that with respect to wealth, ***"no citizen should be so opulent that he can buy another, and none so poor that he is constrained to sell himself."*** The quest for social justice over many centuries is worked out in the open spaces of that proclamation, in the concrete struggles of human beings constructing and contesting all kinds of potential meanings within that ideal. Nothing is settled, once and for all, but a different order of question presents itself: Who should be included? What do we owe one another? What is fair and unfair?

Of course the quest for social justice is worked out within political, legal, and budgetary limitations. The important thing is to live with one foot in the actual world of the here and now, and with the other foot striding toward what could be, but is not yet.

We need a concrete analysis of real conditions, but we also need a vision of where we might go.

The U.S. - given its history - must reject war, conquest, and aggression on principle as a step to becoming a just society; it must commit its considerable wealth and resources to healing the racial nightmare that is at its core. This means reparations, redistribution, reinvestment. It means popular mobilization for full participation in democratic life, and the creation of institutions that encourage the engagements of citizens. And it means reversing the current treacherous tendency —instead of retreating from education and promoting a criminal justice solution to every problem, we must embrace education in all its forms as the great humanizing enterprise that it is, and reject the criminalization of society.

The criminal justice system should be based on principles of fairness, equity, and democratic participation. Concretely, every effort should be made to divert citizens from prison. Principles of restorative justice should guide us, and institutions like peer juries and community councils should be generously supported. Prison should be the last resort, not the first option, reserved for violent offenders, and still built around notions of participatory democracy, community-building, and engaged human capacity. There should be a commitment to education, to creating art and culture, to community craft, to treatment and counseling. Prisoners should emerge more able to participate in all the decisions that affect their lives—economic, social and emotional, rather than scarred and disabled.

****

ERNIE PREATE, ESQ.

Former Attorney General of Pennsylvania

507 Linden, Suite 600, Scranton, PA 18503 (570) 346-3816

With the election of Ed Rendell as Governor of Pennsylvania, Ernie Preate is convinced that as he promised to inmates, Rendell will make the Board of Pardons more functional and he also supports the Parole for Lifers movement. Based on these hopes, inmate James Taylor,

($1,050,000) founder of People Against Recidivism, PAR, has raised $10,000 through his supporters to hire Preate to take his case before the revamped Board of Pardons when that occurs. All Lifers in Pennsylvania are watching carefully.

"JAILHOUSE SHOCK"

Ernest Preate was one of the nation's toughest Attorney Generals. Then he went to prison and learned how justice really works. A new view of justice: once a prosecutor who sent defendants to long prison terms and even death row, Ernie Preate is now a defense attorney who works for prison reform. These are some excerpts from an article in the positive-focused HOPE MAGAZINE, May/June 2002 by Scott Westcot, reporter for the Erie Times-News.

Ernie Preate's epiphany came the first time he entered the mess hall of the federal prison camp in Duluth, Minnesota. After shuffling through the chow line, Preate turned to find a seat. What he saw stopped him cold. Table after table was filled with African American and Hispanic men. As Pennsylvania's Attorney General, Preate was aware of the disproportionate number of minorities behind bars. While serving time himself for mail fraud, he saw it firsthand. "It was just a sea of black faces," Preate recalls of that January 1996 day. "I said to myself, Oh my God, I helped create this." The moment was pivotal in Preate's transformation from Pennsylvania's top law enforcement official to the vocal prison-reform advocate he is today. Preate still believes that criminals, particularly violent offenders, should serve prison time. But his own jailhouse experience convinced him that our criminal justice system largely warehouses human beings, discriminates against minorities, and is pathetically inadequate in its rehabilitation efforts.

Preate's life veered sharply. His first reckoning with the skewed aspects of criminal justice came in the months leading to his guilty plea. The charge of mail fraud - a federal felony - hinged on campaign contributions he had not disclosed a decade earlier, and it reeked of political maneuvering. It might have been reduced to a charge of campaign violations, all that Preate would have been guilty of if he had hand delivered his finance report, instead of mailing it. But when the feds threatened also to charge Preate's brothers in the case, he began to see the difference money makes in our legal system.

"If you have money you can get a fair fight in court," says Preate. "If you're poor, forget it. I wasn't poor, but I by no means had the resources to take on the government. I talked it over with my family and said let's end this right now. We don't have the money to fight it." Preate pleaded guilty and was sentenced to 14 months in federal prison. While in prison he soon learned "...While the system claims it's trying to rehabilitate, it's really about tearing people down. What I was finding was there are a lot of good people in prison that made mistakes. Contrary to public perception that they are a menacing evil, the vast majority are not. Frankly I was shocked by the number who had not received effective counsel," says Preate. Even the simplest things some of those lawyers didn't do. They didn't ask for discovery; they didn't call witnesses; they didn't make the appropriate motions. Our whole system is based on advocacy, and it was clear many of these prisoners had not had competent advocates."

Once he gained his freedom, Preate acted on his promise. "There were some people who knocked me as having a so-called jailhouse conversion," Preate says. "When you've fallen as far as I fell, it's not that you're a bleeding heart. It's that your eyes are opened. Going to prison was a freeing experience for me. For the first time I could think without constraint and without jeopardizing my political career." His main thrust is that the criminal justice system stacks the deck against minorities, the poor, and the disenfranchised. Preate thinks the first imperative is to concentrate on education and prevention.

“What I see is America being destroyed from within. We haven’t built a single new university in Pennsylvania in decades, but since 1984 we’ve built 19 new prisons, expanded one, and have two more in the works. We know that the greatest preventer of crime is education. If we truly committed ourselves to education we would have a much safer society. But we are investing in warehouses of humanity instead of investing in people.”

“My life is no longer about achieving power or political success,” Preate often tells people. “It’s about bringing hope to the hopeless. The most rewarding thing is I am getting to see that I can be an agent for change,’ says Preate. ‘I think our country is at stake, and we have a system that is breaking down.....I'll never stop fighting to change that. Never.”

Lobbyist Coalition
103 N. Main St.
Hatfield, PA 19440-2419

David Mandeville

DN-7632
1120 Pike St. Box 999
Huntingdon, PA 16652

With more than 85% of inmates returning to prison, the current system is an obvious failure. No business with this high a rate of failure would survive.

1) The current attitude of hatred and anger society feels about inmates must change, for it only creates rage among inmates that is projected onto other inmates, those in authority and society as a whole.

2) The attitude needed is one of love, acceptance and understanding. Humankind's greatest teachers all taught that love is the most powerful force that exists, and its transformational power is greater than anything.

3) Prisoners should not be isolated from their communities. Families and communities should be key in their rehabilitation so both parties in a conflict face their responsibilities for bad behavior and make necessary restitution so forgiveness can take place. This will lead to a strengthening of community. When people feel isolated and afraid, they act out against their community.

4) Education in institutions should be focused on self-discovery, helping prisoners identify their values, their physical and emotional needs, their dreams and so forth. Education should be like therapy, helping prisoners better understand themselves and why they act in certain ways. The focus should be internal, with one-to-one interaction at first with the teacher/counselor. Initially I think group settings do more harm than good as people are too influenced by group leaders, and try, out of fear, to protect their images in group settings.

5) Counselors should have very small caseloads and see their assigned prisoners weekly. I see my "counselor" for fifteen minutes a year, when I have my annual review. How can she know me in just fifteen minutes a year?

6) The goal of incarceration should be to enlighten, not punish. Any student of psychology knows that punishment is very dangerous. Positive reinforcement for good behavior is much more effective.

7) Incarceration should work. Prisoners should come out reborn, responsible and wise, full of love and compassion for others. But they will have to be treated differently by prison officials and COs. The way society and the Department of Corrections treat prisoners, it's no wonder both violent and non-violent offenders project their anger onto society once they're released. The only way is to break the cycle by the Department of Corrections. Let them learn how to correct, not just punish.

There is no need to incarcerate non-violent offenders; they belong in rehab or community programs. Only violent and explosive offenders need to be incarcerated, and the family and community should be active in their habilitation.

Long-term sentences should be done away with. No one should spend more than ten years in prison unless he refuses to change his behavior and continues to be a real and violent threat. Most will change their behavior if they are habilitated properly, and their understanding of themselves and life are expanded.

Politics should be left out of the process. The system should have only pure intent: to heal.

I would start a new system by changing the approach taken to prosecute an offender. Instead of a myriad of charges, there would only be two possible charges, violent and non-violent unacceptable behavior. Cases would be prosecuted

for the best outcome for the offender, the victim, the community and the family. Upon conviction, violent offenders would be sent to a habilitation center. This center should be followed by a period of house arrest and then a parole-like system.
Non-violent offenders would be sent to a 3-6 month educational program, like a boarding school but focused on reflection, self-seeking and internally-focused education so the offender can understand himself and what led to his past unacceptable behavior. He should take full responsibility for his behavior and make restitution. Escapism and outward distractions should be minimized, so the offender can look within in peace and quiet. TVs, radios, and sports should be accessible during recreational times but not all day.

Offenders would have to do community service and go to town meetings in addition to weekly counseling sessions with psychologists. They would be praised for their good efforts and encouraged to live up to their potential and fulfill their dreams. The whole process should last about two years, 3-6 months in the center, three months house arrest and eighteen months on some sort of parole.

Violent offenders would go through the same process after their incarceration. The staff would be well-trained and well-paid, treating prisoners with love, respect and understanding. I think these ideas would work, though they need more fine-tuning and deeper exploration. This system would not only be more effective but would cost much less as well. Once people increase their understanding of life and get to the real issues, they will see the truth and will know why their behavior was unacceptable. They will not commit the behavior again but will try to embrace life and live it to the fullest.

I have faith in the resources of this country. Psychologists, former prisoners, behavior specialists and social workers have much experience which could be utilized to fix this horrible problem.

I live in prison and understand its effects. Prisoners walk around full of fear, anger, hate, misery, bitterness, hopelessness and negativity. Their lives are clearly fruits of 'evil'. Christ said that we can only battle evil with good; the current system fights evil with evil, thus creating more evil in the world. Some say, "Look at all the programs and groups; there should be so much good." But what rose can reach its potential in the midst of darkness? Not one! In this environment of rage, helplessness and loneliness, it's no wonder prisoners return to society and commit worse crimes. It would take a miracle for someone to learn to love others in this environment of hate.

Many people give of themselves to help us. They are truly blessings. But many working for the system plant seeds of 'evil' through poor medical treatment, uncaring attitudes, the phone system and power trips. Society's attitude of hatred and vengeance toward prisoners breeds 'evil' also.

If we would only treat people like the animals on television's 'Animal Planet'. A loving, caring attitude and much patience helps mistreated and abused animals come around. Why can't we treat our mistreated and abused humans the same way? We currently use the same methods dog fighters use to train fighting dogs. To make them vicious you must isolate them in a cage, treat them with meanness, tease them, mess with their minds, abuse them and beat them. They will then internalize their anger and project it wherever they can, usually on other dogs, sometimes on their owners, with frequent deadly results.

Can we not see similarities in the current handling of prisoners? Most will return to society with the harvest of the fruits planted in here, a frightening thought. If we plant good seeds and provide them with much light and love, we will ensure that prisoners leave with a bountiful harvest.

The prison system affects everyone in society whether they realize it or not. We are all one humanity, including our lowest and highest members. We need to be reminded that along with being criminals, we are also mothers, fathers, sons, daughters, brothers, sisters, friends, and lovers. But before we were any of these roles, we were humans.
The Department of Corrections has not rehabilitated me. Through my own efforts I've come to understand life differently. I've found meaning and the key lies within my own heart.

****

William DiMascio, Executive Director
Pennsylvania Prison Society

2000 Spring Garden St.
Philadelphia, PA 19130
215-564-6005

The *war on terrorism* is an affair of the heart. It's driven by emotion and fueled by passion. For the moment, at least, it feels wonderful – full of self-righteousness and flag-waving pride, not to mention innocence borne of a simplistic view of the tragedy of September 11th.

I find the whole thing troublesome, however, fraught with the prospect of a darker side filled with far-reaching, unanticipated consequences.

Especially relevant to the Prison Society is the way our response to the tragedy parallels our reactions to the situations that impact our criminal justice system, our *war on crime*.

In fact, it seems that many of the "tough on crime" policies adopted over the last decade have helped to pave the way, or at least condition us to respond as we have in our current international conflict. In the name of protection against crime -- public safety -- we have discredited the judiciary and adopted mandatory sentences, weakened prisoners' constitutional access to redress of abuse, and accelerated an execution process that continues to display its defects.

The American public has heartily supported the war in Afghanistan, perhaps because the military operations were so spectacularly successful but also because the civilian population has not been asked to take part in a military draft or sacrifice any creature comforts. But the defeat of the Taliban and al Qaeda as well as any other terrorism-supporting nations is unlikely to change any of the underlying causes of the terrorist attacks. Some might say our relentless, if not ruthless pursuit of war is likely to further embitter our enemies.

In the same way, our battle against illegal drugs has focused the overwhelming portion of its effort on interdiction with relatively few resources devoted to combating root causes. As a result, we arrest and incarcerate thousands of street corner dealers only to find an endless stream of replacement drug vendors emerging from the ranks of the socially and economically disadvantaged.

A similar dynamic seems to be in play in the terrorists' arena. Writing in *The New York Times*, correspondent Thomas L. Friedman observed: ***"Here's the truth: What radicalized the Sept. 11th terrorists was not that they suffered from a poverty of food, it was that they suffered from a poverty of dignity. Frustrated by the low standing of Muslim countries in the world, compared with Europe or the United States, and the low standing in which they were personally held where they were living, they were easy pickings for militant preachers who knew how to direct their rage."***

As long as we let vengeance and retribution guide our war against terrorism or against crime, meaningful solutions will remain elusive. Worse yet, if we become obsessed with the fear of being attacked, we will surrender those characteristics of our culture and our governance that are most popular around the world and most deeply valued at home.

Lewis H. Lapham, editor of Harper's, has written: ***"Like an Arab jihad against capitalism, the American jihad against terrorism cannot be won or lost; nor does it ever end. We might as well be sending the 101st Airborne Division to conquer lust, annihilate greed, capture the sin of pride."***

Terrorism and crime are not geographic entities with physical features that can be occupied. They are concepts -- often arbitrarily defined in political or partisan terms -- and acts that violate the dignity and vitality of humankind.

No amount of military might will eradicate terrorism any more than unlimited police powers will eliminate all crime. Look at the never-ending violence in the Middle East where military force and terrorism seem to feed on each other. Look also at the criminal justice system in this country where decades of prison building and incarceration have done little to assuage the public's fear of crime.

The time has clearly come for us to consider other strategies in both these conflicts. Shore up our defenses, improve our policing and security, but then let's also address the root causes of these problems. Let's put our sense of fairness and equality to use in leading nations of the world to recognize the problems that breed the kind of hatred that led to the September 11th attacks. And let's also understand that demonizing people caught up in the criminal justice system does nothing to repair the damage done by crime.

The legacy of the United States is steeped in humanistic ideals, ethical and moral values, and democratic principles. These are the armaments of the citizenry. They help to keep us focused when terrorism or crime fan emotions that blind us to the benefits of dissent and compassion. They are all the armaments we need to take the high ground against the "poverty of dignity" that motivates criminal activity nationally and internationally.

****

"Powerlessness is the recruiter for religion, blind faith leading to blind hope, political anesthesia and terrorism. If people took off their sacramental blinders they'd either be moved to action or resigned to slow suicide by dulled environmental poisoning. When religion and culture entangle, everyone sighs with relief, for now an 'US' vs. 'THEM' has been created, and the righteous bore us at all levels of public discourse." El Shabbaz

****

"No man can put a chain around the ankle of his fellow man without at last finding the other end fastened about his own neck." Frederick Douglass (1883)

****

"My life is no longer about power and success. It's about bringing hope to the hopeless." Ernie Preate

****

Bonnie Kerness, Co-Director American Friends Service Committee, Criminal Justice Program

972 Broad St., 6th floor
Newark, NJ 07102

Bonnie and I met when we were both presenting at a conference "From Cellblocks to City Blocks: Building a Movement in Search of Freedom," SUNY Binghamton, March 16, 2002. She is a strong supporter of SageWriters.

There is no way to look into any aspect of prison or the wider criminal justice system without being slapped in the face with the racism and white supremacy that prisoners of color endure. If we dig deeper into these practices, the political function they serve is inescapable. Police, the courts, the prison system, and the death penalty all serve as social control mechanisms. The economic function they serve is equally as chilling. I believe that in the US criminal justice system the politics of the police, the politics of the courts, the politics of the prison system and the politics of the death penalty are manifestations of the racism and classism that govern much of our lives. Every part of the criminal justice system falls most heavily on the poor and people of color, including the fact that slavery was guaranteed in the US by the 13th amendment of the Constitution. Involuntary prison slavery is real.

I've heard people say that the criminal justice system doesn't work. I've come to believe exactly the opposite. It works perfectly as a matter of both economic and political policy. I don't believe it is an accident that the young adolescent of color worth nothing in the country's economy suddenly generates between 30 and 60 thousand dollars a year once trapped in the system.

The expansion of prisons, parole, probation, the courts and police systems has resulted in an enormous bureaucracy which has been a boon for everyone from architects, plumbers and electricians to food and medical vendors—all with one thing in common—a paycheck earned by keeping human beings in cages in human warehouses. The criminalization of poverty is a lucrative business and we've replaced the social safety net with a dragnet. I doubt if this would be tolerated if we were talking about mostly white folks or rich folks.

What's going on in the name of all of us needs to be stopped. Poverty and prisons are state-manifested violence. I think that whites have to consciously wash off the racism that infects us daily in a society where we are privileged in relation to people of color. I think people of color have to become specifically involved in fighting the bottom line expression of racism, classism and oppression that the prison system represents. Until prison activists and outside organizations begin opposition on a more serious level, neither prison administrators nor the U.S. government has to respond to our complaints. Each of us needs to use any forum that we have available to describe the connections between slavery and the criminal justice system, between U.S. domestic policies toward people of color and U.S. international policies towards countries of color. We need to stand up and say "Not in my name!" will you commit these atrocities anymore. There are many reasons to get involved in these issues—human decency being one of them.

We need to organize, organize, organize. We need to find a way especially to reach into women's prisons. I particularly urge free women to form monitoring and advocacy alliances with women in prison. I have worked with many United States political prisoners and their families for decades. I have never seen anything like what I'm now seeing in U.S. prisons. My soul is shaken by what I read in my daily mail.

Many years ago, a Vietnamese sister noted that, "When women become massively political, the revolution will have moved to a new level.

****

Joan Gauker, Director of Volunteers, Graterford Prison Founder and Editorial Writer, *Graterfriends*

As the wealthiest, healthiest and most progressive nation on earth, we should hang our heads in shame for the way we've developed and maintained prison systems that are unhealthy and unenlightened for prisoners and for those still on the street. We have the know-how to do a better job of caring for those who offend and preparing them to return to society (and most prisoners will return) as responsible citizens. Yet, we squander that know-how to salve our need for punishment and retribution – which ultimately harms the prisoners, those who guard them and the society to which they will return. The continuance and expansion of our uninspired, punishment/retribution-oriented prison systems are fueled by unenlightened politicians, a complicated intertwined social justice political agenda, and an apathetic, uninformed electorate.

The new system I would build would be a Day-One system. The concept is that from Day-One of an offender's confinement, everyone in the system, including the offender, is working on a program that will prepare that offender to return to society as an emotionally healthy, contributing member. In this dream, governments would define the object of imprisonment to be removal from society for the purpose of providing the offender with the incentive, the skills and the support system to return to the community as a responsible person able to work, be a good family member, and have a healthy outlook toward society's rules of behavior. The government would implement restorative justice programs, help people work at reconciliation, and provide the treatment and support programs needed in and out of prison. If there were a parole system in this dream, it, too would be a Day-One system, in that from day one of a person's release everyone, including the offender would be working to keep the offender from re-offending. Such a parole system would be staffed by people who care about helping, not policing, those in their charge."

****

Elizabeth Quigley, Coordinator, Pennsylvania Association of Learning Alternatives

Box 201 Quakertown PA 18951

We have the best justice system in the world. On paper. In theory. No other country in the world has a better record for the promise of justice, yet we have the worst justice system in the world. When the rich buy justice. When the corrupt walk. When a parent grieves and an abuser goes free. How can we change so that our justice system lives up to our ideal? By becoming activists. By speaking out. By letting our legislators know that we expect the system to work. By living and practicing justice in our own lives.

With no limitations, financial or otherwise, I would start with the children. I would see that each child was fed, sheltered, loved and listened to, and then a sane justice system could begin. It is the inequities of our larger system that corrupt our justice system. We all have to work on ourselves like Buddhists in order to fix our larger social system, we have to listen deeply like Quakers, and we have to love all society's children so much that we never let any child be hurt. That is where and when justice will begin.

****

A PRISONERS' RIGHTS BILL: LONG OVERDUE

By Joan Gauker

GRATERFRIENDS, SEPTEMBER 2001

At the opening of Israel's Tzalmon Prison in 1996, High Court President Aaron Barak said: "A society is judged by the quality of its prisons. An enlightened society is judged by the treatment of its prisoners The prisoner has committed a crime and has been punished accordingly; his liberty has been taken away, but the human essence still remains. Prison walls separate the prisoner from freedom. But the prison walls must not come between the prisoner and human dignity."

What a premise! Maybe, we could build such enlightened thinking across our land. We could say the words over and over so they finally reverberate in peoples' hearts, are internalized, appreciated for their sensibleness, and finally implemented. And, maybe not!

While we believe laws don't change hearts— that hearts change laws—we also believe in this case, as with the civil rights effort, America's cold hearts need a legal nudge to begin to change. So we too call for legislation to do what should be done under already existing laws.

This is not far-fetched. If one looks to other Western nations or even at the smattering of U.S. efforts to provide for prisoners' 'human essence,' there are models. The trick is to collect these models of progressive thinking, compile them into one document and implement them across the land. We need a national document prohibiting folks from doing more than separating prisoners from freedom. We need a document forcing states to let go of the need to punish beyond separation from freedom.

Black Americans had the Constitution's guarantee that 'all men are created equal.' Yet, separate legislation was needed to enforce their equality. So we propose a prisoners' rights bill rooted in Constitutionally-afforded human dignity—which must not be stripped when a person is separated from freedom as punishment for a crime.

Early on, our nation's founders hoped to thwart the need to punish excessively with the Eighth Amendment: "Excessive bail shall not be required, nor excessive fines imposed, nor cruel and unusual punishment inflicted."

Even as they wrote the Constitution's preamble, these drafters had lofty ideals for us: "...in order to form a more perfect union, establish justice, insure domestic tranquility, provide for the common defense, promote the general welfare, and secure the blessings of liberty to ourselves and our posterity..."

Establish justice? We've established revenge. Promote the general welfare? We keep more than two and a half million of our people warehoused in prisons while their families dissolve or become destitute.

Over time, legislation and courts eroded much of the founders' dreams for justice and general welfare in favor of punishment and revenge.

But it can work both ways. Legislation and the courts can rebuild those dreams, as was the hope (and success) of civil-rights legislation.

We need a prisoners' rights bill that has as its premise the preservation of each person's dignity throughout incarceration, and lists the ways this will be done. While we don't believe we can legislate morality, we find we may have to legislate a process that brings us to humane and sensible treatment of the incarcerated. If we each followed our faith or if we followed the spirit of the laws in place, such legislation would be unnecessary. But we are a people of punishment—and that leads us to excess.

And, possibly on a par with our cold hearts is our indifference. The majority of our citizens have no first hand knowledge of our prison system—its abuses or whom it primarily serves. The public's major sources of information are the stereotypical depictions supplied by books and movies. The enormous discrepancy between the image and real life is not understood by the average citizen. Thus, ingrained apathy also must be overcome.

We must understand an enlightened society is judged by its treatment of prisoners—its treatment of those most detested. Sadly, America's global image is greatly diminished in this area. However, we can respond to our founders' expectations and improve our global image with the implementation of a prisoners' rights bill that recognizes separation from freedom **AS** the punishment.

****

"If there is any kindness I can show, or any good thing I can do to any fellow being, let me do it now, and not deter or neglect it, as I shall not pass this way again."
William Penn

****

John Griffin, author,
Letter to My Father (Xlibris, 2001)

AM 8535
1111 Altamont Blvd.
Frackville, PA 17931 ($1,050,000)

The current prison system is the result of centuries of hate and ignorance. This system is maintained by lies and deceit. The walls that keep us in also keep John Q. Public out.
The state and federal governments have a captive audience. Yet they can't educate these people properly? Can they motivate men, women and children who desperately want to contribute to society in a positive way? Sure they could if they really wanted to. But instead, prisoners are constantly being programmed, through abuse and neglect, to return to prison after their release. Society has turned its back on us by not calling for a system of checks and balances.

Who holds the wardens and superintendents accountable for the failures they release back into society?

This country's hatred and total disregard for minorities and the poor has led to the greatest deterioration in history: the mass incarceration and neglect of its own citizens. As Wall St. benefits from the growth of the prison industry, politicians pass laws to insure that those prisons are filled to capacity.

In order to build a more humane and effective system, one must tear down the old one, brick by brick, exposing the antebellum criminal justice mentality that was created at the end of slavery and is continued under present-day legislation. Realistically speaking, of all the political and social burdens weighing heavily on minorities and the poor, none is as onerous as the impediment to equal justice under the law.

Any new system has to avoid the problems of the old one. Those released from confinement wouldn't be referred to as ex-convicts and denied the rights of full citizenship

My first act would be to establish a criminal justice system that operates within the community. Those individuals found guilty of non-violent crimes would be indebted to the community for service. Those with drug addictions would be given treatment instead of incarceration. There would be effective follow-up programs.

Those committing crimes requiring incarceration would be placed in community owned and operated facilities. These would be retraining centers with both educational and vocational courses, which are updated as there are advances in technology. To assuage cries of those who feel prisoners should not be getting a free education, I'd require that all prisoners work and earn a wage adequate enough to pay their own way.

Prisoners would also have to meet their responsibilities toward their families by paying reduced child support and taxes.

However, without a fair and unbiased court system, judges who are willing to review the progress of those they confine, and a community willing to get involved and hold accountable those superintendents and wardens entrusted with the care of our young men, women and children, no change will be effective.

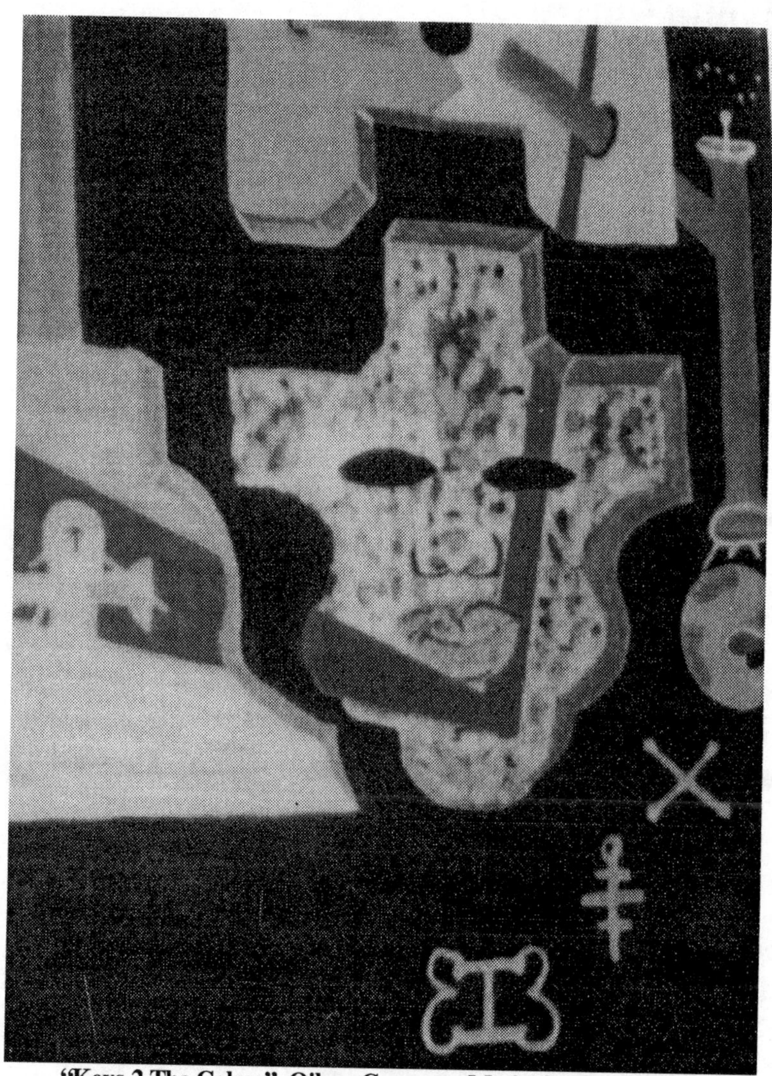

"Keys 2 The Colors" Oil on Canvas Muti Ajamu-Osagboro

Philip Curcio

#AS-0634
1000 Follies Road
Dallas, PA 18612-0286

The current system cannot function as intended because it's inconsistent. State institutions are labeled "rehabilitative" and 'correctional', while the incarcerated are labeled 'filthy' and "incorrigible." Prisoners internalize the revenge that society administers through ostracism and law. "Restoration" is the politically correct term to use when presenting prisons and prisoners.

There are too many mixed messages. The only way a broken relationship can be restored is by incorporating a method that classifies prisoners according to background/history, education, age and disposition. Rather than indiscriminately forcing the younger inmates to house with the older ones or the violent kind with the docile type or allowing the outgoing personality to override the reflective one, I'd organize units (like learning centers) that are conducive to each group. Incorporated in each "grade level" would be academic education, social etiquette and ample opportunity for creative expression.

Another common misconception is that by releasing "non-violent' offenders on parole and denying parole to 'violent offenders," society is safer. Non-violent offenders can be more destructive to communities — not only as drug dealers or burglars, but also as the ones who most often return to prison. Violent offenders usually act out of passion and rarely re-offend when released. Prisoners need to be evaluated on a case-by-case system rather than by categorization. Shortsighted judgment by an impersonal Parole Board must be improved.

SALLY SCATTERGOOD

A longtime activist who inspires many, Sally serves on the board of PAR, and is the co-founder of "Educating Children for Parenting," a unique national program based in Philadelphia that teaches parenting skills at the middle school level.

My vision of a new system would be to have small prisons, no more than 50-60 inmates in each, divided into small groups. Inmates would do their own housekeeping, buy their food in the community, study with nutritionists and cook their own food. Educational opportunities, including college courses would be offered. Everyone would learn skills relevant to the current economy and how to budget. They could be mentored and return to prison at night. The focus would be on conflict resolution, practicing non-violent methods in groups. Children would be in treatment with their parents, for I believe it's terribly important for children to be with their parents. Even abused children would benefit.
For the hard-core inmate and the mentally ill, I'd create hospital-like treatment.

****

Tony Harper

AF-6000
Box 244
Graterford, PA 19426 ($875,000)

As for the healing process in building a legal system from the ground up, Afrocentric and cultural education is the moral fabric from which most people of color get their direction, such as knowing where the great building blocks of our society came from.

Society's power brokers have turned this country into a pig pen because they've lost the true meaning that what we should want for our friend is the same thing we want for our self. We need to keep God at the top of our lives so our decision will be based on wanting the best for one another.

From the dawn of society, racism has been practiced to enslave people from the middle passage, where so many slaves died, to freeing the slaves and promising them forty-acres and a mule, which was nothing but a lie.

But no one has asked the real question: Where did racism come from? How can it be healed? The government has pitted rich against poor for so long to keep the poor in check, so that we will not rebel against a system whose only interest at heart is its own.

Prisons have the same effect as slavery.

Yes, there are many people of color in prison, but if one would reflect on the employment records of each one arrested, one would find that a lack of jobs for years played a part with prisons being filled by people of color. There are some people behind these walls whose only crime was they were in the wrong place at the wrong time, and with dark skin color, which always plays a part in someone's presumed guilt. The states, along with the U.S. government, despite mandates to rehabilitate, refuse to educate people in prison because what better way to employ its masses than by keeping them coming back, keeping men/women locked up until their dreams die behind these walls. Some prisoners have gotten the picture and are doing something about their situation for the better.

Most of us won't be put off and will continue to fight the good fight. Look at the average place where people of color live: the housing is in deplorable shape, there are drug markets and gun shops. On every corner there is a bar or some place selling spirits to people. People of color don't have ships or transports to bring drugs into the country. The recent sniper rampage is what daily life is like for poor people. The government is always there with its hand out indirectly helping to bring the drugs and guns into the black community. Racism is alive and well and will continue to be so until we shed this wrong way of living life.

****

Emmett Fulford

AP-9111
SCI Smithfield
Box 999 1120 Pike Street
Huntingdon, PA 16652

When I watched "The Men Who Killed Kennedy" on the History Channel last night, I was reminded that in many cases, those addicted to power in this country will do the unthinkable to have things their way. They will tell any lie necessary in an attempt to cover up their sick and evil deeds.

I had nightmares most of the night. When I woke up, I grabbed a cup of coffee and the April 2002 issue of *Gratefriends* and read that SageWriters.com was asking for ideas from prisoners in answering the two questions. As a long-time convict, I want to answer these very important questions. I commend and admire SageWriters for the noble effort of changing a system that actually creates the very problem it publicly claims to solve, people committing crimes.

What do I think of the current system? There is a book, Justice For None, written by, in my humble opinion, one of the truest American statesmen there is, Jerry Spence from Wyoming. In the book, Spence lays out the problems, failures and reasons our civil justice system has denigrated into a greed-fed circus, with power-mad tyrants who have only their love of money as their motivation, manipulating 80% of the system. By extrapolating Spence's perspective to the criminal justice system, one is able to discern that the problems are the same, that our Department of Corrections, our Parole Boards, our Board of Pardons, our halfway houses, and our criminal courts have degenerated into a bunch of greedy, vindictive, hateful people. We allow ourselves to be manipulated by our own anger and frustration because when all's said and done, we elect these little Hitlers to carry out our hidden, hateful retribution insead of electing people who, like Jerry Spence, not only can identify the problems but offer counsel and form solutions to these devastating problems

Since I'm currently in prison, I'm going to confine my answer to question two to the Department of Corrections, as one could write several books on the wrongs of the criminal courts alone.

What we need now is human beings working within the operational apparatus of the DOC to implement progressive policies instead of manipulating them in a cynical and sometimes sadistic manner.

Another suggestion for improvement is to look at the model of Dr. Mimi Silbert at the Delancey Street Foundation, 600 Embarcadero, San Francisco, CA 94107, 415-957-9800. Her program has managed to help thousands of born losers since 1971, turning them into productive, responsible, mature and moral members of our American society, paying $9 million in taxes last year!

They have certain principles in the program such as each one teach one, there will be no violence, no threats of violence or intimidation at Delancey Street. You must learn three marketable skills, get a high school diploma, have steady employment, and not hang around glorifying criminal behavior.

May the Lord God bless you all at SageWriters because you are attempting to treat your brothers in prison as you would want to be treated, and in my book, there is no greater command of God than to love your neighbor as yourself

****

"The Importance of Cultural Education" by Robert Muhkam Hagood ($1,085,000)

"When people went to schools and became scholars in Greek, and scholars in Latin, and scholars in the ancient civilizations, but with total ignorance of their own civilization, those people were miseducated." - Dr. Carter G. Woodson (Miseducation Of The Negro, 1930).

The importance of a cultural education is that it prepares one to move through the socialization process of one's tribe, village, or nation, equipped with the knowledge of the "Ways" of ones ancestors. By having the ability to apply the knowledge and learn the arts, skills and crafts, one is accepted and acknowledged as a social peer with both the ability and commitment to make a difference in the lives of one's own people.

As a descendent of African People who were the slaves and property of European Americans, and as a student of both the parochial school and the public school systems during the 1940's and the 1950's, I never saw an image of myself or someone that I could identify with ethnically in the center of the education process. Nor did I hear a discourse in any of the schools that I attended about African people being contributors to civilization.

Studying and learning something of my own culture after fifty years of total ignorance, I viewed a taped lecture by Dr. Leonard Jeffries, who stated that he had a "million dollar White Boy Education, and a million dollar African Education." Dr. Jeffries has the ability to maintain his own self identity, teach African Culture, and still be consciously aware of the wholeness of his academic back ground. No matter what the demands of universities, Dr. Jeffries will always interpret and reevaluate the values of society based upon his own African culture and his own values as a human being.

All education is cultural. Thus I am compelled to ask: In which culture has one achieved his or her education? Also, does their education adequately define the genetic and hereditary nature of the human being that he or she was created to be? Likewise, did he or she learn to think, believe, speak and perform academically and socially in a manner that alienates one from his or her true self? Or did he or she learn the history, values, music, religious and tribal rituals that guide one toward their own cultural identity through the education process?

Armed with the knowledge of one's own culture, he or she redefines themselves and has the tools to re-evaluate the society that they live in.

The importance of a cultural education is that one receives the skills and the knowledge necessary to make a difference in their own lives and the lives of others. One is accepted as a social peer based upon what he or she achieves as opposed to just being born.

Thus a lack of a cultural education will cause one to live a life time mimicking, emulating and serving a people other than one's own. In other words, African people who are descendants of slaves should not be "American as Apple Pie." Instead, the descendants of African people should make a conscious effort to bring their own culture into the center of the education process, thereby preserving and defining their own cultural identity.

****

"We need a history in which we can see ourselves reflected…It is absolutely beautiful because it reveals what people know in their souls…" Kathryn Morgan, Ph.D., Professor Emeritus, Swarthmore College

****

Chaka Turner

BW6610
Box 1000
Houtzdale, PA 16698 ($350,000)

Unfortunately, the present criminal justice system is not a just one. Statistically, there are more deals made simply to attempt to decrease caseloads rather then actual consideration of guilt or innocence. However, these facts primarily pertain to those citizens who can afford private lawyers. Legal research and preparation take immense amounts of time, effort, and resources, all of which a private firm can provide compared to most overworked and underfunded public defender's office.

For example, a person is charged with a murder and there is one witness and the crime took place at night. If the person has the means to mount a defense, their lawyer will investigate the crime scene, the background of the witness, etc. They might discover that the witness wears glasses but did not have them on that night, or perhaps they lied once before in an official proceeding. The public defender may already have 100 clients to defend. Automatically, s/he may be inclined to attempt to plea bargain without having even interviewed a single person, etc.

The present criminal justice system is in need of replacement.

I would not build a new system from the ground up for it already exists. It is known as a THEOCRACY. Government ruled by God. Jesus Christ preached of this government throughout his ministry on earth and referred to it as the Kingdom or the Kingdom of God. It is based on the foremost attribute of God, which is love. God is love. The quality of love is really and truly remarkable. In the Greek that the New Testament was written it, it is called Agape love. This is a special kind of love that while it includes basic affection is more motivated by principle, a sincere appreciation for God, his purpose, and his fellow man. "Love is long suffering and kind. Love is not jealous, it does not brag, does not get puffed up, does not behave indecently, does not look for its own interests, does not become provoked. It does not keep account of the injury. It does not rejoice over unrighteousness, but rejoices with the truth. It bears all things, believes all things, hopes all things, endures all things. Love never fails."

Jesus said, "You must love Jehovah your God with your whole soul and with your whole mind.' This is the greatest commandment. The second, like it, is this, **'You must love your neighbor as yourself.'** On these two commandments the whole Law hangs. If every person loved God and other people with an Agape, or unselfish love, there would be no need for a criminal justice system.

Aaron Wheeler is serving a life sentence. One of his crimes? He was in a sandwich shop with another guy who got angry at the clerk and pulled out a gun and shot him without warning. Aaron had no idea he was going to do this, has never held a gun in his life, and due to mandatory sentencing laws, is considered a co-conspirator. In Pennsylvania, his only recourse is the Board of Pardons.

Aaron Christopher Wheeler

BZ-2590 D-B1-059
P.O. Box 244
Graterford, PA 19426 ($420,000)

I. BACKGROUND:

I am a Black male who first got involved with the Criminal Justice System when I was 15 years of age. I served about 2 to 3 years off and on in various juvenile facilities. As a juvenile, I noticed how the Criminal Justice System was biased against people of color. I saw how a white youth could commit the same crime as a person of color and the white youth would get probation while the person of color would always be sent away for months at a time

In 1991, at the age of 22, I came to prison and have been here ever since. I am not convicted as the perpetrator of a crime, but as a co-conspirator. I never killed, shot or robbed anyone in any of the crimes I am convicted of. I never even touched or possessed a weapon in these crimes. There was no money taken and the majority of the witnesses do not even remember me being present at these crimes (I also said or did nothing at these crimes that they say I was at). However, despite all of this, I am convicted of two counts of second degree murder, robbery, aggravated assault, possession of an instrument of crime and criminal conspiracy which has resulted in a sentence of double life imprisonment with a consecutive sentence of 27 1/2 -55 years. ($945,000-$1,825,000)

Unless the system changes dramtically, I will die in prison.

Caryl Clark, writing for the *York (PA) Daily Record* on February 14, 2001 in an article about why the criminal justice system is the way it is stated: Shelly Todd, PA House Legal Counsel, told a Committee of the Supreme Court, "You must determine whether you will be engineers or parasites. This body is the oldest Supreme Court in the Western Hemisphere. It was established for the benefit of white men. There was no thought of anyone else. You must do the hard job of seeking truth." State Rep. Tom Armstrong (R-Lancaster) testified that his brother's imprisonment enlightened him about the overwhelming numbers of minorities in prison, and the rampant racism and brutality. "We have to shine a big light on this problem," he said.

The Criminal Justice System was created to benefit white men. That includes law enforcement agencies, police, the Courts, the legislature, prisons and all other establishments that have anything to do with the System. We must remember that people of color had no rights when this system was created; we were considered property. Only the owner had rights (even in the Commonwealth of Pennsylvania).

As years went by, we were given certain rights (supposedly the same rights as everyone else), but institutions (within the system) that were created to benefit white men remain the same to this very day. None of these institutions' prisons know how to deal with people of color. Despite the fact that there are now Black judges, jurors, prosecutors, police, correctional officers, legislators, security guards and lawyers, all were trained by the old supremacist policies that have been embedded in these institutions since their creation to benefit white men. No one has ever changed any of these policies that the system was founded upon. The way that the system deals with people of color now is the same way that they dealt with us when we were considered property!

The only way that the system can be improved is if the old foundation is destroyed and a new foundation is created where both whites and men and women of color are treated exactly the same for offenses committed. However, this will never happen, because if the old foundation is ever destroyed, then everything in society that is built on the Criminal Justice System would totally collapse due to the deeply imbedded biasness, unfairness, corruption and racism

For these reasons, there will always be a disparity in a system that benefits white men and discriminates against people of color. For example, look at the case of Thomas Druce, a PA politician, who killed a Black man in a hit and run, left the scene of the crime and covered it up for months. He received a 2-4 year sentence in prison for insurance fraud and leaving the scene of an accident, but after two weeks in SCI-Camp Hill, his case miraculously made it to the Pennsylvania Supreme Court, the oldest Supreme Court in the Western hemisphere (even though it takes everyone else three years to get there after conviction, excluding death sentenced persons) and Druce was granted bail pending his appeal even though the Supreme Court prohibits persons who are serving two or more years in prison from being released on bail pending appeal. Druce served his entire two years on house arrest (which he violated several times) and even when his appeal was denied, he was not returned to prison. He served exactly two weeks in prison for killing a Black man who also was a U.S. Marine.

Marie Noe killed eight of her ten children over a 50 year period and covered it up. *Philadelphia Magazine* did a feature about her and there were rumors of a Hollywood movie. She received a sentence of twenty years probation and five years house arrest (which she violated several times)

for pleading guilty to eight counts of second degree murder. Second degree murder carries a mandatory sentence of life imprisonment in Pennsylvania. (From 1860 to 1974 a person had to commit second degree murder twice before receiving a sentence of natural life in prison, but in 1974 the legislature, over the objection and veto of Governor Shapp, made the sentence for second degree murder mandatory life imprisonment). Marie Noe had eight counts of second-degree murder and she did not spend one day in jail even though she took the lives of eight babies.

Three white teenagers raped an eleven-year-old Black girl at a stadium in Philadelphia. They were given house arrest until a hearing in Juvenile Court. Judge Reynolds (a Black judge) found two of the white teenagers guilty because the eleven-year old could identify two of the three even though all three admitted having sex with her and DNA technology is available for sex crimes. There was community outrage when he sentenced them to four months of treatment.

The above are just three examples of how the system benefits whites as it was created to do. If a person of color would have committed the Thomas Druce crime, s/he would have been tried for first degree murder and probably would have been lucky to receive a life sentence. If a person of color would have committed the Marie Noe crime, s/he would have been tried for capital murder and given the death penalty for all eight counts. If three Black teenagers would have raped an 11-year-old white female, they would have been certified as adults, tried as adults and more than likely would have received at least 40 years in prison. Just take a look across the nation at all of the Black juveniles being tried as adults and being given life sentences.

If a white person commits the act of murder, s/he is charged with and tried for third degree murder or one of the various degrees of manslaughter. If a person of color commits the act of murder, s/he is charged with and tried for first-degree murder regardless of the circumstances surrounding the murder (i.e. self-defense, in the heat of passion, by accident, etc.). All this means is that the white person will be coming home to their family and community again one day in the near future while the person of color will either be executed or die in prison.

The entire world knows about the disparities in drug sentencing (i.e. for **one vial** of crack you get five years in prison, but you need either **five to 500 pounds** of powder cocaine to receive the same five year sentence in prison). You cannot make crack without powder cocaine! If you give me some: powder cocaine, a box of baking soda, a hanger and a pot of boiling water, then I will give you some crack! But people of color are usually the ones caught with crack cocaine, while white people in business suits are usually caught with powder cocaine. Therefore, the disparities remain the same because they only affect people of color and benefit white men/people.

To improve the system would take a lot of doing, which society as a whole will never do, because people of color and the poor are the only ones affected.

The government is in the business of exposing, disrupting, misdirecting, discrediting, or otherwise neutralizing people of color or people who speak out against its actions. The local news is still being used as well to publicize the negative actions of people of color. These actions must be stopped in order to break down the foundations that were created to benefit white men. Only then will the system be improved.

First, as a human being, I would recognize that we all make mistakes and, with that in mind, I would construct a system that is not based on the color of ones skin or on one's financial status. The system would treat everyone the same (i.e. if a white person commits murder and a person of color commits murder, they would both be charged, tried, convicted and sentenced the same). All persons would be treated as human beings who just made a mistake at one time or another rather than as outcasts [criminals/felons/ex-cons/ex-felons], banned from ever enjoying life again after they have paid their debt to society. They are currently: disenfranchised for life [can never vote again], can never hold certain jobs, must tell everyone about the mistake they made [employers, credit agencies, the military, etc.], have their faces and mistakes posted on the internet or a website, cannot live in certain places, etc., which leaves them with no other options but to resort to a life of crime for their survival.

Second, there would be no life sentences, death penalties or parole. No person would be sentenced to more than 10 years in prison at one given time, despite the crimes s/he has committed. Any sentence given would have to be served in its entirety and would require the person's family and community to play a valuable part in his/her rehabilitation and recommitment back into society (rather than the current system that ostracizes the person's family and community from them during incarceration). It would also require the offender to make amends with the victim where possible or the victim's family (i.e. repay anything stolen or damaged; seek forgiveness or at least ask for forgiveness from a victim's family when possible).

Third: If the constitution is the basis of our system, then I would adopt the bedrock view of interpreting the constitution (which means what it says is what it means and we are going to stick strictly by it for all persons) and not the living-document view that currently has the world in chaos (which means that even though it is written, the meaning changes with the times; what it meant yesterday is not what it means today).

Fourth: There would be no classification of crimes such as felony or misdemeanor, and once you pay your debt to society, that crime will never be held against you again. It would be like a bill that has been paid, "Gone Forever" or "Paid in Full," and a person could never lose his/her rights no matter where they are at or what they have done.

Fifth: There would be no such thing as conspiracy. A person would only be held accountable for his/her own actions and not the actions of another. If five people are hanging out together and one of the five happens to kill someone or steal something, then only that one person would be held accountable for his/her own actions and not as it is now that all five would be held responsible for the act of one, especially if they are all people of color and young.

Sixth: Rather than being removed from the community, people would be sentenced to community work, such as picking up trash, painting houses and buildings, cleaning houses and creating gardens and parks, driving, coaching, etc. This way they will be an asset rather than a liability to the community they were helping to destroy.

Finally, there would be a juvenile system where children are treated as children and keeping the family united is strongly practiced despite any crime that a child has committed. The current juvenile system is designed to destroy families and geared towards sending children of color to institutions).

CONCLUSION

"When you control a man's thinking, you do not have to worry about his actions. You do not have to tell him not to stand here or go yonder. He will find his 'proper place' and will stay in it. You do not need to send him to the back door. He will go without being told. In fact, if there is no back door, he will cut one for his special benefit. His education makes it necessary" *Carter G. Woodson*

This is to say that despite Blacks being allowed to be a part of the system now as judges, jurors, legislators, prosecutors, police, law enforcement officials, correctional officers, security guards, wardens, lawyers, etc., the system remains the same because it was built on the premise of benefiting white men and it does not know how to deal with anyone else. These people are now trained and educated in these policies and still follow them fàithfülly. Their minds are so controlled by these policies that they do not even see the wrong in them and what it is that they are doing to their own people.

I know that none of these things may ever happen to change the system, but if they were to happen, the system still might not be perfect because there will be people running it, but it might be more just than the current one, which includes 28 state prisons, 76,553 persons detained in halfway houses, federal, state and local jails in Pennsylvania, and 6,987 juveniles in juvenile facilities. Communities are robbed of their men; families are destroyed; children are left fatherless and motherless; thousands are on parole, probation or under some type of court supervision; legislators are being convicted daily; police scandals are frequent; prosecutors withhold evidence for years at a time and are committing all types of misconduct to obtain convictions and sustain wrongful convictions without any consequence to prosecutors once they are caught. Commonwealth witnesses are being paid with money or leniency in exchange for their testimony against another; courts are turning blind eyes to all of the corruption committed right in front of them daily to protect their political careers while leaving hundreds of thousands of wrongfully convicted and innocent persons behind bars for decades, and the list goes on. There are entirely too many people in prison or who are under the control of the system.

Rev. Peyton Craighill, former President of the Board, Graterfriends; board member, PA Prison Society

The present system is inherently dysfunctional. Its purpose is to reduce the amount of crime in society. But instead it promotes the growth of crime by turning loose people who are, if anything, less capable of coping effectively with life in society than they were when they were brought into the system. It wastes huge quantities of taxpayer money and chews up the lives of millions of people inside and outside the system, with little if anything to show for all the resources committed to it.

Any new system should include the following:

1. Crime prevention
This focuses on youth-at-risk, especially in districts with high rates of juvenile delinquency. Prevention includes efforts such as programs for alternatives to violence, after-school education, family counseling, anti-drug campaigns, and job opportunities.

2. Community policing.
Young people often develop self-destructive attitudes towards social responsibility and authority as a result of what they perceive to be the misuse of power by the police in their neighborhoods. Community policing has been developed as a way to improve relationships between police and the communities they serve. Efforts need to be made to strengthen these programs and to relate them more closely to families and young people.

3. The judicial system.
I am a strong supporter of the move from retributive justice (read "revenge") to restorative justice (read "healing") Support must be given to efforts under way promoting systemic changes in the judicial system. In particular, these include citizens' reparative boards and conferencing. As long as the victims of the present judicial system experience justice primarily as a system used by the dominant authority in society to oppress them, they will have great difficulty developing positive attitudes and actions in dealing with that authority.

4. Corrections.
We call the system "corrections" - but where in the system do we find any "correcting" happening? 96% of the budget for corrections goes into custody and security. Only 4% goes into programs that help prisoners move towards greater success in dealing with their lives in society. We need to find examples in the most effective corrections systems of programs already functioning that serve as alternatives to the present dysfunctional system and then adopt them widely. The absolute minimum would be to supply literacy and GED programs for all prisoners who need them.

5. Post-release support
What can be done to reduce an 85% rate of recidivism? How can parole and other post-release programs become more supportive than punitive? These questions merely open the discussion of how the 600,000 prisoners a year coming out of our prisons can be helped to move more smoothly back into the wider society.

Beyond this bare bones outline of reforms needed in each of the five areas listed above, I have another proposal that I believe to be of great importance.

A major problem with efforts in the criminal justice system to bring about reform is that they are almost always focused on one of the areas listed above without reference to the other four. Because all five are so closely interlinked, such efforts have little hope of success. Due to ignorance, indifference, and protection of bureaucratic fiefdoms, each of the five areas tends to be isolated from the others. An endeavor to break through these barriers and to develop a comprehensive approach to justice reform encompassing all five in relationship to each other is greatly needed.

****

Joseph Betz, PhD,

Department of Philosophy
Villanova University
Villanova, PA 19085

Since the Enron scandal broke, it is hard to think of the American criminal justice system in the same way as before the scandal broke. In the old way, one thought of cops and robbers, drug dealers on city street-corners, dramatic arrests, pictures of the African-American suspects on the front pages of the newspaper, convincing police testimony at the trial, then conviction with a long sentence to wrap up the publicity about the case. If the system needed improvements, our political representatives "fought crime" and proved that they were "tough on crime," by legislating longer sentences, instituting mandatory sentences, building more prisons, reducing funding for legal assistance for the poor, and making it harder for those convicted to file effective appeals. Crime was decidedly "blue collar," a phenomenon of the bombed-out inner city.

Now, after Enron, the American public has been forced to notice that the really hurtful recent crimes were "white collar." These crimes occurred in the executive suites of the new, impressive, center city office buildings, or in the mansions of the CEO's or CFO's in the suburbs outside the city, not in the doughnut of poverty between city center and suburbs. Ken Lay of Enron, aided by Certified Public Accountants from prestigious firms like Arthur Andersen, had falsified company earnings in order to give themselves obscenely large stock options. They had created hard-to-detect partnerships, with them as partners, clear instances of conflicts-of interest, which subtracted from the company's profits but added to theirs. When the public began to suspect that there were lies on Enron's balance statement and the company's stock price started to fall, the Ken Lay's of prestigious American businesses issued more lies about good earnings to keep the stock price up. But, at the same time, they sold the stocks in their stock options because they knew the stock price would quickly and totally collapse. One such company's stock of which I read recently, had been at about $80 a share and now sells for something like $.80 a share, one-hundredth of its former price. Ken Lay, previously a guest at President George W. Bush's ranch, has now been indicted for his crimes, but many of his associates are untouched by the law and government and are even <u>thriving in new careers as members of the federal government</u>. One is Secretary of the Army, Thomas White, a former Enron affiliate company executive, who made a fortune by selling his stock immediately before its price collapsed. The victims of these "white collar criminals" included: 1) the many Enron employees who lost their jobs; 2) the many Enron employees who had all their pension monies, as the company required, in Enron stock; 3) the average Californians and others who were hurt during the winter of 2001 by dishonest Enron manipulations of the price of heating oil and gas in deregulated and vulnerable California.

The government tends not to prosecute "white collar" criminals. The criminals are investigated, and sometimes some attempt is made to discipline them, but what happens to them is unlike what happens to "blue collar" criminals. They might be tried and fined, but they have deceptively obtained so much money that they can well afford to pay a fraction of it in fines. Thus, even after punishment, the crime has paid handsomely. Something like this happened when Michael Millken and Ivan Boesky made fortunes by manipulating the "junk bond" market. The Securities and Exchange Commission and other governmental units investigated and disciplined them with fines they could easily afford to pay. At any rate, such "white collar" criminals do not wind up in jails, or wind up in jail for only brief sentences, often in federal country club- like jails. The title of this book, "Celling America's Soul" should really be "Celling America's Poor and Black Souls."

The contrast I am drawing, then, is between poor, often ghetto-reared, often African-American "blue collar" criminals in the state prisons like Graterford, and rich, born-with-a-silver-spoon- in-their-mouths, often WASPish, "white collar" criminals, like I believe the Enron executives are, who are not serving sentences or not serving them in places like Graterford. I am a teacher at Villanova University who began teaching philosophy courses in Graterford Prison thirteen years ago. I have gotten to know a little about the prison and about my students, some of whom I have taught in five different courses. The overwhelming impression that one gets is that this prison is only for "blue collar" criminals, that crime is only "blue collar" crime, that the institution is only for members of one social and economic class, only for poor urbanites, mostly African-American and Latino, many of whom are school-dropouts who can barely, or, only at a very low level, read or write. Of perhaps 3300 in the prison, only about 125 can qualify for and are enrolled in our Villanova college-level courses.

When I think of why this is so, I am forced to imagine the following. These inmates are examples of what is likely to happen to a person who, through no fault of his own, grows up in urban poverty. It is the poverty left behind when the "white flight" from Philadelphia began occurring after World War II. As the whites left for the suburbs, they took with them their stores, factories, businesses, and ability to pay taxes, and left behind a vacuum empty of all of these. The poor, often Black or Puerto Rican, were sucked into the vacuum, for there were old and inexpensive row-homes there, but they could not get jobs or could not get good jobs, for the white employers were gone. When jobs disappear, crime appears. When jobs disappear, fathers disappear from their wives and children. If men cannot spend their time working, they will spend it drinking, gambling, and finding ways to make a quick and often dishonest dollar. If one in the ghetto cannot get work, he can still get drugs, and opportunities with drugs replace opportunities with working for Fortune 500 companies, which the Ken Lay types had.

One way out of the ghetto is the army, and I have taught many prisoners who were in the army, but the army usually lasts only a few years, and then, back to the ghetto. And for Vietnamese War vets, back to a poorer ghetto without a good job and no thanks for serving one's country. Speaking of the class difference a middle-class teacher like me encounters with his students in prison, many of them had been in the army, but I have yet to meet one who was an officer in the army like my friends or classmates were.

Not all of the inmate-students I have taught at Graterford came from absolute poverty. Some came from more prosperous families in nicer neighborhoods. But, even so, the ghetto and its ills often affected them, because they dared to experiment with the drugs that they learned were for sale in the poor neighborhood which they visited on drug-shopping expeditions. And, yes, I admit it, not everyone is in prison because of sociology, not everyone is "depraved because deprived" as the song goes in "West Side Story."

Though the United States economy is plagued by some of the most extreme economic inequality in the capitalist world, the well off can have their own temptations to crime. I have encountered a few imprisoned because of the lust, greed, anger, sloth or other Capital Sins which can ruin lives in every social class. But, overwhelmingly, to visit the prison is to visit a poor neighborhood. To concentrate the poor in a prison like Graterford, just as they were concentrated in their old inner-city neighborhoods, is to continue the criminogenic conditions which caused their crimes in the first place.

I feel much more concern for the conditions in American society which have brought so many members of our lowest socio-economic classes to prison, and concern for the continuation of concentrated poor people in prison, than I have for the conditions which the prison authorities create within the walls of their institutions. Political authorities external to the state prison have already determined that it is an institution for members of the lowest socio-economic classes, and there will be no country-club-like frills. But I can recommend changes, and one can think of them as treating those in our lower socio-economic classes as if they are invited to enter the middle class when they leave prison. And 95% of the American prison population does get out of prison eventually. Here are my recommendations.

* The federal government should adopt something like the "Freedom Budget," which A. Phillip Randolph, Jr., head of the black Brotherhood of Sleeping Car Porters, designed for the Johnson Administration but which was put aside to pay for the Vietnamese war. In Randolph's vision, however the federal government decided to spend its money, it would do it in such a way that it generated the maximum number of jobs for those who really needed them, especially in economically depressed parts of the country. We would spend our money on labor-intensive projects, and employ the labor of the poor recompensed by a living wage.

* Control the flow of capital in the economy so that it is prohibited from leaving the cities or the country. This can be done, not necessarily with the stick of regulation, but perhaps by the carrot of tax breaks, low taxes in enterprise or

development zones, or the like. There are many ways a strong government could bargain with business to get jobs back into the inner city.

* Realize that drug selling occurs in its most virulent form only where there is no other employment, and drug using only where there is no opportunity or demand to use one's time productively. Treat drug users, not punish them, and give decent jobs to ghetto residents so that they can make a living without drug selling. This should come when good business and employment opportunities for all, regardless of race, return to the inner city. Then, the work ethic will crowd out the drug ethic as it has for most suburbanites.

* If prisons are bad because they continue to concentrate the poor in the same criminogenic conditions which the ghettoes had which originally caused the problem, then this sort of concentration in isolation should be broken up by various sorts of integration. Get more concerned, successful citizens into the prisons to work with the inmates. Get the non-violent inmates out of the prisons to mix at work with people from whom they will acquire the habits of solid citizens. In fact, get all of those whose future conduct is not likely to be a threat to society out of prisons quickly, with shorter terms, or perhaps with half-way houses. Many religious groups, especially the Quakers or others with a pacifist bent, would love to experiment with this quick or partial release. Another form of desirable social integration is more and closer contact with the convict's family members, including conjugal visits.

* My vision, more integration of those without with those within prisons, for quicker release and partial release and for the treatment rather than imprisonment of drug addicts, means two other changes—shorter sentences and fewer prisons. Since we made the wrong decision over a decade ago, and since all states have been building more and more prisons to accommodate those given mandatory and long

sentences, there now exists a vested interest which will resist fewer prisons. Guards do not want to lose their new jobs, legislators do not want to admit to foolish waste of tax monies. Maybe we could keep those prisons as bedrooms and cafeterias for those convicted of crimes, but more visitors would be coming in and more inmates would be going out, and, in my scheme, more substantial jobs and employment would be found in them. To suit me, prisons would be better integrated with decent society in dozens of new ways. But there would have to be fewer prisons in any case, I think, because we would have fewer convictions resulting in incarceration and shorter sentences. The U.S. needs to consider carefully why we are the highest in the nations of the world in the percentage of our population held in prisons. What length sentences for what crimes do other more enlightened nations regularly assign?

* In recommending shorter sentences, I very much have in mind to shorten the life sentences which Pennsylvania gives. They are real-life sentences, death by incarceration, life-sentences without parole, without "good time" (meaning no disciplinary violations) or "earned time" (meaning good behavior allowed to reduce sentence length). Only a few other states refuse to give lifers hope by allowing parole. In my teaching for Villanova at Graterford, I have gotten to know many lifers. They are the ones who finish their B.A. degrees while they are incarcerated, because it might take 10 or 12 years to get in all the needed courses, and they can well afford the time. Lifers who have been in prison for 15 or 20 years seem much different to me from the unstable, perhaps dangerous youths that they were when they committed their crimes and began their sentences in their 20's. They are calm, decent, thoughtful, civil, cooperative, people. They are well worth taking a chance on by returning them to society. They have already paid for their second-degree murders with 15 or 20 years, a sentence for the crime longer than most European countries give. Parole them. **We need a far more generous, less punitive parole board in Pennsylvania.**

* In the 1960's, Governor Milton Shapp announced that there would be no execution of death sentences while he was governor. He dismantled and put into storage the electric chair, and returned the death-row inmates previously awaiting execution to the general prison population. This magnanimous act should now be repeated. The isolation of death-row incarceration is inhumane. Inmates condemned to death should be given a chance to prove they are not dangerous to the other inmates in the general prison population. Having done so, they too should enjoy more integration with the decent and concerned citizens from outside now more present in the prison.

To whatever degree the old unreconstituted prison remains after my previous recommendations are accepted or rejected, the prison should become more and more a place of possible reform and rehabilitation. Prison should be a place where there is a more effective and sincere chance of correction. There should be meaningful work for all in prison related to occupations in demand in the outside world. There should be more mentoring, with training related to the newest tools and techniques now used on the outside. The 70% in prison who cannot read or write on an adult level should get the literacy training they so desperately need to be productive and responsible citizens. Having learned to read, they need better instruction to get their G.E.D.'s, to pass their high school equivalency exams. For several years in the 1990's, there was no instructor on the school staff at Graterford competent in both English and Spanish, capable of preparing the Latinos for the G.E.D. exam. This had a most pernicious, snowballing effect, some Latino inmates claimed. Unable to get their G.E.D.'s, the Latinos were unable to impress the parole board with their accomplishments while incarcerated. Unable to impress the parole board, they were serving time well beyond their minimum sentences before they were released unlike many non-Latinos.

Is there really any hope that my suggested reforms will be instituted in the American prison system? There is the present opportunity to go in directions favoring them because of the widespread anger at "white collar" criminals and the new realization of the enormous financial harm they have done to the whole economy. Those reflecting on these "white collar" criminals, and their favorable treatment compared to that of "blue collar" criminals, might indeed act to reduce the punishment differential in the two social classes of criminals. Since it is unlikely that we will begin to treat the influential "white collar" criminals as badly as we do the "blue collar" criminals, maybe a sense of fairness will induce us to treat the "blue collar" criminals as gently as we treat the "white collar" criminals. However, this could only happen if we gave the Enron-like scandals the attention they deserve. The president has called our attention away from these scandals involving his friends and away from our domestic inequality and injustice, and has concentrated our attention on foreign wars. The war on Afghanistan has become a war on terrorism so broad that it might never end. When things are going badly at home, when the population is divided and one part suffering, start a war to unite them and silence those complaining about domestic circumstances by coercing them with the threat of being called unpatriotic.

****

Carol-Anne Riddle, PhD, who has served on the boards of Graterfriends and PAR, wonders why the media has focused so little on what goes on in prisons.

REPARATIVE BOARD PROCESS
By Carol-Anne Riddle, Ph.D.

I have been a volunteer in prison reform groups in Pittsburgh and Philadelphia for over 20 years and one thing I have learned is that the DOC - Department of Corrections - the perfect oxymoron - is in desperate need of an intense examination:

A $1,925,000,000 budget for this year. How can it cost almost $2 billion to support 28 prisons with a population of 35,000 men and women in a system defined as a failure? The first thing I think of is the amount of corruption there.

One odd side issue of that budget is that the DOC receives money for each telephone call made by inmates to their families and friends. All calls must be made collect. So we see largely poor families subsidizing the imprisonment of their fathers and sons, mothers and daughters.

Bo Lozoff of the Human Kindness Foundation wrote "Prisoners currently sleep on floors, in tents, in converted broom closets and gymnasiums or in double or triple bunks in cells that were designed for one inmate. For the most part, prisons are barbaric, terrifying places...We offer convicts no opportunities to learn compassion or take responsibility for what they have done, nor make restitution or offer atonement to their victims in any practical ways."

Supermax. The new super maximum isolation prisons from which "no one leaves alive." How many have been built in Pennsylvania? What does each one cost and does the state totally fund it or does the federal government pay part? Why has the media not investigated this whole idea? Have state legislatures had any voice in the planning and building of these concentration camps?

Addiction to drugs and alcohol. Inmates who are addicted to drugs and alcohol, estimated to be 70% of the incarcerated population, continue to use them in prison. Who brings them in - the guards? Vendors who deliver trucks full of goods? Who else? How much treatment is available?

What does a life sentence mean? In all states except Pennsylvania and two others, lifers can be considered for parole after some years served and a clean record in prison. In Pennsylvania, a life sentence means the rest of your life and leaves lifers totally without hope except for the Parole & the Board of Pardons; the past two governors have declared no possible parole or probation for lifers. We are paying to keep more and more elderly men in prison at a cost of over $65,000 each. They are unlikely to commit any further crimes and requiring increased medical care each year –

Real job skills in a real work environment. Unfortunately, decades ago the labor unions fought against implementing job training and doing real work in jails and prisons. Now there is some small amount of job training with salary ranges of 25 to 61 cents per hour.

And 95% of inmates are released from jail and prison. Margaret Thatcher said, "Prisons are an expensive way to make bad people worse."

Since the American prison system is widely regarded as a failure, what would an adequate criminal justice look like? One possibility is the Reparative Board Process.

The Reparative Board Process sets up goals for avoiding the corruption of the whole criminal justice system. This is a process of dealing with law-breakers now being used in Vermont, parts of Canada, Australia and in some other nations. It is based on how some native cultures deal with the problem. The philosophy of Reparative Boards is the opposite of "correction" which is the process of warehousing humans with a minimum of preparation for their return to the outside.

In the reparative process, inmates have four jobs to perform as restitution:

1. They have to do something to indicate they realize and acknowledge their wrongful actions.

2. They have to make restitution to their victim, if there is one, by expressing remorse - in a letter, phone call, personal meeting or through another person, etc.
3. Some restitution has to be made to the community as a whole.
4. They have to work out a plan for a course of living to avoid previous failure, i.e., entering a drug program.

One of the best aspects of this Reparative system applies if this is a first offense for the man or woman. In such cases s/he can start with a clean record after going through this program. This requires effort by the offender and needs support during the process but it has been very successful in stopping recidivism. We are spending almost $2 billion in Pennsylvania alone for our current failure. Why not try a pilot program?

There are a variety of educational programs offered mostly by volunteers but the basic foundation of prison life is cruel, vile and immoral. *Prison* exists as an unknown world for the average American, an underground horror rarely examined.

The most vile aspect is death row. In Illinois during several years time, the governor realized that a total of 13 men on death row had been released because they were found to be innocent and at the same time 11 had been put to death. Illinois has stopped putting people to death. Only those of us who are concerned about prisons pay attention to what happens on death row. State officials want to do their killing silently and out of sight.

Internationally renowned artist, teacher and community builder, Lily Yeh, founder of the Village of Arts and Humanity has been working with artists at Graterford for several years. The work of one of her students, Muti Ajamu Osagboro, is shown throughout this book. A documentary of her work has been done by Glen Holsten, of WHYY-TV, one of Philadelphia's public television stations. The photos of Muti, Anton/Trevor and Muhkam are from stills taken from Holsten's video of the Graterford artists in the program.

"ART IN PRISONS"

by Lily Yeh, Founder, Village of the Arts and Humanities
2506 N. Alder St. Philadelphia, PA 19133 (215) 225-7830

Lily Yeh and Muti's sister, Rosalyn Payne wearing a "Free Muti Now" t-shirt that he made for her to wear at an opening of an art exhibit at Eastern Penitentiary

I have been involved with prison inmates in Pennsylvania since 1991, first corresponding with them and then conducting art workshops in prisons. In 1997, I had the good fortune of seeing "The Red Clay Country," a video by Kevin O'Neill, who is an artist, film maker, and poet. The tape contains interviews he had conducted with prison inmates in Graterford and his own poems about prison. I remember vividly how I was struck by the power of the images of the prisoners in brown uniforms on the screen and the urgency and immediacy of their words. I felt compelled to go into Graterford to meet these men and to hear their stories.

In April 1998, working with the prison authority and Lifers, Inc., in Graterford, I formed an artist team composed of Gerry Givnish (visual art), founder of The Painted Bride Arts Center in Philadelphia, Glenn Holsten (video/film) of WHYY-TV, and myself (multi-media) to go to Graterford to conduct workshops. We named our workshops "Story-telling through painting and video."

The continuous three-year effort of the artists and lifers working together has resulted in a stunning exhibition that was on display in the historic site of the former prison, Eastern State Penitentiary, from May to November, 2001. This show was one of four parts of the city-wide exhibition titled "Unimaginable Isolation, Stories from Graterford." The other three parts opened that fall in Philadelphia at the University of the Arts, the Painted Bride Art Center, and the Village of Arts and Humanities.

The reason we are taking on the highly controversial prison issue at the Village of Arts and Humanities is because we see that the prison population is an extension of our community and communities similar to ours. The Village is located in inner city North Philadelphia, the so-called "The Badlands." We have so many families torn apart by poverty, crime, and incarceration. I witness mothers and fathers pining for their sons and daughters, and I see our children crying for their parents locked away in prison. The purpose of the Village is to build community through innovative arts, education, construction, and social programs. Yet, as we work hard to build people, strengthen our youth, reconnect families, and reconstruct this community, we witness powerful forces at work tearing our community asunder. The mission of the Village is to do justice to the people we serve. There is no choice but to look at the prison issue face-to-face. Thus, the purpose of this and other city-wide exhibition is to make the invisible visible, to reconnect the broken, to heal the wounded, and to know that we are all connected. We feel that prison system is a reflection of us and our society at large.

Through this project and through art, we aim to explore the issues of crime and punishment. We aim to honor the humanity and talent of men in Graterford, people who think, reflect, feel, and have the capacity to love. In this process, we do recognize the pains and sufferings of victims of crimes and their families.

****

"Healing is work, not gambling. It is the work of inspiration, not manipulation. If we the healers are to do the work of helping bring our whole people together again, we need to know that such work is the work of the community. It cannot be done by an individual. It should not depend on people who do not understand the healing vocation...The work of healing is work for inspirers working long and steadily in a group that grows over generations, until there are inspirers and healers wherever our people are scattered, able to bring us together again."
Ayi Kwei Armah, The Healers

****

"Trying to change a culture is lonely work, but this is more important than anything now." Vina Drennan

****

Robin Casarjian, Founder

Lionheart Foundation
Houses of Healing
National Emotional Literacy Project For Prisoners
P.O. Box 194 Back Bay
Boston, MA 02117
781-444-6667 www.lionheart.org

With more than 70,000 copies of her Houses of Healing distributed to state and federal prisons nationwide, Robin Casarjian is a well-respected international leader in bringing powerful and effective emotional literacy rehabilitation curricula to prisoners and prison staff across the country and abroad. This prisoner's guide to inner power and freedom, also available in Spanish, has brought both hope and powerful, practical tools for rehabilitation to prisons since 1995. The book, which has an accompanying training manual for facilitators, offers hands-on exercises for developing emotional literacy skills, which helps break the cycle of violence and addictions. In addition, the foundation offers an educational and training video series and free professional training at institutions. They are currently working on an edition dealing with juveniles which will be distributed free to every juvenile detention facility in the U.S. Massachusetts is now implementing the first "Houses of Healing Therapeutic Community" in the country. This is an intensive, contained unit of 32-40 men within the larger inmate population of 1,000. Over twelve weeks, these men will participate in a comprehensive Houses of Healing Emotional Literacy program which will include a research component measuring behavioral change and recidivism.

Robin Casarjian has sent copies of the book to the current 40 members of SageWriters at various prisons around the country, where it is hoped that seeds of empowerment and change will be planted and blossom

Vipassana Prison Project

info@prison.dhamma.org

Imagine a consecutive 10-day silent retreat being held for twenty inmates at a maximum security prison in the deep south. In January 2002 at the W.E. Donaldson Correctional Facility in Bessemer, Alabama, 20 inmates successfully completed the Vipassana course. Vipassana, also known as insight or mindfulness, means to see things as they really are, and is a logical process of mental purification through observing physical sensations. The non-sectarian technique enables one to achieve peace and harmony, freeing the mind from deep-seated causes of suffering. The practice, which is being studied for effectiveness by the National Institute of Health, is taught in 10-day courses where participants sit in silence, learning the step by step technique for eleven hours a day. The goal is freedom from mental negativities. While the course considers the essential teachings of Buddha, it is taught in a universal, nonsectarian and non-religious fashion and does not require one to be a Buddhists. Priests, nuns, rabbis and imans all benefit from learning the technique, which is now a part of many prisons in India. Thousands of police cadets also take the course as part of their training. There are two videos about Vipassana in prisons: "Doing Time, Doing Vipassana," an award-winning documentary about prisons in India, and "Changing from Inside," about women prisoners taking the course at Seattle's North Rehabilitation Facility. The technique can be practiced by people of any culture, race, religion, nationality or sexual orientation. All courses are free, led by volunteers.

"Of hatred and ill will may not a trace remain. May love and goodwill fill body, mind and life." Dhammapada

Alternatives to Violence Project

15 Rutherford Place New York, NY 10003

The Alternatives to Violence Project, Inc., is an organization of dedicated volunteers formed by Quakers to help people develop effective ways of dealing with conflicts creatively and without violence. Its courses are offered only to voluntary participants. Each course consists of a 22-hour intensive program of exercises and discussions designed to develop self-esteem and self-confidence in a trusting and supportive atmosphere, which creates a sense of community. The courses teach principles of cooperation with co-workers, skills in listening, speaking, and observing and explore the many nonviolent solutions that are possible in almost every conflict when approached with a caring attitude toward others.

****

"May it be, oh Lord, that I seek not so much to be consoled as to console, to be understood as to understand, to be loved as to love. Because in giving oneself that one receives; it is in forgetting oneself that one is found; it is in pardoning that one obtains pardon." St. Francis of Assisi

****

The course of human history is determined not by what happens in the skies but what takes place in our hearts."
Sir Arthur Keith

****

WHAT OTHER COUNTRIES DO

*The following reports about international prison conditions are taken from articles from the February 2002 Corrections Today, a publication of the American Correctional Association. (reprinted in **Graterfriends**)*

FINLAND JUSTICE NOT POLITICIZED

By Tapio Lappi-Seppala, director of Finland's National Research Institute for Legal Policy.

The Finnish criminal policy is both humane and rational. Elsewhere in the world - most notably in the United States and the United Kingdom - criminal policy is less rational - a toll of general politics, a way to transmit symbolic messages, take a stand, etc. Instead of balanced reasoning and weighing pros and cons of different strategies, criminal justice interventions often are decided by a simple political authority, the more simplistic the approaches advocated - thus one sees programs and slogans compressed into two or three words, such as "prison works," "war on drugs," and "zero tolerance."

This, then, leads to a tendency to offer simple solutions to complex problems and to pander to a punitive (or presumably punitive) public opinion with harsh tough-on-crime campaigns. A common feature of these campaigns is that the solution to social problems is sought in places where it cannot be found - the penal system.

However, the ongoing total reform of the Finnish Penal Code has been executed throughout in the spirit of "humane neoclassical crime policy," regarding principles of due process and legal safeguards. The penal system reform moves in the direction of the expansion of community-based measures and focuses on situational and local crime prevention. For now, it still is difficult to imagine that the claim that "prison works" will find its way into Finnish political campaigns.

AFRICAN REFORM: PARALEGALS

By Adam Stapleton, a UK criminal lawyer working for the past six years in Malawi with Penal Reform International as a consultant. He has consulted on human rights and penal reform issues for donor agencies in other African nations.

Prisons in Malawi, an English-speaking country in sub-Sahara Africa, are antiquated, fortress-like structures where men dressed in rags sit in the sun with nothing to do; where more than 100 men sleep on the floor of a dormitory, packed in like sardines in a space designed for 30; where windows are two or three slits high on the walls, and the air is stale; and where the toilet is usually a bucket by the door. The smell is stunning, as is the human degradation and the poverty of it all. More than 50% of the prisoners are remand prisoners awaiting trial - some have been waiting for years. Women prisoners are separated from men, and have their children with them, but have no special treatment or diet provided, unless from outside sources.

In 1996, 40 African nations' representatives met to discuss the continent's prison conditions. Heads of prison services, law commissioners, police officers, judges and governmental officials sat with non-governmental representatives to discuss problems, which boiled down to just one: crowding. The conference produced the **Kampala Declaration on Prison Conditions in Africa**, whose preamble calls African prisons "inhuman." With it was drawn a plan for penal reform in Africa that highlights the "special role" of nongovernmental agencies (NGOs) in safeguarding inmates' human rights. It also urges inmates' access to lawyers and accredited paralegals; special attention to vulnerable inmates such as juveniles and females; and regular reviews of the time detainees spend on remand -- recommending closer attention to alternative sentencing such as the use of local, customary practices for settling disputes through restorative justice processes.

This declaration, adopted by the UN in 1997, and others developed throughout Africa, influenced a 1999 UK international penal reform conference when representatives from more than 50 countries called for a new agenda on penal reform. **The document's common theme is that criminal justice systems worldwide need reform and prison services are in crisis.** The new agenda for penal reform developed at the UK conference argues that criminal justice should have a "well-defined and limited role to play in any democratic society and should not be use to resolve problems not relevant to it."

In May 2000, the Para-Legal Advisory Service (PAS) was created in Malawi as an innovative project seeking to apply the principles and recommendations of the declaration, and to give poor people access to the formal justice system. Since then, paralegals have instituted positive changes, earned the trust and respect of prisoners and criminal justice professionals and made themselves indispensable.

CANADA:
ENCOURAGING COMMUNITY CORRECTIONS -- LESS PRISON

By David Daubney, general of criminal law policy and coordinator of the Sentencing Reform Team in the Policy Sector of the Department of Justice of Canada in Ottawa.

Canadian ministers, made aware of the increasing numbers of Canadian prisoners, in 1995, called for a strategy to contain the prisoner growth rate and associated costs. They chose one that combines crime prevention, tough treatment of serious crime and greater use of community sanctions for low-risk offenders, over a shift toward a crime control and punishment policy. The legislative centerpiece of this Canadian venture, Bill C-41, also created the "conditional sentence of imprisonment." Given a conditional sentence (less than two years), the offender is permitted to serve in the community with certain conditions.

Among other versions, framers of Bill C-14 noted more than **30% of prison admissions were for failure to pay fines. They established two alternatives to prison for failure to pay fines**: the non-issuance/renewal of licenses or permits and streamlined ability to register the outstanding fine as a civil judgment. Several provinces have fine-option programs for offenders to work off fines through community service. Also, it is required the judge inquire into the offender's ability to pay before levying a fine; the fine be calculated on a formula that reflects minimum wage levels; and there must be a default hearing to determine if the offender has a reasonable excuse for nonpayment before a warrant of committal can be issued. These changes contributed to dramatic decreases in the number of offenders imprisoned for fine default.

Canada's revisions also reformed aspects of probation, parole (accelerate it), and prison **(moving to a restorative justice model).** Among the new principles are: to assist in the rehabilitation of offenders; to promote a restorative sense of responsibility in offenders and acknowledgement of harm done to victims and the community; to not deprive an offender of liberty if less restrictive sanctions may be appropriate in the circumstances; and to consider all available sanctions other than incarceration for all offenders, with particular attention to the circumstances of Aboriginal offenders.

SCOTS INDEPENDENT PRISON INSPECTIONS: Aim for Decency; Changed Lives

by Clive Fairweather, Scotland's Chief Inspector of Prisons.

The principle of independent prison inspection has a long history in the United Kingdom, but some might ask why this should be of any relevance to corrections in the United States. The answer is **the inspection reports inform the community, which is unable to see what is going on behind prison walls, while highlighting poor performance and good practice at the same time.** This approach is an important tool for promoting correctional excellence.

Its origins in the UK can be traced back to at least 1773, when John Howard was appointed high sheriff, or judge, of Bedfordshire. Along with magistrates, he was responsible for prison inspection, and was appalled by the conditions and injustices he found. Consequently, he became an advocate for the reform of the penal establishments, and began to visit prisons, not only in the UK, but also around the world, in a quest to improve standards.

After the Napoleonic Wars ended in 1815, the Quaker Movement, which included Elizabeth Fry, persuaded a parliamentary select committee to agree that one uniform system of prison discipline should be established in every jail and house of correction in England and Wales. Also, prison inspectors were appointed to visit and report on them. Howard and Fry's vision of reform through independent inspections, enshrined in the Prison Act of 1835, still is relevant in the 21st century.

In 1981, a non-governmental independent inspectorate for English and Welsh prisons was formed, and a similar body was established in Scotland. The objective given to the chief inspector is a deceptively simple one: "To inspect or arrange for the inspection of prisons in Scotland and to report to the secretary of state on them...In particular, on the treatment of (inmates) and conditions in prisons."

The chief inspector, appointed by the queen, is independent from those in prison operations. His or her inspection team consists of several inspectors or consultants, and two advisory senior prison governors, and a $300,000/year budget. The inspection process is dynamic. It reflects the nature of each particular establishment, while retaining a core set of issues for use at all inspections. When a particular issue arises from a certain inmate group, the inspectorate examines it in detail and, if required, carries out an inspection focusing solely on that issue. Following the inspection and weeks of redrafting, detailed reports are published and made available to prison management, staff and prisoners, and distributed to the wider public via nationwide media outlets.

Each penal establishment, even private ones, receives a full formal inspection every three and one half years, which can last between seven and 14 days depending on the size and complexity of the establishment. All aspects of the prison are examined for safety, decency and its contribution to crime prevention. The team is interested in assessing outcomes from the public's point of view. **The reports that emerge, therefore, are a detailed snapshot of the establishment and, although politicians and prison authorities may not always act on their contents, the subsequent media coverage can be a powerful instrument for change. Eventually this gets officials' attention.**

Full inspections are followed each year by intermediate visits, which may be unannounced. These reports are made public, ensuring that progress is continually monitored. The chief inspector is required to submit a written annual report to the Scottish Parliament and may be called in to provide verbal evidence.

Some reports in recent years led to wider improvements, for example, in conditions for remand prisoners - those awaiting trial or sentencing. Through inspectorate pressure and the efforts of individual governors, remand prisoners throughout Scotland now receive the best of prison conditions, whereas previously they were a disadvantaged group.

There also are improvements in conditions for women prisoners - who until recently in Scotland had an appalling record of suicides. **Scottish politicians now accept that the number of women in prison should be greatly reduced - dealt with in the community through alternatives such as electronic monitoring, which allows mothers to look after their children.**

The main female prison itself has been transformed, with its health center now entirely restructured to address the physical and mental health needs of the vulnerable and often bewildered women who regularly arrive at the prison from court. Better working conditions have been introduced, as well as televisions in every cell to reduce the time for morbid contemplations. This may seem incredible, but it is only during the past year that prisoners have had access to TV because of public disquiet about an apparent luxury. Also, prison authorities are uniformly concentrating their efforts on measuring and dealing with individual drug problems.

The first questions any chief inspector of prisons must ask when stepping into a jail are brutal: Are they injured? If so, why and what can be done to prevent this?" This applies equally to staff and prisoners. To the questions: "Are conditions decent here?" inspectors use the rule of thumb that **prison conditions should be no better or worse than those found in public institutions such as schools or hospitals.** However, increasingly, the inspectors are asking: "What does this particular establishment try to do to prevent future victims or crime?" This refers to escapes and rehabilitation.

The one thing prisoners have is time, and such time should be used constructively to help offer individuals new opportunities and change inappropriate behavior patterns. Prisoners need to learn to lead more useful lives and to be properly prepared for release. **Here the importance of role models in the shape of experienced and mature correctional officers cannot be underestimated.**

Thus, the central aim of imprisonment and inspection is not only about incarceration, but also about **trying to change behavior as a practical crime-prevention measure**. This requires careful assessment of offenders at the start of their sentences to determine their problems, their histories of offending and reasons behind it, as well as if there is any family support and whether they will have accommodations after release, etc. Induction should not be regarded as an event, but rather as an ongoing process. Staff must keep returning to "measure" and obtain more detail from offenders regarding what will help bring about significant change. They should create a sentence plan for the individual who, while in prison, tries to address these issues, ending up with a workable release plan.

Each prison also has an independent body (descended from the original magistrates of the 1700's), now called the Visiting Committee. This body scrutinizes its prison on a regular basis and members are appointed by the first minister or local authority. **They represent a cross-section of the community, are volunteers, and organize their visits in such a way that someone is inside a prison each week to monitor the treatment of prisoners and report to the governor or politicians what is found.** These laypersons lack detailed training, but more than make up for it through their fair, open-minded approach. These watchdog are by no means "toothless and barking," and the concept of independent prison inspection is as applicable elsewhere in the free world as it is to the UK. Visit website: www.scotland.gov.uk/hmip for ideas.

SWEDISH PRISONS: POSITIVE

By Bertel Osterdahl, formerly a Major General in the armed forces who in 1994 became Director General of the Swedish Prison and Probation Administration.

It is an important aspect of Swedish criminal policy to reduce the suffering that is inescapably linked to deprivation or restriction of liberty. It clearly is beneficial for inmates to return to the community as law-abiding citizens. To achieve this, their time in prison must be used positively and creatively so they have more of a chance to do so. This requires an investment in a range of active treatment programs that allows them to address their offending behaviors.

Also, it is well known that incarceration has damaging effects. While incarcerated, inmates tend to discuss crime, improve their knowledge of ways to commit crimes, enlarge their criminal contacts and plan future crimes. Thus a prison can become unsafe for inmates and staff. Further, prison life is highly regulated and tends to remove opportunities for personal responsibility. **Prisons can become colleges of crime that reinforce criminal identity and diminish capacity to adjust to the demands of community life.**

An initial task for the Swedish Probation and Prison service is to counteract these negative effects. Prison leave and visits are granted to maintain contact with families and community organizations. Correctional staff develops relationships with inmates to have a positive influence in their lives. Specific programs are developed to allow inmates to address their social inadequacies. **Life in prison should approximate as**

closely as possible to the social conditions of the community so inmates can maintain a sense of personal responsibility.

Alternatives to incarceration are used to the greatest possible extent. Incarceration not only puts offenders' capacity for leading law-abiding lives at risk, but also is an expensive sanction.

Legislative changes were made recently to reduce incarceration by wider use of probation and community service. **Life-sentenced inmates rarely serve their entire sentences.** The practice is that government, following the granting of a request for clemency, usually transforms the indeterminate life sentence into a fixed term. Thereafter, the provisions on conditional release apply. Since 1995, life sentences have been commuted to between 18 and 25 years of fixed incarceration.

The role of the prison officers is changed. Formerly, the uniformed officer staff only had custodial duties. Social work assistants and psychologists carried out social work and treatment activities. A late 1980s study showed prison officers often manifested stress symptoms as a result of being seriously under-stimulated and uncomfortable in their passive role. Consequently, social work assistants were transferred to other branches, and prison officers staff given new tasks with greater responsibility. Staff has become contact persons for granting prison leave, entry into personal change programs, etc.

In their new role, prison officers resolve conflicts among inmates which threaten prison security and order. Close contact with inmates allows staff to know the underlying reasons for inmates' negative actions. Hence technical security in the form of high walls and closed-circuit TV, alarm devices, etc. now is supplemented by knowledge derived from closer inmate-staff contact -- dynamic security.

As a result, escapes diminished steadily and the home-leave misuse rate is low.

NETHERLANDS: NEIGHBORHOOD PRISONS

By Kees Boeij, General Director of the Penitentiaries Noord-Holland Noord in the Netherlands.

In the Netherlands there is an increasing effort to detain offenders in their neighborhoods, rather than the former practice of detention where the crime was committed. Also, placing detainees near their home facilitates family visits.

This effort stems from the realization by penitentiary leaders the system had to come out of its isolated position—where everything was done to build small societies within the prison walls—which had its own kitchen, library, educational staff and employment provisions. Once officials realized this was not always efficient, and by no means a guarantee of good quality, they started looking for partners in society who were willing and able to provide these services.

When they realized they were not only isolating the detainees but the prison itself, they began putting new prisons in industrial areas—where citizens rarely try to prevent their presence. The search for partners was based on the understanding prison governors cannot rehabilitate or reintegrate inmates into society alone. In fact, prisons do not want to do it alone because a variety of authorities and people are needed during detention to assist and guide detainees. Also, for the system to do it alone makes it too easy for society to hold the prison system solely responsible.

In the Netherlands, ex-detainees are entitled to housing and government benefits. Municipalities like to cooperate to arrange this. Moreover, there are subsidies from the Ministry of Social Affairs to the municipalities to compensate the

costs for former detainees assisted with housing, benefits and education.

KAZAKHSTAN:
From Totalitarianism in Prisons to Human Rights

By Pyotr Posmakov, chairman of the Committee for the Penal System of the Republic of Kazakhstan.

During the Soviet era, Kazakhstan was a land of forced labor camps. The republic's prison service, a component of the Soviet Union's system, had a punitive criminal policy that caused severe crowding. After the 1991 Soviet Union breakup, Kazakhstan became independent and established its own penal system. In 1984 the number of prisoners surpassed 100,000. Since then, three amnesties and decriminalization of about 70 criminal code articles caused the number to stabilize at 84,000 in recent years.

Studies show no direct connection between the number of crimes and the amount of incarceration. The incarceration rate is determined more by general conditions of reliance in society and balance of political forces. Indeed, the rate of imprisonment seems to depend on criminal policy, the application of laws and traditions that have taken root in public consciousness. An offender eventually will be released, and it is no secret that incarceration does not help re-educate inmates. In fact, during incarceration inmates become saturated with criminal ideology and take it with them upon release. **Thus, by passing a significant part of the country's population through detention facilities, the society deteriorates.** It is not difficult to calculate the continuation of such a criminal policy toward incarceration during the next 10 to 20 years may result in irretrievable consequences.

Thus, "Limitations of Freedom," a new kind of punishment that does not require the offender's isolation, will be introduced in Kazakhstan by 2003. Those sentenced to limitations of freedom retain their active and passive electoral rights to the state and local government bodies as well as the right to participate in the republican referendum.

Currently, Kazakhstan is making efforts to humanize its approach to punishment and move closer to the international standards and norm, but the changed socioeconomic situation in Kazakhstan limits the work. Still, officials and non-governmental organizations interested in penal reform are exploring many options. For the past two years, Prison Reform International has been working on a Kazakhstan project that includes prison reform; alternatives to prison; and tuberculosis treatment and control.

"LAND OF THE FREE" DEPRIVES MANY"

By Andrew Coyle, director of the International Centre for Prison Studies, University of London, U.K., formerly a prison warden for 25 years in Scotland and England.

With less than 5% of the world's population, the US has 23% of the world's inmates – more than 2.6 million men, women and children in federal and state prisons and local jails. This is a greater proportion than any other country in the world. Include those on some sort of parole, and the figure rises to 6.6 million. 3.8% of all US residents.

These figures set the US apart from the democratic world and are a constant source of wonder for academics, correction professionals and public commentators in other countries. Why should it be necessary for the "land of the free" to deprive so many citizens of their liberty? Who are these two plus million men, women and children? What happens to them while in custody? What happens to them after their release?

If a correctional system exists to serve its community, then it makes sense that this community should be able to judge the extent to which this mandate is being observed. For better or worse, prisons are a part of the democratic process in all countries. Those of us who work in them carry a heavy burden on behalf of our fellow citizens. The world of corrections is generally self-contained, with practitioners rarely looking beyond their own borders for points of comparison or learning.

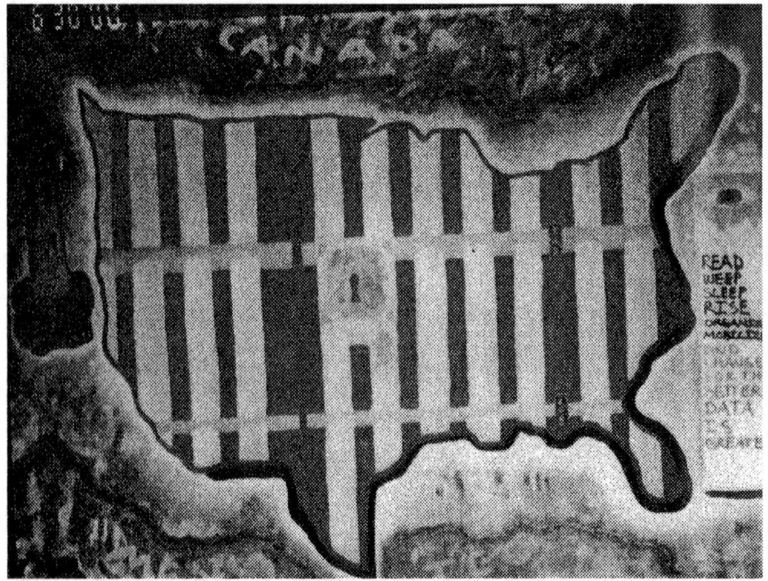

Celling of America Oil on Canvas Muti Ajamu-Osagboro

"All that is necessary for evil to flourish is for good men to do nothing" Edmund Burke

AFTERTHOUGHTS: THE EFFECTS OF WRITING THIS BOOK

Each of the seven core contributors answered the following questions:

**When we first started talking about the book project, do you remember how you felt? What you thought?*

**What were your doubts about: yourself? The project?*

**What was it like for you to write your story?*

**What was the hardest thing for you to write about?*

**How did you push through your internal resistance?*

** What was the most healing part of doing this work?*

**Have your perceptions of yourself changed in any way since doing the work?*

**Any new dreams?*

**Your criticisms/kudos about the project and the process?*

** What do you see as the next step for SageWriters?*

JAMEEL SALAHUDDIN
($840,000)

My initial encounter with Judith Trustone and her Creative Writing course was quite serendipitous in that I simply stumbled upon it one evening. I'll never forget how it happened. I was on my way to a college-level English course held in the prison's education department. As I made my way to the English class, I saw an astonishing sight. From the corner of my eye as I walked past a room, I saw what appeared to be a tiny little woman sitting in a circle with a group of prisoners. Without pausing, I walked on until the impact of what I'd just seen hit me. I stopped, turned around and walked back for a second glance. Sure enough, there they were, sitting in a circle rather than the usual rows of chairs in the middle of the room. What caught my attention the most was Judith, sitting in a chair with her legs tucked up under her like one of those meditation gurus. She appeared to be almost levitating, and she radiated light. It was like a bright oasis in this dark place. Amazed, I tapped on the door and asked if I could enter the room. Once inside, I apologized for the interruption and inquired about what kind of a class this was. After being told it was Creative Writing, I then asked if I could have a seat and join in for a moment.

As I sat in the midst of that circle, I listened with fascination as each prisoner in turn read something he had written about fatherhood. Genuinely moved, I was impressed with the depth of feeling and emotion present in the readings. I just happened to have with me a copy of a letter I'd sent to my cousin earlier that day sharing with her memories of my father. I asked Judith if I could read the letter to the group, and she said ok. As I began reading it aloud, I became so caught up in the intensity of what I was sharing that I almost started crying. Although the letter was brief, I feared I wouldn't make it through the reading, as my voice began to crack and my emotions overwhelmed me. When I finished, the room was silent and everyone just sat looking at me, speechless, their own father issues stirred.

I never made it to the English class down the hall.

The Creative Writing class met weekly, and although I had another course on the same evening, I split my time between them. I'd sit in Judith's class for an hour and then go to my English class for the remainder of the evening. In this way, I still managed to get good grades in my college courses as well as hanging out with Judith and her squad.

Prior to meeting Judith, I had never been involved in anything like what I experienced in her class. From her I learned there is much more to the writing process than simply using words in a descriptive way. Under her guidance, we underwent all sorts of meditative and healing exercises long before we got seriously down to the task of writing.

When we first started talking about the possibility of a book project, I, like many in our group, didn't really take the idea seriously. We simply viewed it as wishful thinking. But once we began writing our individual stories, several men dropped out of the group. It's one thing to think or talk about what you've experienced, but when it comes to writing and finding the proper words to convey those experiences to others, it can be difficult, especially when those experiences were painful.

I have always longed for the ability to write. There have even been times when I've sat in a dark cell during the night pleading with God to give me a voice capable of conveying to the world who I am and what I've been through. Yet I had no idea what the process of telling my story would be like. Sitting alone, thinking about and reliving my past was an emotional roller coaster ride. While writing about the happier moments in my life, I was filled with a warm sense of joy. But while writing about the darker times, I plunged into deep bouts of depression. Most difficult was writing about the sexual and physical abuse of my childhood. Long-buried thoughts and memories came to the surface.

There was one occasion, while I was writing about my childhood abuse, that an intense rage began boiling inside me, a rage so strong I thought I would explode. I had to stop writing for several days. I wrote to Judith (she'd been banned from the prison by then) and cussed her out for stirring all this stuff up inside me. I even asked her what was I supposed to do with all this rage? I called her and she gently suggested some techniques for handling the anger.

I stayed in my cell for days, too afraid to come out, fearing I might snap out at someone, anyone. I was forced to examine my past and come to grips with the fact that these abuses were not my fault, and if I wanted to heal and grow, then I had to move beyond the pain and rage.

I did move on, and resumed writing. Having somehow worked my way through the rage, I began to feel a certain lightness in my heart and soul. And my willingness to share my story opened me to a new level of freedom I'd never felt before.

After mailing my story to Judith, I felt a genuine sense of accomplishment. Soon the world would know who I am.

But as the months passed and Judith told us of the many challenges she faced putting this book together, I and many others in the group began to doubt if it would ever be a reality. The whole idea just seemed too good to be true. And, like everything else good that happens in here, nothing positive would come of it.

Then September 11th happened, causing our hopes to plummet. We were sure no publisher would touch us now. But Judith kept leading the charge, telling us to just keep pressing forward.

Now, almost two years since we first began this book project, it looks like it's finally going to be published. It appears that Judith has pulled off a miracle. I don't even know what to say.

Although neither Judith nor I are at Graterford any longer, my experience in her course has had an incredible impact on my life. Here, in another prison, I spend a lot of time and energy talking with some of the younger prisoners about writing. I even function as an editor for many of them, assisting them in creating short stories and other works.

It seems as if our SageWriters group has grown so much larger than its founding members. The spirit of Judith Trustone and our small group is touching more lives than I ever thought possible.

****

"While there is a lower class, I am in it; while there is a criminal element, I am of it; while there is a soul in prison, I am not free." Eugene Victor Debs

****

"Millions of Americans from all points of the political spectrum are feeling off-balance, unsure, upset or unglued. The rest are in prison." Michael Moore

****

"When the prison gates slam behind an inmate, he does not lose his human quality; his mind does not become closed to new ideas, his intellect does not cease to feed on a free and open interchange of opinion." Thurgood Marshall

TONY
($875,000)

When the topic of the book first came up, I was a bit hesitant to relate my life to outsiders because it would leave my personal experiences open to criticism. Through the course of writing about myself, I learned that we all suffer from what others think of us. Most of my life has been closed to everyone but my family because of the state of the world in which we live. Opening up to strangers, I was afraid of what they'd think about me and my family. What I've learned through writing this book is that there is rain in everyone's life. The point is how we deal with situations.

I really didn't think I had enough knowledge and information to put pen to paper. Life experiences, yes. But as I worked, I taught myself the most important lesson of all, that I am a human being and, if I want to be heard, I will lend myself a voice. Judith just kept encouraging me to write, and that was the best advice.

Writing my story awakened so many painful memories about my young life that it hurt to reflect that far back. When I looked at how my parents raised us, I disliked the way they did it. But after feeling angry for awhile, something else kicked in and I realized that back then children didn't come with an instruction book, and my parents, kids themselves, did the best they knew how to do. I'm grateful that the most important thing my parents taught me was how to love.

Putting my story on paper was a healing process for me. It helped me put both my life and my parents' lives into a form I could understand. But there are some things I can never understand or accept, like why my mother abandoned us to go to raise someone else's children when her own kids had not grown up yet. We are handed so many choices in life;

sometimes we make the wrong ones for what we think are the right reasons without considering the outcome.

What helped me push through my resistance was that I kept getting encouragement and came to feel that what I had to say had value.

Now I was seeing myself more as a man with something good to say to the world.

Since writing my story, I have grown more comfortable with who I am as a person. I don't blame myself anymore for the course my life has taken. I have new confidence, and I realize that my lifelong shyness has disappeared. I'm no longer afraid to talk on any subject.

I have new energy to bring about the most important thing, to get on with the rest of my life. I am now a writer.
I've become a much stronger person through my writing.

I can see that most of the SageWriters are eventually going to write their own books, and Judith will have lots of little babies running around the world. They will owe a deep thanks to this special lady who saw that there is more to us than just our labels and numbers

Peace be with all of us.

****

"If now is not a good time for the truth, I don't see when we'll get to it." Nikki Giovanni

****

MICHAEL
($770,000)

Part of me has always dreamed of having a book published. It has been along the lines of fiction/fantasy, so I was a bit apprehensive about a group book. I'll admit I was skeptical but hopeful. The skepticism came mostly from my judging the capabilities of the other inmates involved.

I wasn't sure about how much I was willing to reveal about myself. I am choosing to remain anonymous because of possible retaliation from the Department of Corrections when I'm considered for parole. I had and still have confidence in Judith's abilities and determination. The project as a whole was under question by me because I felt that many of the others involved couldn't or wouldn't pull their own weight.

While I was writing my story, a lot of memories came up for me the more I wrote. Many of my personal experiences were forgotten until I actually started to write. Some of the more painful ones were difficult, but in a way it has helped me to cope in a positive way by writing and revealing them to others.

The hardest thing to write about was the time of my life with Uncle Warren when he sexually abused me. I felt such shame and betrayal. Even though it wasn't an extreme form of abuse, it was a very big turning point in my life. I believe it created in me a deep distrust of people and their true motives.

After I decided to reveal all, it became easier for me. Once the pen started to flow, I was able to write smoothly. I think a writer has to be decisive and know where he or she wants to go. After that, at least for me, it just happened.

Being able to walk through my most painful issues from the past was a healing process for me. It triggered memories, both good and bad.

My perception of myself has changed. My self-esteem has improved. I realize that after writing my story, what happened to me wasn't so bad. It allowed me to compare my relatively small issues with other people's huge ones.

One of my dreams has always been to write a novel. Now I have a better idea of what it takes. I don't have any new dreams as I'm still trying to achieve my old dream of peace of mind.

I wished the students had shown more enthusiasm for the class. When assignments were given, not everyone complied in a timely way. I didn't care for the way this institution conspired against the Creative Writing class and our teacher. Eventually they succeeded in removing both from the grounds.

I'm grateful for the ongoing correspondence with Judith, which has kept me writing, for that kind of support and encouragement can be in short supply in here. Without her drive, determination and organizational skills, none of this would have happened.

I'm a bit skeptical about SageWriters chances for survival beyond this project. I say this only because of the conditions under which we live. For the most part, most of the members of the group itself are preoccupied with their own problems and lack of liberty. I've displayed this on several occasions, and my situation is minor compared to some of the others. I will be getting out of here someday. I'd like in the future to see a monthly publication by SageWriters consisting of who prisoners are and what they've done to change themselves. Until and unless the public has a better understanding of prisoners as human beings, this will always be a hostile environment for us.

****

Anton Forde/Trevor Mattis ($455,000)

I don't recall exactly how I felt when the book project was first discussed, but I know I was supportive of anything that gives us prisoners a voice.

My only doubts were about revisiting the past. Though my story is always in my head, and I plan an autobiography, writing it was, I don't know, maybe cathartic. I was just hesitant about reliving the past and that moment that brought me here, since I tend to compartmentalize my experiences and rarely visit my pre-incarcerated life.

Nothing was really hard for me to write. The worst of my experiences, that of being charged and convicted for a crime I didn't commit, is a thing I've written about over and over as I litigate my case in my fight to obtain justice.

I liked revisiting my college years. I'm not sure about healing aspects, but I truly appreciate getting the opportunity to show who I am as a person.

My perceptions of myself have not changed, but I think I've become a better writer, though I do procrastinate. I am proud of publishing <u>Contemplations of a Convict</u>; I'm working on the second edition right now, as well as a book of poetry.

I have no new dreams; I have a laundry list of old dreams yet untouched.

The next step that I see for SageWriters is taking on the issue of prison reform and contributing a voice to the political and social issues of the day.

My admiration and respect go out to Judith Trustone for her compassion, dedication and tenacity in seeing such an arduous task as the compilation of this book through to the end. Congratulations to all of us SageWriters!

****

Muti Ajamu-Osagboro
($735,000)

When the book project began, I felt it was just another project for me. One of perhaps fifteen that I was juggling. It is but a slice of the quadruple layered cake I will eventually present to the entire world.

Writing "Portrait of Innocence" was deeply spiritual. Another step on the road to cathartic liberation.

I had no doubts about myself. My doubts about Judith were: Will her brainwashed upbringing allow her to accept the ugly truth about the country's judicial system, and just as important, how much of it will she actually present to the public? Could she really grasp the reality of Black lives?

The hardest thing for me to write was how the entire system routinely gang-raped the so-called rights that I had, all in a day's work. They didn't even stop to burp.

There was no resistance, just pain. I've told my story thousands of times before, and each time I do, it's less painful. Each time it is cathartic. The funny thing with "Portrait" was that it was the first time I'd written it all out from start to finish and to actually see all the treachery the injustice system has taken me through. It's unreal.

According to their plan, I was supposed to be dead years ago. If I never thought miracles existed before, I now know that my being alive is a miracle. That's what I see every time I look in the mirror…a breathing miracle.

Every time I read my story in its totality it was a healing experience.

I don't have dreams. I have visions, and this is just one page in the book of my life.

I appreciate Judith's willingness to learn, her caring and her kindness. Her ability to come out of her comfort zone and risk being "niggerized." Her willingness to challenge wrongs as she is blessed to understand them.

The next step for SageWriters is whatever we decide.

The revolution will be visualized…in literary excellence.

****

Muhkam
($1,085,000)

When the men in our creative writing circle sat down to discuss the possibility of a collective book project, I aligned myself with the group decision as a gesture of support for the group's efforts to extend their horizons of communications with what we prisoners call "The Outside World." I realize now that I should have participated more in these group discussions and paid more attention to what was being agreed to, for at no time had I entertained the possibility of ever being called upon to write about myself. After all, everyone in the SageWriters group knew that my writing skills were limited to the writing of poetry, or so I thought. Also, I was most comfortable with the thought that I would leave the serious writing for the book project to the men who had ambitions to be novelists and playwrights, as well as the academic types who enjoyed endless discourses on the subject of writing styles and which author wrote what a hundred years ago. My thoughts were that I would write what I see, think and feel, and be free from the box of academia. Nevertheless, the time did arrive when I either had to shit or get off the pot. I had to honor my word.

After evaluating my concerns about my own writing ability, there remained a consideration that was like a straight arrow destined to penetrate the core of my being and honoring my word.

During the years of interacting with Judith in our SageWriters group, I developed an intense respect for her as a result of her dedication and loyalty to the prisoners, to prison reform issues and our efforts to maintain human dignity.

Also, when she sent the urgent message, “Come on, Muhkam, I’ve heard from everyone but you,” my thoughts were that although I had been the ninth man called to the plate, there was no way that I was leaving the game without taking my turn at bat. No way!

We’ve all heard that in the final seconds of life, a drowning man sees his whole life flash before him like a film being projected upon a gigantic movie screen. To my knowledge, the drowning man has never told anyone about this peculiar experience that so many believe to be true.

However, my experience of three decades of imprisonment has resulted in my revisiting the events and circumstances of my life over and over again. Thus the call for me to begin writing about myself was the inevitable revisiting of my sinful past, over and over again.

Writing about myself compelled me to recall memories of my childhood, the escapades of a too curious and fearless teenager, and the young adult who didn't quite find his way to manhood until after he had experienced all of the chastisements of living, and then finally learning the cold, often cruel reality lessons of life.

Aside from the remembrances of the mundane events of my life, there were several pleasant revisits of that most memorable and joyous experience of meeting, knowing and loving the gracious and beautiful Doris Dean Hagood, my beloved wife, God's blessing to my life. She brought me years of comfort, encouragement, love and happiness, until she died of a brain aneurysm on June 28, 1997.

The process of writing for the book carried me to that place where I was no longer talking to someone else about me, rather, Muhkam was talking to Muhkam, re-evaluating, resolving, becoming and perhaps, as Judith always says, being in beauty.

****

Jameel Whitaker ($525,000)

Because I was a part of this project from its very inception, I felt that our writing group (SageWriters) would get authentic exposure. Also, our collective talents would serve to build a bridge between prisoners who are sincere and utilize their time well with citizens who are willing to listen to various shades of a prisoner's mind.

I had no doubts about the book's success; I hope it will gain the necessary momentum needed to open doors for other endeavors like this one. My writing suffered when society's pressures distracted me from working with the same intensity and passion as when I was confined at Graterford. Though in prison your day is dictated by prison officials, one can concentrate more because prisoners are not being bombarded with everyday societal pressures like paying the rent and car repairs.

I pushed myself to write when I fell into a writing slump by thinking about the men I left behind. I knew I had the other SageWriters' vote of confidence and they expected me to stand tall and resolute in the world after serving a lengthy prison sentence.

Submitting my work, usually late, to Judith, who showed so much patience and support with my procrastination episodes was rather healing. My perception of myself always changes when I undergo a difficult challenge and meet it successfully. For me and I'm sure for many, inertia is the true enemy of creativeness.

There is so much opportunity in anyone's life if they can learn to tap into that creative force. I'm still exploring this process. I've had glimpses, however brief, of my own creative genius.

I see some very heavyweight SageWriters coming from Graterford and other prisons.

I thank Judith Trustone for sharing her light with me.

"When it shall be said in any country in any world, my poor are happy; neither ignorance nor distress is to be found among them; my jails are empty of prisoners, my streets of beggars; the aged are not in want; the taxes are not oppressive...when these things can be said, then may that country boast about its constitution and its government."
Thomas Paine

Judith Trustone

While this is the end of the book, it really is a beginning. With the exciting new technology of print-on-demand publishing there will be room in later editions for many of those whose work was not included, those who promised to write but haven't yet, and for reactions from readers. It is apparent that as a nation we must begin honest conversations minus political posturing and take actions to change this dysfunctional, barbaric, and extremely expensive system. The bottom line is what are we going to do about the injustice created by poverty and racism. With the growing gap between the haves and the have nots, Shadow America grows larger and darker each year as the prison industry grows and grows like a tough weed, choking the life out of everything and everyone in its path, especially fragile seedlings.

Hopefully at this point the reader has come to realize the tragic waste of the human beings whose voices are heard on these pages and will do whatever possible to remedy conditions in Shadow America.

Personally, this was a difficult project to complete as I couldn't visit the SageWriters, all mail comes under the eyes of censors and all phone conversations are monitored and recorded. In the group we developed a kind of code so we could talk more freely. For instance, the book was called "Nelly" after Nelly Bly, the 19th Century journalist from Pennsylvania who got herself admitted to the Belleview mental asylum in New York, spent two weeks there and then got out through the intercession of a colleague. Her book about conditions in mental asylums was a wake-up call for making American mental asylums more humane.

While reading what the SageWriters wrote was exciting, especially as they grew more confident and assured, I was at times overwhelmed at the responsibility of editing Black English from a white perspective. And their sense of time was quite different from mine. If I asked for immediate responses through the mail I was certain to get them at least three weeks later. Dealing with prison life consumes them and makes them unaware of deadlines or the different kinds of pressures we feel outside the walls. Because of the Chronic Traumatic Stress Syndrome from which they all suffer, they tend to be self-absorbed. Yet each in his own way has been illuminating, amazing me with their strength and courage. I doubt if I could survive one day of their lives.

On a deep level, my painful awakening to the truth about the criminal justice system shook my view of the rest of the world. Yes, I am more cynical than ever, yet knowing what they've survived and achieved has given me inspiration and an incredible perception of gratitude for the abundance, privileges and freedoms that I have. Whenever I feel weary or sorry for myself, all I have to do is think of my imprisoned "brothers" and "sisters" and I immediately stop my internal whining. There are times when I have a beautiful experience that I yearn to share with them. My capacity for joy has grown, and I am much more patient.

When I travel or shoot a spectacular sunset, I send them pictures. I have a series of "Skyscapes" currently on exhibit that came about when Muti once asked me while I was flying to the west coast to take pictures above the clouds as he'd never been on a plane.

When I eat a succulent mango I wondered if Anton will ever again taste the fruit that grows abundantly in his native land. In a way that's hard to explain, the two years of getting this book together has made us a kind of family, an odd one for sure, but a family nonetheless.

I have tried as much as is possible under such malevolent scrutiny to share my life, my struggles and my triumphs.
I feel honored to have worked with these prisoners and for having earned their not-easily-won trust. I pray I have given their voices the accuracy and the honesty they demand.

I fear for the harm they may experience as a result of being openly involved with this project. As soon as I learn of any retaliation against them by guards or administration, the information will be posted on our website, SageWriters.com along with names and numbers of who to call to protest. I will also alert the media.

Just as we were going to press, I got a call from Jameel Salahuddin, who was terribly upset. It seems he was emptying a waste basket into a larger container when an apple rolled across the floor and then fell five tiers down, splattering at the feet of some guards. Jameel immediately put up his hands and yelled down that it was an accident. Within minutes he was shackled, and while standing and trying to explain, one of the guards picked up an apple and threw it at his chest as hard as he could, almost knocking Jameel over. Demanding medical attention and a chance to write up the guard who injured him, he spotted a lieutenant walking nearby with some men in suits. He meekly called out could he talk to the lieutenant and proceeded to tell what had happened and that he wanted to file a complaint against the guard. Calling the guard a "known hothead," the lieutenant asked Jameel to not file a complaint and that the guards accusations that he had assaulted them with an apple would also be dropped. So instead of being sent to The Hole for six months or more, Jameel was unshackled and released into his cell. All he was trying to do was clean his "house." He could have been badly beaten like Anton was. Or had years added to his time.

Such is the daily life of terrorism in our prisons.

Let us join together to shine a light into Shadow America and create a new system that gets rid of poverty, treats, trains and rehabilitates, a healing system that brings out the best in all who enter. If half the folks in prison were released tomorrow with no threat to the community as the experts *state, imagine what $23 billion could do for rehabilitation, treatment and training. We need to explore becoming more of a social democracy rather than the arrogant empire that the rest of the world is coming to despise. Ending poverty and changing prisons needs to be declared a national emergency.*

"Never doubt that a small group of thoughtful committed citizens can change the world. Indeed, it's the only thing that ever has." Margaret Mead

THINGS YOU CAN DO RIGHT NOW

The resources and recommended reading listed in this book are but a small sample of what's out there. Go to your library, get on the internet and explore the world of alternatives to this terrible system. Educate yourself, and as you learn, educate those around you, especially when you hear someone saying something that in no way reflects the reality of prison life, like: "They're all getting a free college education, and I have to work hard to pay for my kids to go to college." Or "They should lock them all up and throw away the key!" And one of the most common, that prisons are like "country clubs." According to inmates, the series "Oz" on HBO in no way presents a true picture of prison life. Most importantly, visit your closest maximum security prison and become a volunteer.

TWELVE THINGS YOU CAN DO TODAY

1. Write to any or all of the SageWriters whose stories have touched your heart. Offer your support in whatever way is appropriate.
2. Identify activist groups in your state or region and join the one that most appeals to you. (see Resources)

3. If you're a member of a church, synagogue or mosque, find out if your institution has a prison ministry. If not, start one.
4. Volunteer to teach/mentor an inmate through local programs. (see Resources).
5. Write to four inmates. This will give you a wider perspective on the issues than just writing to one.
6. Find out your state's laws on mandatory sentencing, the death penalty, life sentencing and aftercare services. If you don't like what you learn, speak out—to politicians, the press, the clergy—get active.
7. Make generous contributions to organizations like the Prison Society, the ACLU and Amnesty International that are working to improve conditions in Shadow America.
8. Speak out when someone makes a joke about rape in prison. Make the truth known.
9. If you're a lawyer, contact Muti, Anton, Muhkam, Tony and the others and help to get them out of there!
10. Write and e-mail letters to television crime shows that falsely portray police brutality, prosecutorial misconduct and inaccurate pictures of prison life as acceptable.
11. Begin ongoing conversations with local and federal politicians about your concerns about the waste of your tax dollar and the destruction of the human spirit and lack of treatment and rehabilitation that characterize our current system.
12. Hold ALL prisoners, but especially those in this book, in your prayers and meditations, so they may survive the physical, mental, emotional and spiritual bites the beast tries to tear daily from their troubled beings.

"A well-ordered police state rests on the cornerstone of a cowed citizenry…an electorate sedated by the drug of fear."
Lewis H. Lapham

****

Creativity

"Writing is external ink sculpting from cerebral clay"

"A sentence is to the pen what a clip is to a rifle and a word is to a sentence what a bullet is to a clip…squeeze tight!"

"The paint brush is more powerful than the pistol."

"Writers' block never visits the homes of those who write with feeling."

Muti Ajamu-Osagboro
from A Prisoner's Soul Survival

****

"Make every effort to send love out in response to hate. This was the message of Christ. If you have love within, it is what you will have to give away. All hatreds, even our seemingly justified hatred in reaction to aggression, is a part of the cancer that destroys humanity. The more we send out harmony and love to others, regardless of their behavior, the more we are living in oneness. Certainly we need jails and other means of protection from those who transgress toward others. What we do not need is hatred as our response to their antisocial behavior." Dr. Wayne Dyer

****

"Prison systems throughout the world are generally ugly, barbaric, counterproductive and insane. Someday our descendants will look back on our time with shock that such sophisticated people could have treated prisoners the way we do." Bo Lozoff, Human Kindness Foundation

****

SUGGESTED READING

Casarjian, Robin. Houses of Healing: A Prisoner's Guide to Inner Power and Freedom. Boston, Massachusettes: Lionheart Press, 1995.

Conover, Ted. New Jack: Guarding Singsing. New York: Random House, 2000.

Dwyer, Jim; Neufeld, Peter; Scheck, Barry. Actual Innocence: Five Days to Execution and Other Dispatches from the Wrongly Convicted. New York: Random House, 2000.

Forde, Anton/ Mathis, Trevor. Contemplations of a Convict: Aphorisms for the Heart and Mind. Haverford, Pennsylvania: Infinity Publishing.com, 2001.

Griffin, John W. A Letter to My Father. Xlibris Corporation, 2001.

Hallinan, Joseph T. Going Up the River: Travels in a Prison Nation. New York: Random House, 2001.

Harnish, John F. Everything You Always Wanted to Know About POD Publishing but Didn't Know Who To Ask Haverford, Pennsylvania: Infinity Publishing.com, 2002.

Hooks, Bell. Salvation: Black People and Love. New York: Perennial, 2001.

Reiman, Jeffrey. The Rich Get Richer and The Poor Get Prison: Ideology, Class, and Criminal Justice. 5th ed. Needham Heights, Massachusettes: Allyn and Bacon, 1998.

Rickford, John Russell; Rickford, Russell John. Spoken Soul: The Story of Black English. New York: John Wiley & Sons, Inc., 2000.

Smitherman, Geneva. Black Talk: Words and Phrases From The Hood To The Amen Corner. 2nd ed. New York: Houghton Mifflin Company, 2000.

Wimsatt, William Upski. No More Prisons: Urban Life, Home Schooling, Hip-Hop Leadership, The Cool Rich Kids Movement, A Hitchhiker's Guide to Community Organizing, and Why Philanthropy is the Greatest Art Form Of The 21st Century. New York: Soft Skull Press, 1999.

Wright, Bruce. Black Robes, White Justice: Why Our Legal System Doesn't Work For Blacks. 2nd ed. New York: Kensington Publishing Corp. 1993.

Abu-Jamal, Mumia Death Blossoms: Reflections of a Prisoner of Conscience, Farmington, Pennsylvania: The Plough Publishing House, 1997

Cleaver, Eldridge, Soul On Ice, New York: Dell, 1968

Jackson, George. Soledad Brother. New York: Coward-McCann, 1970; reprint ed., Chicago: Lawrence Hill Books, 1994

Mitford, Jessica. Kind and Usual Punishment: The Prison Business, New York, Knopf, 1973

National Insitute for Justice, Convicted by Juries, Exonerated by Science, 1996

Borchard, Edwin M., Convicting the Innocent, DaCapo Press, 1970 (c. 1932)

Cutler, Brian C. and Penrod, Steven D., Mistaken Identification: The Eyewitness, Psychology and the Law, Cambridge University Press, 1995

Protess, David and Warden, Rob, A Promise of Justice: The Eighteen Year Fight to Save Four Innocent Men, Hyperion, 1998

Cole, David, No Equal Justice: Race and Class in the American Criminal Justice System, New Press, 1999

Jackson, Rev. Jesse, Marlowe and Co., Legal Lynching: Racism, Injustice and the Death Penalty, National Press Books, 1996

Christie, Nils. Crime Control as Industry: Towards Gulags, Western Style. New York, Routledge, 1993

Pisciotta, Alexander W. Benevolent Repression: Social Control and the American Reformatory-Prison Movement. New York, New York University Press, 1994

Gilligan, James, M.D. Violence: Reflections on a National Epidemic and Its Causes Grosset-Putnam Books, 1996

Gilligan, James, M.D. Preventing Violence Thames and Hudson, Inc., 2001

Donziger, Steven R., The Real War on Crime: The Report of The National Criminal Justice Commission, Harper Perrenial 1995

Mauer, Mark, The Race To Incarcerate, New Press, 1999

RESOURCES

Pennsylvania Prison Society
2000 Spring Garden Street
Philadelphia, PA 19130-3805
215-564-6005 www.prisonsociety.org

Center for Restorative Justice and Peacemaking
University of Minnesota School of Social Work
105 Peters Hall 1404 Gortner Avenue
St. Paul, MN 55108-6160
612-624-4923 ssw.che.umn.edu/rjp

The Human Kindness Foundation
Rt. 1 Box 201-N Durham, NC 27705
919-942-2540

Justice and Mercy, Inc.
Box 223 Shillington, PA 19607
610-208-0406

SageWriters.com
Box 215 Swarthmore, PA 19081
610-328-6101
www.SageWriters.com

Lifeline PA
Box 61 Bensalem, PA 19020

Graterfriends
C/o Pennsylvania Prison Society
2000 Spring Garden Street
Philadelphia, PA 19130
215-564-6005
DonnelBrown@PrisonSociety.org

The Fight For Lifers
Box 7691 Philadelphia, PA 19101

Books Through Bars
4722 Baltimore Ave., Philadelphia, PA 19143
215-727-0882 x 2 www.booksthroughbars.org

American Friends Service Committee
National Criminal Justice Program
1501 Cherry Street Philadelphia, PA 19102
215-241-7130

National Clearinghouse
for the Defense of Battered Women
125 South 9th Street Philadelphia, PA 19107
215-351-0010 or 800-903-0111 ext. 3

TOVA
Theater of Witness
"Living with Life" (video)
126 E. Baltimore Pike Media, PA 19063
484-444-0418

THRESHOLDS, Delaware County, PA
Cheyney Road Thrornton, PA 19373
610-459-9383

www.prisonactivist.com

The Sentencing Project
918 F Street N.W. Suite 501
Washington, DC 20004
202-628-0871
www.sentencingproject.org

Campaign for an Effective Crime Policy
918 F Street N.W. Suite 505
Washington, DC 20004
202-628-1903

"It is from numberless diverse acts of courage and belief that human history is shaped. Each time a man or woman stands up for an ideal, or acts to improve the lot of others, or strikes out against injustice, s/he sends forth a tiny ripple of hope, and crossing each other from a million different centers of energy and daring, those ripples build a current which can sweep down the mightiest walls of repression and resistance." Robert Kennedy

"May the bonfire of hatred burn down to nothing but ashes. May a river of love spill over and flow through the hearts of all." Buddha